Unity Metaphysics

As taught by the Unity School of Religious Studies

Rev. James R. D. Yeaw, D.Div., Editor

Unity Spiritual Center

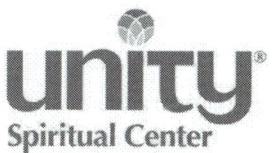

Portions ©2015 by James Yeaw. All rights reserved.

Unity Metaphysics is a work developed by the Unity School of Religious Studies of the Unity School of Christianity. It has been edited for clarity with notes added pertaining to modern scholarship.

Acknowledgment

This material was written by Marvin Anderson and Ed Rabel sometime in the early 1990's. Marvin chose the citations and Ed wrote the commentary. Known as "the Tan version was followed by what has come to be known as the "Blue" version a few years later. The Blue version was put together by Leona Stefanko and Susan Downs. Both the Tan and Blue versions had two books which we have combined into one.

The questions in the appendix are from the Unity Correspondence School annotations.

First Edition, 2015 021516

Library of Congress Cataloging-in-Publication Data

Yeaw, James, ed.
Unity Metaphysics
 P. cm
Includes index
 ISBN-13: 978-1519103680
 ISBN-10: 1519103689

Contents

Introduction v

Part I – The Nature of God 7

Chapter 1 - Truth: What is Truth? 9

Chapter 2 – What is God? 19

Chapter 3 - The Divine Paradox 29

Chapter 4 - The Trinity 35

Chapter 5 - The Problem of Evil 43

Chapter 6 - The Kingdom of God 53

Chapter 7 – The Creative Process 63

Part II – The Nature of Humankind 79

Chapter 8 - Self Knowledge 81

Chapter 9 - Consciousness 91

Chapter 10 – The Trinity in Us 99

Chapter 11 – Mind - The Crucible 107

Chapter 12 – Personality and Individuality 115

Chapter 13 – Spiritual Evolution 123

Chapter 14 - Salvation 131

Chapter 15 - Denials and Affirmations 139

Chapter 16 - Understanding Faith 149

Chapter 17 – Co-Creation 157

Part III – The Relationship between Us and God 165

Chapter 18 – Jesus, the Christ 167

Chapter 19 – Prayer and Meditation 175

Page | iii

Chapter 20 - The Twelve Powers 187

Part IV – Practical Application of Metaphysics 201

Chapter 21 – Metaphysical Basis for Health and Healing 203

Chapter 22 – Metaphysical Basis for Prosperity 247

Chapter 23 - Keys to Demonstration 277

Section V 285

Chapter 24 – Hebrew and Christian Scriptures 285

Appendix - Answers to Advanced Discussion Questions 287

    Chapter 2 287

    Chapter 3 312

    Chapter 4 312

    Chapter 6 315

    Chapter 7 316

    Chapter 8 321

    Chapter 10 327

    Chapter 11 335

    Chapter 14 351

    Chapter 15 357

    Chapter 16 360

    Chapter 17 362

    Chapter 18 363

    Chapter 19 368

    Chapter 24 385

Index 397

Introduction

This is a course in Unity Metaphysics designed to provide the background, understanding, and frame of reference necessary for metaphysical thinking. The course provides an overview of the basic concepts and ideas found in the writings of Charles Fillmore grouped under the following main categories:
1. The Nature of God.
2. The Nature of Humankind.
3. The Relationship between God and Humankind.

We have added part IV – Practical Application of Metaphysics to further present Fillmorian materials on Healing, Prosperity and Demonstration.

More than 600 footnotes have been added to provide sources in Hebrew and Christian Scriptures as well as the original Unity books. We would suggest referencing these works in your studies so that concepts are placed in context:

Metaphysical Bible Dictionary
Fillmore, Charles, *The Revealing Word*
Cady, H. Emilie, *Lessons in Truth*
Shanklin, Octavia *What Are You?*
Lynch, Richard *Know Thyself*
Fillmore, Charles, *Christian Healing*
Fillmore, Charles, *Talks on Truth*
Fillmore, Charles, *Keep a True Lent*
Fillmore, Charles, *The Twelve Powers of Man*

This book is meant to be a life-long reference book as you study the essence of self. It is designed to be studied, subject by subject. Each chapter includes key questions to look at while you need. An online test is available if you wish to test your knowledge of these concepts. Memorization of words and phrases, however, will not, in the long run, lead to the abundant life that Jesus mentioned.[1] It takes a deep understanding, a willingness to learn from life lessons, time spent in meditation, and a discussion of the application of Truth with your spiritual community. There are suggested discussion questions in many of the chapters. Some applicable answers to these questions are found in the appendix starting on page 287.

If you have questions, comments or desire clarification you may also email us at info@unitysc.org. We will attempt to clarify or to refer you to sources for greater understanding.

> Rev. Jim Yeaw
> Sun City, Arizona
> 2015

---

[1] John 10:10

Part I – The Nature of God

Supplementary Reading

- Cady, H. Emilie *Lessons In Truth,* Chapter 2
- Fillmore, Charles Christian Healing, Chapter 1
- Fillmore, Charles *Talks on Truth*, Chapters 1 and 11
- Fillmore, Charles *Keep a True Lent*, Chapter 2
- Lynch, Richard *Know Thyself,* Chapters 2, 5, and 13

This part will give the basic foundation for Truth, including what God is; how God works in your life; what the kingdom that Jesus spoke of is in your life; the illusion of good vs. evil and how to create a life because of what God is.

You will experience a new vision of what God is, releasing many concepts of what God isn't. This, for some, will be a difficult journey. You will struggle with these concepts if you hold to a view of a God somewhere else, maybe in a place called heaven. If you are a Trinitarian Christian you will find a new way of looking at the Trinity. If you are a fundamentalist Christian that has come to believe that all truth is in the Hebrew or Christian Scriptures, you may see that Truth a little differently. You may also want to look at *A Spiritual Interpretation of the Hebrew Scriptures* or *A Spiritual Interpretation of the Christian Scriptures: The Gospels*. We have included hundreds of Biblical footnotes in this work to help you. Jeremiah said it well:[2]

> *"This is the covenant I will make with the people of Israel after that time," declares the LORD. "I will put my law in their minds and write it on their hearts. I will be their God, and they will be my people.*

More questions may arise than answers. This is good. It is better to live with a question than dogmatic certainty.

Those who have already carefully studied spiritual Truth will find that they can bring any desired good into their lives by persistently affirming it is there already. All Truth is already in your heart. Watch for it. Affirm it! Later on, their own personal experiences and inward guidance will lead them to an understanding of divine Truth making it easy to follow simple rules which, at first, seemed difficult and confusing.

Trust the presence of Spirit. Remember that "God's presence (word) is a lamp to guide your feet and a light for your path."[3]

An affirmation for you as you study:

> *I only see Truth and beauty and love that is life. I see it present in every atom of my life and every entity. I see it manifested at this very moment, and in every moment.*

---

[2] Jeremiah 31:33
[3] Psalm 119:105

Chapter 1 - Truth: What is Truth?

Questions from the Lesson Text
1. Define the following:
    - Divine Ideas
    - Truth
    - Absolute Truth
    - Relative Truth
    - Metaphysics
2. What is the Church of Christ?
3. What does Charles Fillmore mean by the "progressive nature" of Truth?

Questions for Advanced Discussion
1. What do you base "truth" on?

Lesson Text

"What we mean by Truth is concerned with the great fundamental questions that have always perplexed and at the same time engaged our profoundest attention:
- What is the character of God?
- How does God create?
- What is the real character of us?
- What relation do we bear to source?
- What is the ultimate destiny of us and the universe?

It is helpful to realize that we have a special meaning for the word Truth as used in Unity. We do not mean "all the Truth there is." Nor do we mean "all the facts that are known." The Unity usage of the word Truth is in connection with divine ideas as they relate to God and humankind. Divine ideas are the spiritual patterns for all that pertains to us. They are all the components known to our mind which constitute what we call good. Anything that acknowledges, verifies, supports, or expresses divine ideas is called "Truth" in Unity terminology. Anything which contradicts or attempts to negate divine ideas is called "error" in Unity terminology. In Bible terminology, the opposites of Truth are called "sin" or "evil." For us, the most essential and basic of all divine ideas are what we now experience as twelve spiritual faculties: faith, strength, love, power, imagination, understanding, order, zeal, will, judgment, renunciation, life.[4]

Absolute Truth and Relative Truth

"It is only from the plane of mind that one can know Truth in an absolute sense. That which we pronounce truth from the plane of appearances is relative only. The relative truth is constantly changing, but the absolute Truth endures; and what is true today always was and always will be true."[5]

Absolute Truth is the realm of divine ideas in all their original purity and power. Our mind does not function in the absolute nor as the absolute. We can only relate the absolute. In order to do this, our mind must draw upon divine ideas, giving them form and relating

---

[4] Fillmore, Charles *Atom-Smashing Power of Mind*, p. 84
[5] Ibid, p. 88

them to time and space. For this purpose we create thought. Thought forms divine ideas into usable concepts. Thoughts change constantly, mostly determined by time, place, and circumstances. Divine ideas (absolutes) never change.

Metaphysics

> "Metaphysics" The systematic study of the science of Being; that which transcends the physical. By pure metaphysics is meant a clear understanding of the realm of ideas and their legitimate expression."[6]

Again, it is useful to realize that we have a special meaning for the word "metaphysics" in Unity terminology. As is the case with the word "Truth" the essential key is acknowledgment of divine ideas. Metaphysics is really the study and science of divine ideas, which may totally transcend the data of existing physical facts. When we use the word metaphysical in Unity, we almost always mean something which is true concerning the inner life of every human being, regardless of time, place, and circumstances.

Examples:
- Forgiveness primarily benefits the forgiver.
- Temptation constitutes an opportunity for choice.
- Health is our true and natural state.

Even if existing facts of the moment seem to contradict any of the above statements, their metaphysical validity remains intact.

---

[6] Fillmore, Charles *The Revealing Word*, Metaphysics

Metaphysical Bible Interpretation

As metaphysical Christians we take the Scripture to be a spiritual history of man as well as a history of outer events. We try to read it in the spirit appropriate to it. Spiritual things must be spiritually discerned. The Bible is a spiritual book.[7]

"In reading the Scriptures we gradually raise our consciousness of them as mere history and begin to apprehend them as setting forth the principle or law of life. We find the great Bible characters fitting into the pattern of our own consciousness, where they represent ideas. This makes the Bible a divine Book of Life rather than merely the history of a people.[8]

This does not mean that a study of the written Scriptures will itself solve your problems unless you come into the apprehension of the real Scriptures, the Bible of the ages, the Book of Life within your own consciousness.[9]

Perhaps the clearest definition of metaphysical Bible interpretation is stated in the preface of the *Metaphysical Bible Dictionary*:[10]

The Bible is, from Genesis to Revelation, in its inner or spiritual meaning, a record of the experiences

---

[7] Fillmore, Charles *Teach Us to Pray*, p. 140
[8] Fillmore, Charles *Prosperity*, p. 70
[9] Fillmore, Charles Prosperity, p. 180
[10] ---, *Metaphysical Bible Dictionary*

and the development of the human soul and of the whole being of man; also it is a treatise on man's relation to God, the Creator and Father... We see in the Bible symbolical pictures showing the growth and unfoldment of the latent spiritual power in man up to the time when he comes into manifestation of the perfect 'image' and 'likeness' in which he was created.

What makes metaphysical Bible interpretation unique is that it allows us to interpret characters and events in Scripture as various aspects of our own consciousness. We then use these insights and the increased awareness they generate to transform our lives.

A New Age

Jesus never taught that God would destroy the earth, but he did teach that collective evolution was being carried forward in great periods or ages, one of which was ending in his time.[11]

All this presages a new state of consciousness for humankind It is the beginning of the visible reign of the Christ, whose seed man was Jesus of Nazareth ... He it was who went into all the domains of thought and formulated ideas that have waited for a people who could comprehend and utilize them. We are that people. The dawn of the millennium is in our keeping. We possess the keys that open the gates of the New Jerusalem ... A higher state of consciousness is bursting full-blown upon the whole

---

[11] Fillmore, Charles *Keep a True Lent*, p. 27

> world. It is everywhere, and those who are most open to its influx are being rewarded. The power is abroad in the earth, and it calls to men and to nations, 'come up higher'.[12]

> We are the posterity to whom Jesus addressed most of his words. Many of the people of His time and place did not comprehend most of the words He spoke. For them, Jesus gave a ministry of works. For the few who had "ears to hear" and for people of the future, He gave His ministry of words. The level of consciousness which can now comprehend Jesus' words could be called the new age. We are now in that age, and the words of Jesus have greater meaning and impact now than they ever had before in history. This is one meaning of the "second coming of Jesus Christ." He has come to us now, two thousand years after His resurrection in the form of his words. Jesus said, "Heaven and earth will pass away, but my words will not pass away.[13]

Charles Fillmore often refers to "the coming of the end of a religious dispensation." Although this term is not entirely clear, it must relate to the cycles or "ages" of certain levels of religious thinking. The level of religious thinking just prior to the present could be designated as the Hebrew Scriptures, "eye for an eye, tooth for a tooth," strict letter of the law of mechanical cause and effect. The current new age could be designated as metaphysical Christianity, forgiveness of sin, grace, and Truth. For those who "have ears to hear," the words of Jesus can come

---

[12] Fillmore, Charles *Talks on Truth*, p. 124
[13] Mark 13:31

alive as the new age religion. Jesus said, "My words are Spirit and they are life."[14]

Church of Christ

> *The church of Jesus Christ still waits for a ministry that will represent it as it is—an organization in heaven without a head on earth, without a creed, without a line of written authority. This church exists, and must be set up in its rightful place—the minds and the hearts of men. It can never be confined to any external organization; whoever attempts such a movement, by that act, ceases to represent the true church of Christ.*[15]

These words were written by Charles Fillmore at a time when he was very much opposed to organized churches if they in any way interfered with the development of greater freedom of individual consciousness. Most existing churches of his time were of that type. So Fillmore was somewhat anti-church. But many things have changed since then. Today, it is likely that Fillmore would relax his views concerning the true church of Jesus Christ. Many Unity churches are churches of Jesus Christ, even though they may be quite organizational. If the actual teachings of Jesus are being presented, then it is a legitimate church of Jesus Christ. Of course, this true church must have its foundation in the mind and heart of each individual.

---

[14] John 6:33
[15] Fillmore, Charles *Talks on Truth*, p. 109

The Progressive Nature of Truth

> *We are receiving new Truth in all fields, and if we are to use it, it seems most important that our religion be progressive, that we get new and higher concepts, and that we see deeper and more scientific relations in the lessons and experiences of those who have preceded us in study and demonstration of spiritual Truth."*[16]

> *Do not dogmatize in creed, or statement of Being, as a governing rule of thought and action. These things are limitations and they often prevent free development because of foolish insistence on consistency. The creed that you write today may not fit the viewpoint of tomorrow; hence the safe and sure religious foundation for all men is that laid down by Jesus, 'The Spirit of Truth... shall guide you into all the Truth.'*[17] *A statement setting forth the teaching of a religious institution is essential, but compelling clauses should be omitted.*[18]

Correct teaching of metaphysical Truth keeps such teachings organic. One correct method of teaching is to always keep an "open door" in all presentations. Knowledge can be a living thing. All living things must be free to grow. Knowledge increases as more light enters the human consciousness. When any system of knowledge contains "closed doors," then the organic quality of such knowledge begins to deteriorate. In religious thinking this

---

[16] Fillmore, Charles *Jesus Christ Heals*, p. 126
[17] John 16:13
[18] Fillmore, Charles *The Twelve Powers* of Man, p. 111

deterioration becomes static dogma, outworn theology, mechanical repetition, and superstition that is out of step with the times. This has happened to almost all important religions in our history on earth. It can be prevented from happening to metaphysical Christianity (Truth) if we preserve its organic quality by keeping the "open door" policy in effect.

Chapter 2 – What is God?

Questions from the Lesson Text
1. What is Unity's first premise concerning the nature of God?
2. Give a brief definition for each of the following terms:
- Principle
- Spirit
- Substance
- Omnipresent
- Omniscient
- Omnipotent
3. Choose one of the paradoxical aspects of God and tell how it helps you to understand God in your life.
4. Are we capable of understanding God?

Questions for Advanced Discussion
1. What is God?
2. Is God a person? Explain fully.
3. What is God as Principle? as Law?
4. What is meant by "God immanent in the universe"?
5. Explain omniscience
6. Explain omnipresence
7. Explain omnipotence
8. How does God dwell in us?
9. Explain God as the one Mind.
10. What is meant by studying Mind back of nature?
11. Are we capable of understanding God?
12. What is our inheritance from God?
13. How are divine ideas brought into manifestation?
14. From what source did Jesus feed the multitude?

15. What idea was back of Jesus' work in healing the sick and raising the dead?
16. How shall we do the works that Jesus did?
17. What and where is the kingdom of heaven?
18. How do we enlarge our concept of God?
19. Why are we not always conscious of our oneness with God?
20. How are we awakened to the knowledge of God?
21. Explain the meaning of the statement, "...in God we live, and move, and have our being...
22. What is "God's will" for us?
23. What is "God's purpose"?
24. How do we come into conscious unity with God?
25. To whom do we refer when we say: "Son of God"; "Son of man"; "son of man"?
26. When and how did you go from a view of God as transcendent to a God as immanent and transcendent?

Lesson Text

> *There is but one Presence and one Power in all the universe: God, the Good, Omnipotent.*

This statement, so famous in the Unity movement, should not be taken as an excuse to call everything God and to call God everything. The one Presence and the one Power refers only to God. God is the only absolute. All else is conditioned and limited. We do not call "things" God. Things formed are not the one Presence and one Power. Only God, the Unconditioned, the Unlimited, the Unformed is the Absolute. As serious students of metaphysical Truth we should have this clarified in our thinking. Otherwise there is the danger of falling into what we call "absolutism," which amounts to exaggerated pantheism. This distorts practical Christianity, which is the outstanding characteristic of the Unity teachings. If one is tempted to think that everything is God and God is everything, it would be good to remember these words spoken by Jesus: "The Father ... is greater than all."[19] If the Father (God) is greater than anything that is, then it is not correct to limit God to things that exist.

God is Not a Person

> *We cannot get a right understanding of the relationship that the manifest bears to the unmanifest until we set clearly before ourselves the character of original Being. So long as we think of God in terms of personality, just so long shall we fail to understand the relation existing between man and God.*[20]

It is very difficult for some to let go of the notion that God is a person. This is understandable. Almost all the words we are accustomed to hearing about God are words we use when we are talking about persons. Even Jesus personified his realization of God by calling Him "Father." But Jesus was not "defining" God when He spoke of the Father. Jesus was naming his feeling of relationship by use of the word Father. He also used the simple word "good" in describing God. Spirit is not a person. Good is not a person. Good is a principle beyond definition. And so it is with God.

---

[19] John 10:29
[20] Fillmore, Charles *The Twelve Powers*, p. 52

Being

> *Being-God the Mind of the universe composed of archetype ideas: life, love, wisdom, substance, Truth, power, peace, and so forth. Being is omnipresent, omnipotent, omniscient; it is the fullness of God, the All-Good.*[21]

Charles Fillmore frequently used the word "Being" as a synonym for the word "God." Fillmore and most of the New Thought teachers and writers were also fond of using divine ideas as synonyms for God. (God is love; God is wisdom, etc.) This practice is quite acceptable, and is part of any good teacher's "poetic license." But we must also keep in mind that in the absolute sense, God is that which is even greater than that which He has created. God created what we call Being. God created all divine ideas, such as love, wisdom, power, etc. But since the essence or omnipresence of God can be seen in these created things, then it is not really wrong to occasionally use them as synonyms for the word God.

Two Aspects of Being

> *Being has two aspects: the invisible and the visible, the abstract and the concrete. The visible comes forth from the invisible, and this coming forth is always according to a universal method of growth from minute generative centers. All forms are built according to this law. From center to circumference is the method of growth throughout the universe.*[22]

---

[21] Fillmore, Charles *The Revealing Word*, Being, p. 22
[22] Fillmore, Charles *Atom-Smashing Power of Mind*, p. 134

Since metaphysics deals mainly with that which is true of the inner life of every human being, then it is not difficult to see that the invisible aspect of being is considered of primary importance. The invisible is the matrix for all that becomes visible, just as silence is the matrix for all sounds that become audible. The invisible is connected directly to the Source of all that comes into existence and the power of our faith should always be in this invisible Source. The visible is legitimate, but it is a product of the Source (invisible). Throughout his writings Charles Fillmore constantly refers to the supremacy of the invisible aspect of Being. Jesus did the same. This is not to imply that the visible aspect of life is not valid or does not exist. Such an attitude is not healthy for abundant living. The visible is merely secondary in priority under the creative law of Spirit.

God as Spirit

> *Spirit is not matter, and Spirit is not person. In order to perceive the essence of Being we must drop from mind the idea that God is circumscribed in any way or has any of the limitations usually ascribed to persons, things, or anything having form or shape.*[23]

This paragraph states, "Spirit is not matter." It also states, "Spirit is not person." So, what is Spirit? It is important that we have some personal comprehension of what is meant, for it is the one and only definition that

---

[23] Fillmore, Charles *Jesus Christ Heals*, p. 29

Jesus gives of God. Jesus said, "For God is Spirit."[24] God is the Presence of a love, an intelligence, and a power that is beyond all defining or explaining. God as Spirit, however, can be acknowledged and experienced.

 God as Principle

> *The fundamental basis and starting point of practical Christianity is that God is Principle. By Principle is meant definite, exact, and unchangeable rules of action. That the word principle is used by materialistic schools of thought to describe what they term the 'blind forces of nature' is no reason why it should convey to our minds the idea of an unloving and unfeeling God. It is used because it best describes the unchanged-able-ness that is an inherent law of Being.*[25]

This paragraph serves a very useful purpose in helping persons who may be troubled over the concept of God as principle. The word principle, as commonly used, denotes an unfeeling set of rigid rules or formulas. However, this is not the meaning when the word is used as an aspect of God. God as principle is not an unfeeling force. The word, principle, as connected with God, pertains to the perfect and unchanging nature of God. God is the principle of Absolute Good. This is quite different from principles of mathematics, chemistry, or pathology. We are a step nearer when we speak of music and art, but that is not quite it. Absolute Good is the only accurate

---

[24] John 4:24
[25] Fillmore, Charles *Jesus Christ Heals*, p. 34

statement, because Absolute Good cannot be defined, and God is always beyond formal definition.

God as Law, Principle in Action

> *The development of man is under law. Creative Mind is not only law, but it is governed by the action of the law that it sets up. We have thought that man was brought forth under the fiat or edict of a great creative Mind that could make or unmake at will, or change its mind and declare a new law at any time; but a clear understanding of ourselves and of the unchangeableness of Divine Mind makes us realize that everything has its foundation in a rule of action, a law that must be observed by both creator and created.*[26]

When we speak of God as law, we must be clear in our thinking (as was the case with God as principle) because we may tend to think of God as law in the sense that we think of man-made laws. This would give a cold and harsh impression of God. Actually, God is not "the Law." God is the creator of laws. These laws serve the purposes of God, which are always good. God's laws are our friends. They work to help us and bless us. The subheading of this paragraph is "Principle in Action." Principle in action is called by Jesus "The Holy Spirit." God's laws work to convert divine ideas into human experiences.

---

[26] Fillmore, Charles *The Twelve Powers*, p. 38

God as Mind

> ...the connecting link between God and man. God-Mind embraces all knowledge, wisdom and understanding and is the source of every manifestation of true knowledge and intelligence. God as principle cannot be comprehended by any of the senses. But the mind of man is limitless, and through it he may come into touch with Divine Mind. <u>The one Mind is a unit and cannot be divided. The individual mind is a state of consciousness in the one Mind.</u>[27]

God as Mind is omnipresent intelligence. Our minds are not Divine Mind, but they are connected to Divine Mind. The Absolute is limitless, and God is the only Absolute. All things that exist have limitations. Our minds are connected with the unlimited Divine Mind, and can receive all knowledge and inspiration from that connection.

God as the Absolute

> *God is substance, not matter, because matter is formed, while God is the formless. God substance lies back of matter and form. It is the basis of all form yet does not enter into any form as a finality. Substance cannot be seen, touched, tasted, or smelled, yet it is more substantial than matter, for it is the only substantiality in the universe. Its*

---

[27] Fillmore, Charles *The Revealing Word*, page 84

> *nature is to 'substand' or 'stand under' or behind matter as its support and only reality."*[28]

God is the creator of substance, it is one of God's divine ideas. Basically substance is, first of all, the divine idea of all possibilities of useful forms. In his paragraph, Fillmore calls it "the basis of all form." Substance is always present. Form is not. Substance cannot be depleted as form can be. Substance cannot be added to or subtracted from. Form can have either done to it. So we see that substance and matter are not the same thing. All divine ideas generate energies which can be appropriated and used by the human mind. Substance is one of these. It is the idea of rightful form. Our minds utilize the energy of this idea in the production of such forms. Consciousness of substance is the surest and most powerful basis for all true prosperity. God is the Source.

God as Love

> *God is the love in everybody and everything. God is love; man becomes loving by permitting that which God is to find expression in word and act. The point to be clearly established is that God exercises none of His attributes except through the inner consciousness of the universe and man.*[29]

God is love, indeed; but God is even more than love. He is the Creator of all love and the eternal Source of all love. For most persons, the most enjoyable of all experiences of the Presence of God is in the form of His

---

[28] Charles Fillmore, *Prosperity*, p. 14
[29] Fillmore, Charles *Jesus Christ Heals*

love for us. "God is love," is a Truth that is being felt more and more strongly in human hearts as evolution proceeds. Religious thinking has reached new heights of spirituality and Truth in our new age. Jesus Christ was the "seed man" of this new age of religious thinking; we are the beneficiaries. God as love is now very, very real.

Chapter 3 - The Divine Paradox

Questions from the Text
1. Give a brief definition for each of the following terms:
    - Grace
    - Principle
    - Personal
    - Immanent
    - Transcendent
    - Father/Mother
    - Law
    - Grace

Questions for Advanced Discussion
1. What, in your experience of spirituality, do you regard as paradoxical?

Lesson Text:
Principle/Personal

> *We shall realize that Being is not only principle so far as its inherent and undeviating laws are concerned, but also personal so far as its relation to each one of us is concerned; that we as individuals do actually become the focus of universal Spirit, of the all-pervading and all-wise Logos, and that through us the universe is formed.*[30]
>
> *God is personal to us when we recognize Him within us as our indwelling life, intelligence, love, and power. There is a difference between a personal God and God personal to us. Since the*

---
[30] Fillmore, Charles *Teach Us to Pray*, p. 169

> *word personal sometimes leads to misunderstanding, it would probably be better to speak of God individualized in man rather than of God personal to man."[31]*

A Paradox is an assertion that seems contradictory or opposed to common sense but is nevertheless true. Paradox is not contradiction nor inconsistency. Paradox is part of the wholeness of God's creation, and we can easily adjust to paradox as well as we adjust to facts. God may be realized as unfailing Principle, and God may be experienced as a warm and loving Presence. This is one example of the divine paradox.

Immanent/Transcendent

> *"God immanent-This refers to the all-pervading and indwelling presence of God, the life and intelligence permeating the universe. Jesus revealed that the Father is within man, forever resident in the invisible side of man's nature."[32]*

> *"Transcendent God-God above or beyond the universe, apart from it. God is more than His universe; He is prior to and is exalted above it, but at once He is in His universe as the very essence of it. God is both transcendent and immanent."[33]*

Omnipresence has to be immanent/transcendent. That is the very meaning of the word. Jesus did say, "The

---

[31] Fillmore, Charles *The Revealing Word*, p. 83
[32] Fillmore, Charles *The Revealing Word*, God, p. 85
[33] Fillmore, Charles *The Revealing Word*, Transcendent God, p. 196

kingdom of God is within you," and many persons jump to the conclusion that Jesus meant that the kingdom of God is only within them. This view tends to overlook the transcendence of God. Only God can be the immanent /transcendent presence. A very important statement is contained within Charles Fillmore's paragraph from *The Revealing Word*: "God is more than the universe."

Father/Mother

> *"In Scripture the primal ideas in the Mind of Being are called the 'sons of God.' That the masculine 'son' is intended to include both masculine and feminine is borne out by the context, and, in fact, the whole history of the humankind. Being itself must be masculine and feminine, in order to make man in its image and likeness, 'male and female'."*[34]

> *"Just as God has been from the beginning so Spirit substance has been from the beginning. This substance is in fact the Mother side of God, the feminine element in God's nature. It is the universal medium in which we plant all ideas of supply and support. Just as the earth is the universal matrix in which all vegetation develops, so this invisible Spirit substance is the universal matrix in which ideas of prosperity germinate and grow and bring forth according to our faith and trust."*[35]

> *"God's love sees you always well, happy, and abundantly provided for; but God's wisdom*

---

[34] Fillmore, Charles *The Twelve Powers* of Man, p. 52
[35] Fillmore, Charles *Teach Us to Pray*, p. 39

> *demands that order and right relation exist in your mind before it may become manifest in your affairs as abundance. God's love would give you your every desire, but God's wisdom ordains that you forgive your debtors before your debts are forgiven."*[36]

The term Father/Mother God is often used in Unity. It is based on very ancient theological insights and metaphysical symbols which had their origin prehistorically. Masculine and feminine are terms which need to be viewed on a level of meaning higher than physical body gender or personality traits. In metaphysical terminology, the masculine principle is the active, energy-generating power. The feminine principle is the more passive aspect—the matrix from which energy can be generated. Both are necessary for existence, for manifestation, and for human evolution. God is the divine Source of the masculine/feminine principles. We relate to that Source, hence we have the beautiful concept of Father/Mother God.

Law/Grace

> *"Law, Divine—Divine law is the orderly working out of the principles of Being, or the divine ideals, into expression and manifestation throughout creation. We, by keeping the law of right thought, work in perfect harmony with divine law, and thus paves his way into spiritual consciousness. Divine law cannot*

---

[36] Fillmore, Charles *Prosperity*, p. 122

be broken. It holds us responsible for the result of our labors."[37]

"The plane of activity for life and strength at a certain stage of man's development is the physical, material plane. During this stage God in God's grace grants to us, when our motive is pure, a degree of immunity from the effects of his ignorant transgression of the divine law.[38]

Grace means good will, favor, disposition to show mercy. Therefore, we do not hold ourselves as bond servants of the law, but as recipients of the grace of God, as sons of the Most High. The grace of God extends to all people, not alone to one sect or creed. All men are equal in favor with God."[39]

"'Grace and truth came through Jesus Christ'[40]*; that is, the real saving, redeeming, transforming power came to man through the work that Jesus did in establishing for the race a new and higher consciousness in the earth. We can enter into this consciousness by faith in Him and by means of the inner spirit of the law that He taught and practiced."*[41]

Jesus taught a new understanding of divine law. He acknowledged mechanical cause and effect, but he knew it was possible to "fulfill the law" by transcending its strictly

---

[37] Fillmore, Charles *The Revealing Word*, Law Divine, p. 118
[38] Fillmore, Charles *Mysteries of Genesis*, p. 138
[39] Fillmore, Charles, *Keep a True Lent*, p. 168
[40] John 1:17
[41] Fillmore, Charles *The Revealing Word*, Grace, p. 89

mechanical repetition. This can be done only by certain changes of consciousness. One of these changes is to let go of the insistence of "even-exchanges" in life all the time. Another change is to be willing to forgive sin instead of insisting on punishment for sin. Grace is the name given to the aspect of divine law which does not deal in "even-exchanging," but in the increase of good through greater giving.

Chapter 4 - The Trinity

Questions from the Text
2. Give a brief description of Metaphysical Trinity.
3. Where, in the Bible, is the Trinity found?
4. What is first in the Metaphysical Trinity?
5. What is second in the Metaphysical Trinity?
6. What is Third in the Metaphysical Trinity?
7. What is the Spirit of Truth?

Questions for Advanced Discussion
1. Give both the religious and the metaphysical terms for the Holy Trinity.
2. Explain how mind, idea, and expression are in all that appears (manifestation).
3. Briefly explain how understanding the metaphysical meaning of the Trinity of God helps you in daily life.
4. What is the meaning of the word "Logos"?

Lesson Text
Metaphysical Trinity

> "The Holy Trinity is known as the Father, the Son, and the Holy Spirit. Metaphysically, we understand the Trinity to refer to mind, idea, and expression, or thinker, thought, and action."[42]

> "All people who have studied metaphysics and understand somewhat the action of the mind recognize that there is one underlying law and that through this law all things come into expression; also that there is one universal Mind, the source

---
[42] Fillmore, Charles *Keep a True Lent*, p. 14

and sole origin of all real intelligence. First is mind, then mind expresses itself in ideas, then the ideas make themselves manifest. This is a metaphysical statement of the Divine Trinity, Father, Son, and Holy Spirit. The Trinity Mind, the expression of Mind, and the manifestations of Mind are found in simple numbers and complex combinations everywhere."[43]

The framework of the Trinity is basic to metaphysical thinking, since it is symbolic of the process wherein manifestation is produced from the invisible energies of divine ideas. In Unity, most emphasis is given to this metaphysical framework of mind, idea, and expression. The theological meaning of the Trinity (Father, Son, and Holy Spirit) is perhaps more complicated, and it is on this approach to the meaning of the Trinity that there exists differences of interpretation.

Scripture Symbols vs. Metaphysical Terms

"The metaphysics of the Hebrew Scriptures are based on this law of the Trinity. They were written far ahead of the collective thoughts, and it is probable that those who wrote them did not understand all that was involved in the word of the Spirit."[44]

"Here are the Scripture symbols compared with modern metaphysical terms: [45]

---

[43] Fillmore, Charles *Jesus Christ Heals*, p. 121
[44] Fillmore, Charles *Jesus Christ Heals*, p. 122
[45] Fillmore, Charles *Jesus Christ Heals*, p. 64

God	Christ	Humankind
Mind	Idea	Expression
Father	Son	Holy Spirit
Thinker	Thought	Action
Spirit	Soul	Body

These two excerpts are good examples of Charles Fillmore's thoughts about the Trinity in both scriptural[46] and metaphysical terms. In some of his other writings he reveals a recognition of the Trinity also in the manifest-physical level of life. In *The Twelve Powers of Man* he writes: "Three primal forces of Being are manifest in the simplest protoplasmic cell ... every atom has substance, life, and intelligence."[47]

Three in One

> *God is the name of the all-encompassing Mind. Christ is the name of the all-loving Mind. Holy Spirit is the all-active manifestation. These three are one fundamental Mind in its three creative aspects.*[48]
>
> *Reducing the Trinity to simple numbers takes away much of its mystery. When we say that there is One Being with three attitudes of mind, we have stated*

---

[46] The doctrine of the Trinity does not appear in the Bible nor did Jesus and his followers intend to contradict the Shema in the Hebrew Scriptures: 'Hear, O Israel: The Lord our God is one Lord' (Deut. 6:4).... The doctrine developed gradually over several centuries and through many controversies.... By the end of the fourth century the doctrine of the Trinity took substantially the form it has maintained ever since in some forms of Christianity. The controversy, indeed, was settled by church councils.
[47] Fillmore, Charles *The Twelve Powers* of Man, p. 54
[48] Fillmore, Charles *Jesus Christ Heals*, p. 63

> *in plain terms all that is involved in the intricate theological doctrine of the Trinity.*[49]

Charles Fillmore refers to overcoming the "mystery" of both the idea of the Trinity and of the "intricate theological doctrine of the trinity." This indicates that he felt the desirability of a more simple and logical approach to this subject. Perhaps the most practical value of understanding the Trinity is simply that it involves all the orderly energy sequences which result in desirable manifestations.

First in the Trinity

> *God is first in the Trinity. God is mind and is everywhere present. God is principle, law, Being, Spirit, All Good, omnipresent, omniscient, omnipotent, unchangeable, Creator, Father, cause, and source of all that is. God as Spirit is forever accessible.*[50]

God as first in the Trinity can be viewed as the Absolute. God as first in the Trinity is totally positive, the ultimate of positive energy expression, what we call absolute good!

Second in the Trinity

> *Second in the Trinity is God's idea of man. It is called Jehovah in the Hebrew Scriptures and Christ in the Christian Scriptures. The second in the Trinity*

---

[49] Fillmore, Charles *Christian Healing*, p. 20
[50] Fillmore, Charles *Keep a True Lent*

> is also called the Word, the Son, the Logos, the anointed One, and the I AM.[51]
>
> Logos—The Word of God; the divine archetype idea that contains all ideas: The Christ, the Son of God, spiritual man in manifestation.[52]
>
> The Christ is God's divine idea of man, the embodiment of all divine ideas existing in the mind of Being.[53]
>
> You are linked with the universal spiritual mind through the Christ Mind. It is through the Christ Mind that all things come to you; it is the channel to the All-Mind of the Father.[54]

This section can sometimes seem confusing since Charles Fillmore uses several terms synonymously. Perhaps the clearest definition is in the third paragraph of this section when he writes: "Christ is God's divine idea of man, the embodiment of all divine ideas existing in the mind of Being."

Third in the Trinity

> The work of the Holy Spirit is the executive power of Father (mind) and Son (idea) carrying out the creative plan. It is through the help of the Holy Spirit that man overcomes. The Holy Spirit reveals,

---

[51] Fillmore, Charles, *Keep a True Lent*, p. 15
[52] Fillmore, Charles *The Revealing Word*, Logos, p. 123
[53] Fillmore, Charles *Keep a True Lent*, p. 10
[54] Fillmore, Charles, *Prosperity*, p. 75

> helps, and directs in this overcoming. 'The Spirit searches all things, yea, the deep things of God.' It finally leads man into the light.[55]
>
> Do not be misled by the personality of the Holy Spirit and the reference to it as 'he'... The Holy Spirit is the love of Jehovah taking care of the human family, and love is always feminine. Love is the great harmonizer and healer, and whoever calls upon God as Holy Spirit is calling upon the divine love.[56]

The Spirit of Truth

> The Spirit of Truth is God thought projecting into our minds ideas that will build a spiritual consciousness like that of Jesus. The Spirit of Truth watches every detail of our lives, and when we ask and by affirmation proclaim its presence, it brings new life into our bodies.[57]

The Spirit of Truth is a spiritual concept very similar to the Holy Spirit. But the Spirit of Truth has more to do with knowledge and understanding, rather than just good in general as is the case with the Holy Spirit. "The Spirit of Truth" is a term originating with Jesus. He designates this Spirit to be the actual conveyor of divine ideas into the level of our current ability to understand. Jesus makes the Spirit of Truth a very personal thing for each person who believes and accepts that Spirit. The Spirit of Truth is

---

[55] Fillmore, Charles, *Atom-Smashing Power of Mind*
[56] Fillmore, Charles, *Jesus Christ Heals*, p. 183
[57] Fillmore, Charles *Jesus Christ Heals*, p. 180

involved in all healing but its primary function is the development of spiritual knowledge and understanding of Truth principles.

The Key to Understanding the Trinity

> *"If you would know the mystery of Being, see yourself in Being. Know yourself as an integral idea in Divine Mind, and all other ideas will recognize you as their fellow worker. Throw yourself out of the Trinity, and you become an onlooker. Throw yourself into the Holy Trinity, and you become its avenue of expression.*[58]

What is said in this paragraph is true of all Truth teachings. You must not think of yourself as one thing and Truth as another thing. You are that truth, and that truth is you! Metaphysical teachings have no real meaning or purpose unless a human being is involved. There is no virtue without a human being involved. There is no sin or evil without a human being involved. There is no healing, no prosperity, and no happiness without human beings involved in either negating them or experiencing and sharing them.

---

[58] Fillmore, Charles *Christian Healing*, p. 20

Chapter 5 - The Problem of Evil

Questions from the Text
1. If God is the only power in the universe, and it is Absolute Good, then where does the appearance of evil come from?
2. Define the following:
- Absolute Evil
- Relative Evil
- Sin
- The Devil

Lesson Text:
Definition of Evil

> *Evil—that which is not of God; unreality; error thought; a product of the fallen human consciousness; negation. Evil is a parasite. It has no permanent life of itself; its whole existence depends on the life it borrows from its parent, and when its connection with the parent is severed nothing remains. In divine Mind there is no recognition of evil conditions. Such conditions have no basis of reality. They are conjurations of a false consciousness. Apparent evil is the result of ignorance and when Truth is presented the error disappears.*[59]

After we have learned something about what sin and evil are not, let us try to formulate some idea as to what those words might be referring to. First of all, they

---
[59] Fillmore, Charles, *The Revealing Word*, Evil, p. 64

have to be connected with a human being and human behavior. Secondly, they have to refer to something wrong, something that is not correct. Since these words are used mostly in a religious sense, they would have to refer to something that is against spiritual Truth or divine ideas. On this basis, the metaphysical meaning of the words sin and evil become quite clear. Sin and evil are the words we use to refer to any human attempt to negate any divine ideas.

Evil, Absolute vs Relative

> *God knows that there is a great negative, which is a reflection of His positive, but He is not conscious of its existence. We know that there is an underworld of evil, in which all the rules of civilization are broken, but we are not conscious of that world because we do not enter into it. It is one thing to view error as a thing apart from us, and quite another to enter into consciousness of it.*[60]

The opening sentence of this paragraph presents the reader with a very challenging paradox. Charles Fillmore first states "God knows that there is a great negative. . ." Then, in the same sentence, "(God) is not conscious of its existence." The big question is: How can we say that God knows something and then say God is not conscious of that same thing? Unity teaches that God is Omniscience, which means all-knowing. All consciousness is contained within Omniscience. So we cannot say that any sort of knowledge can be lacking in God's consciousness. Another way of stating the idea Charles

---

[60] Fillmore, Charles *The Twelve Powers*, p. 42

Fillmore had in mind might be thus: God knows of the existence of the negative, but God does not react in any way. God remains the absolute good, the one presence and power. God is in no way affected or influenced by the existing negativity manifested through us.

Origin of Evil

> *By and through the imaging power of thought, we can produce illusions that confuse him. This occurs only when he fails to look to Divine Mind for the source and nature of his ideals. Obviously, many are deceived into thinking that they are indeed bound, and the unhappy conditions claimed do show forth in them. This is only consciousness entangled in its own effects.*[61]

There can be no question that the origin of what we perceive as evil is in human nature itself. As long as we identify with negative emotions by connecting our sense of I Am to them, our minds will be attempting to negate divine ideas. There are countless reasons why many continue to do this, and as long as anyone is doing it, sin happens and evil continues to exist. The level of human consciousness where most negating of divine ideas is attempted is the level generally designated as "false personality." This is the area of lies and illusions within human nature where most of our negative identifying occurs. In Bible symbolism this is called Satan, the devil, the adversary, the tempter, demons, evil spirits, etc.

---

[61] Fillmore, Charles *Keep a True Lent*, pp. 63-64

Free Will and Evil

> *It is possible for man to form states of consciousness that are out of harmony with the God principle, but these do not endure, and through experience man learns to adjust his thought to that of God… God is free to do as He wills, and He has implanted that same freedom in man. When we understand this ego-forming capacity of man and even of nature, we have the key that unlocks the many mysteries and contradictions that appear in every walk of life.*[62]

Misuse of freedom of thought, belief, and will are the mainsprings of our continued sojourns into evil and useless, unnecessary suffering (hell). Freedom of choice in how to think, what to believe, and how to react gives us a unique place in the universe. We generate our own heaven or hell. We may continue to blame God for creating heaven and hell, but God has only given us the resources and the freedom to use those resources in any manner we choose.

Separation from God

> *We came out of God, are of the same mind elements, and exist within the mind of God always. Yet by thinking that we are separate from omnipresent Spirit we set up a mental state of apartness from our source and we dwell in ignorance of that which is nearer to us than hands and feet. A few moments of thought daily directed*

---

[62] Fillmore, Charles *Atom-Smashing Power of Mind*, p. 18

> *toward God in acknowledgement of God's presence will convince anyone that there is an intelligence always within us that responds to our thought when we direct our attention to it."[63]*

A sense of separation from God is the result of sin, not the sin itself. Numerous things may have caused this, but, whatever the cause, it can be corrected. Forgiveness of sin (any sin, whatever sin, no matter who, what, why, when, or where) is essential. Forgiveness of sin will restore the sense of unity with God.

Sin

> *Sin—Missing the mark; that is, falling short of divine perfection. Sin is man's failure to express the attributes of Being — life, love, intelligence, wisdom, and the other God qualities.[64]*

> *Transgression of the law brings its own punishment. We are not punished for our sins but by them.[65]*

The Bible word for sin ("amartia" in Greek) means literally to "miss the mark." In the Hebrew Scriptures, the corresponding Hebrew word is "net." It is the same word that an archer would have used if he missed the target. While this may seem like a surprisingly benign meaning, it does accurately describe the condition brought about (lack of perfection). For a metaphysical definition of the word

---

[63] Fillmore, Charles, *Teach Us to Pray*
[64] Fillmore, Charles, *The Revealing Word*, Sin, p. 179
[65] Fillmore, Charles *Keep a True Lent*, p. 32

"sin," however, we need to relate the term to human consciousness. Thus, metaphysically, sin is the word we use that refers to any human attempt (conscious or unconscious) to negate or distort divine ideas.

Sins of Commission and Omission

> *All the ills of humanity are the effect of broken law, of sin. That word 'sin' covers more ground than we have usually granted it. There are sins of omission and commission. If we fail to cultivate the consciousness of the indwelling spiritual life, we commit a sin of omission that eventually devitalizes the organism.*[66]

Omission and commission are two methods we use in our attempts to negate divine ideas. We can try to ignore them, refuse to learn about them, withhold our belief from them, are unwilling to experience them; or, we may even try to pervert them into harm-causing expressions. We may try to use divine ideas to satisfy selfishness, cruelty, or any negative impulses that arise from false personality. Sin is different from mistake if the mistake was a result of pure ignorance. We designate sin as an attempt to negate divine ideas.

The Devil[67]

> *Devil—The mass of thoughts that has been built up in collective consciousness through many generations of earthly experience and crystallized*

---

[66] Fillmore, Charles *Jesus Christ Heals*, p. 17
[67] See the footnote with a definition of Satan in chapter 23

into what may be termed human personality, or carnal mind, which opposes and rejects God. The 'devil' is a state of consciousness adverse to the divine good. . . There is no personal devil. God is the one omnipresent Principle of the universe, and there" is no room for any principle of evil, personified or otherwise.[68]

Some metaphysical schools warn their students against the development of power, because they fear that it will be used in selfish, ambitious ways. It doubtless is true that the personal ego sometimes lays hold of the power faculty and uses it for selfish aggrandizement; we can readily see how what is called the devil had its origin.[69]

The devil as a literal personification of evil is totally rejected in the Unity metaphysical theology. Yet the devil is a metaphysical symbol which cannot be ignored. It exists. It causes harm. But it is also something which can be dealt with in a manner which prevents further harm. All this is beautifully symbolized in the Gospel accounts involving Jesus and the devil. The devil is a personified symbol of a human tendency — the tendency toward negativity. There seems to be a trace of this in everybody, more strongly active in some than in others, but it is a collective phenomenon and it is strictly a human consciousness phenomenon which has no existence in pure spiritual principle.

---

[68] Fillmore, Charles *The Revealing Word*, Devil, p. 54
[69] Fillmore, Charles, *The Twelve Powers* of Man, p. 66

The Key to Understanding Evil

> In metaphysics the beginning students insist upon having evil explained to them — how it originated, and why it has place in existence — when good is the origin of all that is. They worry and they play their thoughts upon this question until in sheer desperation they, as a rule, give it up. The tangle of a good God and a bad devil will not straighten itself out from their plane of perception. The trouble is that they do not know enough about the good. . . To know about evil we must first become thoroughly familiar with good."[70]

Our purpose is to understand Truth — to learn to accept, believe in, and become willing toward God's divine ideas. In the gaining of such understanding mastery of existence is gained, including mastery of those existential factors called sin and evil.

Reconciliation of Good and Evil

> *When one understands the creative processes to be the working of the various principles of Being in our development, many inexplicable situations are cleared up. God cannot bring forth without law and order. To produce a man, there must be a combination of forces that at some stages of soul evolution may seem to work against one another; but when one understands that the great creative Mind brings forth under law, reconciliation and*

---

[70] Fillmore, Charles *Prosperity*, p. 39

consistency are found where inharmony and contradiction seemed dominant.[71]

Charles Fillmore often speaks of a combination of forces in his teachings which are based on the Trinity. Through understanding this principle, forces which appear contradictory are creatively reconciled, and a higher synthesis emerges. Resistance or opposition makes effort necessary in life. It can come in many forms and we often label these forms "bad," "evil," "the devil," etc. Jesus named it "the adversary." When we understand the character of, and necessity for, this "combination of forces," we are able to make room in our attitudes for their existence. We do not need to get negative or violent.

We learn how to agree with "the adversary," (nonresistance). This is followed by the manifestation of new blessings, answered prayer, and further opportunities. It's important to remember that the apparent opposition force itself is not evil or sinful. It is only our wrong interpretation of it, our negativity about it, and our attempt to misuse it that causes the harm and suffering brought about by such "sin."

---

[71] Fillmore, Charles *The Twelve Powers*, p. 54-55

Chapter 6 - The Kingdom of God

Questions from the Text
1. What and where is the kingdom of heaven?
2. What is the definition of the following:
   - Fourth Dimension
   - God's Will
3. How do we attain the kingdom?

Questions for Advanced Discussion
1. What and where is heaven?

Lesson Text
Planes of Life

> There are many planes of life, one above or below another, yet not conflicting. All creation is based on life activity, or as it is called in physical science, rates of vibration. A certain activity in the life current forms worlds on a plane, which we may call the physical; a little increase in the vibratory rate makes another system, which we may designate as the psychical; a still higher rate makes a universe where spiritual ideas prevail. These are all interlaced and interblended in the presence around and within us, hence the 'Kingdom of God is within you,'[72], or 'among you', as one translator gives it.[73]

---

[72] Luke 17:21
[73] Fillmore, Charles *The Revealing Word*, Planes, p. 150

> *"'The Kingdom of God is within you.' The pivotal point around which Spirit creates is within the structure of consciousness.*[74]

These paragraphs are especially helpful in clarifying the confusion which sometimes occurs when people believe that because God is the one Presence and one Power, because God is Omnipresent, and because God is our Creator, everything in existence is one in the sense of all being on the same scale. This is not metaphysically correct. True, there is the essence of oneness which binds, blends, and harmonizes all things. But there is the fact of differences in scale, different planes, and different vibratory rates. These differences are what require recognition of polarity and scale of being. To overlook this is to call everything the same in all respects, which is not practical Christianity. The only thing we know of which is able to cope with the paradox of the oneness of God's creation and all of being with the polarity and diversity of planes of existence is consciousness. In our existential universe consciousness is the key that unlocks all the mysteries of paradox.

Fourth Dimension

> *All persons in rare moments catch glimpses of this creative plan as a whole, and of man's importance in its beauty and perfection. But this subject is so deep and so far-reaching that it can be realized in small degree only by those who have developed*

---

[74] Fillmore, Charles *Jesus Christ Heals*, p. 76

> *spiritual sight and feeling, and practice thinking in the fourth dimension.*[75]

One of the problems connected with thinking about the fourth dimension is that some persons tend to think of the fourth dimension as the Absolute. It is not the Absolute, but only a dimension which transcends most of the current limitations of three-dimensional existence. The Absolute is not any dimension.

Recognition of the Kingdom

> *It is not a question of geographical locality but of mental recognition. Seeking the Kingdom of God within changes our whole mental viewpoint. We find ourselves right in the presence of creative Mind, and seeking to co-operate with this Mind, we receive spiritual inspiration and are guided in even the minutest details of life.*[76]

It is wonderful and exhilarating thought that the Kingdom of God is within us. The Kingdom of God is a term used by Jesus which has the same meaning as Omnipresence. As far as an individual human being is concerned the very heart of Omnipresence is within our own being. Since God is beyond all dimensions and all limitations of space and time, it is correct to say that the very center of Omnipresence is wherever any person becomes centered in that Presence. A person can only become centered in self. Hence, Jesus states, "For lo, the Kingdom of God is within you." We may take Charles

---

[75] Fillmore, Charles *Atom-Smashing Power of Mind*, p. 62
[76] Fillmore, Charles *Teach Us to Pray*, p. 87

Fillmore's words quite seriously when he tells us that "Seeking the Kingdom of God within changes our whole mental viewpoint." It is vital to believe this and understand its implications. A person's mental viewpoint before seeking the inner Kingdom might be mediocre, or even lacking. But by making the sincere effort to center oneself in Omnipresence wonderful changes of consciousness will occur. These good inner changes will find ways to manifest into the outer, beginning with the health of the body, and then into the many affairs of daily existence.

Externalization of the Kingdom of God

> *This is no fanciful sketch, nor does it refer to a theoretical place or condition to be reached in some future state or under circumstances more propitious. This kingdom of God is now existing right here in our midst. It is being externalized little by little.*[77]

The externalization of the Kingdom of God is one aspect of our purpose on earth. In order to do this, we must learn how to grow in dominion and mastery of existence. We cannot demonstrate the Kingdom of God if we have not first learned to be useful and dependable in the down-to-earth business of ordinary existence. Charles Fillmore correctly states that the externalizing of God's Kingdom is being accomplished "little by little." This is true, and we must learn to reconcile ourselves to this fact. Otherwise we become impatient and seek shortcuts and artificial methods.

---
[77] Fillmore, Charles *Jesus Christ Heals*, p. 115

The Kingdom of Heaven

> *Heaven is everywhere present. It is the orderly, lawful adjustment of God's kingdom in man's mind, body, and affairs; it is the Christ consciousness, the realm of divine ideas, a state of consciousness in harmony with the thoughts of God. Heaven is within every one of us; a place, a conscious sphere of mind, having all the attractions described or imagined as belonging to heaven.*[78]

Metaphysically, the Kingdom of God and the kingdom of heaven are not exactly the same things. The Kingdom of God is the Absolute. It is Omnipresent, Limitless, Changeless, and Pure Being. The kingdom of heaven is relative to us. It encompasses the very highest levels of our being. Also, it is a process within us. It is our growing and unfolding consciousness of Truth and oneness with God. It is within, but it is in different stages of realization for each person and not a fixed absolute, as is the Kingdom of God. In Unity, there is a tendency is to speak of both kingdoms without any distinction of meaning. This usually causes no problems, for they are so closely interrelated that it seems unnecessary to separate them.

Science and Religion

> *The kingdom of the heavens, the new dimension of mind and energy that is being unfolded today in the spiritual ethers by the discoveries of the scientists, should not be divorced from the kingdom of heaven*

---

[78] Fillmore Charles *Keep a True Lent*, p. 177

> *taught in parables because His listeners were not trained in science.[79]*

Charles Fillmore was a strong advocate for the validity of both religion and science, and the connection between the two is becoming more and more apparent. True metaphysical revelation always precedes the development of greater technology in science, medicine, and the arts. Greater technology is a furthering of the process of manifestation, which always begins in consciousness. But all are under the same system of principles and laws that are spiritual in origin, character, and purpose. Religion and science already are one, but our consciousness still needs to become more correctly aware of why and how.

Kingdom of Heaven on Earth

> *The real of the universe is held in the mind of Being as ideas of life, love, substance, intelligence, Truth, and so forth. These ideas may be combined in a multitude of ways, producing infinite variety in the realm of forms. There is a right combination, which constitutes the divine order, the kingdom of heaven on earth. This right relation of ideas and the science of right thought is practical Christianity.[80]*

Divine ideas constitute the kingdom of heaven. But they are formless and intangible as long as they remain just ideas in the higher levels of being. As our minds appropriate these divine ideas, we give them form and

---

[79] Fillmore, Charles *Atom-Smashing Power of Mind*, p. 58
[80] Fillmore, Charles *Christian Healing*, p. 14

location in time and space. Under the law of mind action these ideas are able to penetrate the realm where they take on form and character. They are able to express their energies "after their kind," and they also are able to transform their energies directly into us as our own experience!

God's Will

> *God-Mind expresses its thoughts so perfectly that there is no occasion for change, hence all prayers and supplications for the change of God's will to conform to human desires are futile. God does not change God's mind, or trim God's thought, to meet the conflicting opinions of humankind. Understanding the perfection of God thoughts, we must conform to them; so conforming, we will discover that there is never necessity for any change of the will of God in regard to human affairs.*[81]

God is the only Absolute Good. Can we even begin to get an inkling of what Absolute Good means? We innately know that it is the ultimate Truth about God. Do any of us really want Absolute Good to ever change? Of course not. Nor do we really want the will of Absolute Good to be altered or modified, even if we temporarily want things to go a certain way. When we recall the many times Jesus speaks of God's will we find that it is always in regard to something good, good even beyond any personal expectations.

---

[81] Ibid, p. 18

The Divine Plan

> *In order to get at the very heart of Being, it is necessary to realize that it is manifesting in the least as well as in the greatest, and that, in the bringing forth of a universe, not one idea could be taken away without unbalancing the whole. This brings us to fuller realization of our importance in the universe and to the necessity of finding our right place."*[82]

It causes a good feeling in a human soul when one realizes that we are all part of a divine plan. The very fact that we have been created means that we are necessary, somehow, even if we cannot as yet begin to see how. What is God's divine plan? We can perceive certain aspects of it and certain details within it but, as to the plan itself, we are just beginning to awaken to the fact that there is such a thing. The divine plan is not the same thing as predestination, because in God's plan there is always the divine idea of freedom. This means freedom of choice. This keeps the divine plan creative and organic. It is not a fixed, static "thing." Does the plan ever change? Not really. But numerous changes constantly take place within the plan. That's what keeps our participation in the plan exciting and beautiful.

Attaining the Kingdom

> *We adjust our thought world to the kingdom of divine ideas through a process of denial by which we eliminate from consciousness all inharmonious*

---
[82] Ibid, p. 11

ideas, and through affirmations of truth by which we establish self in harmony with divine ideas... The kingdom of heaven is attained, first, by one's establishing in one's mind the consciousness of the truth of Being; second, by one's adjusting one's outer life to Truth."[83]

The one way in which we will surely attain our right place in God's kingdom is by conditioning our consciousness continuously. Charles Fillmore believed and taught that the most effective way to do this is through correct expression of the powers of denial and affirmation. The formula is simple: You deny correctly by letting go of anything in consciousness which seeks to negate any divine ideas. You affirm correctly by stating your belief and willingness toward any divine ideas.

---

[83] *Metaphysical Bible Dictionary*, Kingdom of Heaven, p. 387

Chapter 7 – The Creative Process

Questions from the Text
1. How does God create?
2. Define the following words:
   - Evolution
   - Involution
3. What is the Law of Cause and Effect? How does it apply to your life?
4. What are the seven steps of creation?
5. Is creation finished? Explain.

Questions for Advanced Discussion
1. From what source did the idea-man spring? What other names are given to this idea?
2. What is meant by the term "the first-born of all creation"?[84]
3. What is a thought center?
4. How are thought centers formed?

Lesson Text
How God Creates

> *God is Spirit. In creation Spirit takes the form of mind, implanting itself in substance and becoming manifest as perfect man. Here is condensed in a few words what would take volumes to describe. Here are epitomized all books on physiology and evolution, mental science and psychology, religion and spiritual philosophy.*[85]

---
[84] Colossians 1:15
[85] Fillmore, Charles *Teach Us to Pray*, p. 67

How does God create? In the book of Genesis the method is symbolically set forth: "And God said, Let there be ... and there was ..." When this is taken literally it only leads to arguments between "creationists" and "evolutionists," but when understood metaphysically it contains much logic. Among other things, the Absolute (God) is the Creative Principle, Power, and Intelligence. The creation allegory depicts the Creative Principle expressing its power and intelligence as "Let there be." This is the Logos, the Word of God, and is fulfilled in God's spiritual creation. God has created wholeness, and wholeness has its components which relate to God's plan for THIS universe. Those components are called divine ideas.

Involution

> *Read in the light of Spirit, the first chapter of Genesis is a description, in symbol, of the creative action of universal Mind in the realm of ideas. It does not pertain to the manifest universe any more than the history of the inventor's idea pertains to the machine that he builds to manifest the idea. First the problem is thought out, and afterward the structure is produced. So God builds His universe.*[86]

The idea that involution precedes evolution must be approached "... in the light of Spirit ..." as Mr. Fillmore has stated in his opening sentence. We do not evolve into something that has no existence before we attain it. It exists prior to our attainment of it, although as a potential

---

[86] Fillmore, Charles *Christian Healing*, p. 31

or as an ideal. The ideal is what God has already created. The attainment of those ideals is what evolution is all about. Charles Fillmore states, "So God builds His universe." The work of building is done through us.

Evolution

> There can be no logical doubt that an all-wise and all-powerful Creator would plan perfection for His creations and also endow them with the ability to bring His plan into manifestation. That is the status of the world and its people. We are God's ideal conception of His perfect man, and He has given us the power of thought and word through which to make that ideal manifest.[87]

> Involution always precedes evolution. That which is involved in mind evolves through matter.[88]

> Evolution is the result of the development of ideas in mind. What we are is the result of the evolution of our consciousness, and that consciousness is the result of seed ideas sown in our mind.[89]

    Evolutionary theories have usually focused on such things as evolution of species, or physical body forms, the survival of the fittest and the selectivity of natural laws. These are true only of life forms below the level of ours. Our evolution is not a mechanical "happening." It is the result of individual and collective efforts. The pattern

---

[87] Fillmore, Charles *Jesus Christ Heals*, p. 16
[88] Fillmore, Charles *The Twelve Powers*
[89] Ibid, p. 39

being followed is a spiritual one. The energy required comes from sources other than nature. There is no fixed or static goal. The goal itself has an open door. The signs of success are not limited to higher physical forms, but are directed toward greater freedom from the limitations of physicality. As in all things that pertain to our highest good, divine ideas are the true keys to our evolution.

The Trinity in Creation

> *"God is the origin of all, and from Him, in orderly steps through His perfect idea (Son) and His wise builder (Holy Spirit) all creation proceeds. The Son (man) looks to the Father for all instruction, and the Father responds to the Son's demands by sending forth the Holy Spirit equipped with the wisdom and power necessary to perform the work.[90]*
>
> *Three primal forces of Being are manifest in the simplest protoplasmic cell. Every atom has substance, life, and intelligence. This corresponds with the symbolical creative process of Jehovah, as described in Gen. 2:7. The "dust of the ground" is substance; "breathed" refers to the impartation of intelligence; and the "living soul" is the quickening life. These three constitute the trinity of the natural world, in which the body of man is cast.[91]*
>
> *God is law and God is changeless. If we would bring forth the perfect creation, we must conform to law and unfold in our mind, body, and affairs as a*

---

[90] Fillmore, Charles *Talks on Truth*, p. 70
[91] Fillmore, Charles *The Twelve Powers* of Man, p. 54

> *flower unfolds by the principle of innate life, intelligence, and substance.*[92]

Here we have another interpretation of the Trinity. This concept may appear to be repetitious but the more a person contemplates its many aspects, the more this framework begins to emerge as something clear and important.

Law of Cause and Effect

> *There are no accidents in the laws of Being. 'Whatsoever a man sows, that shall he also reap'*[93] *is another way of saying that for every cause there is an adequate effect. This law of sequence is like all other laws that inhere in Being, it is good.*[94]

There are many aspects to the law of cause and effect, some much higher and finer than others. When Charles Fillmore states "there are no accidents in the laws of Being", he is stating a principle that is true in the absolute. On the relative plane of existence, however, there is a valid meaning for the word "accident." It does not mean something that happens without a cause. It means something that has happened that was either unforeseen, or unnecessary, or caused by a mistake. Would one then say that there are no "mistakes?" Again, that is correct only in the absolute. On the relative plane of existence mistakes are happening all the time. Mistakes need correcting, just as accidents need preventing.

---

[92] Fillmore, Charles *Prosperity*, p. 58
[93] Galatians 6:7
[94] Fillmore, Charles *Talks on Truth*, p. 78

Certainly we are now talking of something that is only relevant on a narrow and limited plane of existence, but these are factors we need to deal with. Although they are not problems for the absolute, the absolute gives itself to us in the form of all needed help. "God is our help in every need."

Two Creation Stories

> *Only through perception of the mental law by which ideas manifest from the formless to the formed can we understand and reconcile these two apparently contradictory chapters.[95] In the light of true understanding everything is made plain, and we discern just how Divine Mind is creating man and the universe: First the ideal concept, then the manifestation.[96]*

Only the first chapter of Genesis is about the original divine creation. This is God's creation of wholeness. Its components are all God's divine ideas that pertain to us. It is finished, whole, and total. The second story is an allegory of something which proceeds within creation. It is the forming of individuality. It is about the beginning of each person as a living individual soul, endowed with great creative possibilities. It depicts the turning point in us from involution (existence in Eden) to evolution (emerging into the world). Our role in creation is to bring forth, to produce, and cause manifestation, and to grow in consciousness.

---

[95] Genesis 1 and 2
[96] Fillmore, Charles *Christian Healing*, p. 32

Stages of Creation

> *The key to the operation of mind is symbolically set forth in the Genesis account of the six days of creation. Our mind goes through the identical steps in bringing an idea into manifestation. Between the perception of an idea and its manifestation there are six definite, positive movements, followed by a seventh 'day' of rest, in which the mind relaxes and sees its work in a process of fulfillment.[97]*

> *In the first chapter of Genesis it is the great creative Mind that is at work. The record portrays just how divine ideas were brought forth into expression. As we must have an idea before we can bring an idea into manifestation, so it is with the creations of God. When we build a house we build it first in our mind. We have the idea of a house, we complete the plan in our mind, and then we work it out in manifestation.[98]*

Charles Fillmore sees a distinct analogy between the symbolisms in the first chapter of Genesis as it pertains to God and creation and to us and manifestation. This can be comprehended only when we view the Creation story in Genesis as an allegory. In the Bible, numbers have symbolic meanings. Seven is the symbol of completion in the manifest realm. The seventh day (Sabbath) symbolizes a period of rest from externally directed attention and effort.

---

[97] Fillmore, Charles *Prosperity*, p. 83
[98] Fillmore, Charles *Mysteries of Genesis*, p. 12

First Step: Light

> In bringing forth a manifestation of God's abundant supply, take the first step by saying, 'Let there be light;' that is, let there be understanding. You must have a clear perception of the principle back of the proposition 'Go d will provide.' The one universal, eternal, substance of God, which is the source of all, must be discerned and relied on, while dependence on material things must be eliminated from thought... If you have established that light, you have begun your demonstration and can go to the second step.[99]
>
> Light is intelligence, a spiritual quality. It corresponds to understanding and should precede all activity. At the beginning of any of our creating we should declare light.[100]

"Let there be light" is an affirmation of illumination. Light is a symbol with many meanings in our Bible, the most important of which is intelligent awareness. In the Silent Unity prayer ministry, the prayer for illumination is always spoken first. Charles and Myrtle instituted this practice from the very beginning and it has been maintained to this present day. Charles Fillmore often stated that the prayer for illumination is the one most quickly and surely answered.

---

[99] Fillmore, Charles *Prosperity*, p. 83
[100] Fillmore, Charles *Mysteries of Genesis*, p. 16

Second Step: Faith

> *The second step in creation is the development of faith or the firmament.*[101]

> *A 'firmament' must be established; that is, a firm place in the mind, a dividing of the true from the apparent. This is done through affirmation. As you affirm God as your supply and support, your words will in due season become substance to you.*[102]

Faith is our supreme affirmative faculty. It is interesting to note that the first Bible symbol for faith is "a firmament" and to notice the similarity between the words "affirmation" and "a firmament."

Third Step: Imagination

> *The third step is the forming of this substance into tangibility. 'Let the dry land appear.' Out of the omnipresent substance your mind forms whatever it wants by the power of imagination... If you have already taken the other steps, you can picture in mind the things you desire and bring them into your manifest world.*[103]

> *The first day's creation reveals the light or inspiration of Spirit. The second day establishes faith in our possibilities to bring forth the invisible. The third day's creation or third movement of*

---

[101] Fillmore, Charles *Mysteries of Genesis*, p. 16
[102] Fillmore, Charles *Prosperity*, p. 83
[103] Fillmore, Charles *Prosperity*, p. 84

> *Divine Mind pictures the activity of ideas in mind.*[104]

It is important to point out that, although this first paragraph sounds as though the imagination actually does the work of bringing forth a desired manifestation, this is not correct. The imagination does not cause manifestation. It only produces the mental image of that which is to be made manifest. In the whole process of manifestation all twelve powers are involved. The imagination does, however, perform the important step of determining the general form of the desired good.

Fourth Step: Understanding/Will

> *The fourth step in creation is the development of the 'two great lights,' the will and the understanding, or the sun (the spiritual I AM) and the moon (the intellect). These are but reflectors of the true light; for God had said, 'Let there be light: and there was light'—before the sun and the moon were created.*[105]

> *The 'greater light,' in mind, is understanding and the 'lesser light' is the will. The greater light rules 'the day,' that realm of consciousness which has been illumined by Spirit. The 'lesser light' rules 'the night,' that is, the will; which has no illumination (light or day) but whose office is to execute the demands of understanding.*[106]

---

[104] Fillmore, Charles *Mysteries of Genesis*, p. 18
[105] Ibid, p. 19
[106] Ibid, p. 20

Will and understanding (two of our twelve powers) are symbolized in the fourth day of the creation allegory. Students often question the reason for metaphysically interpreting the allegory in the step-by-step manner which Charles Fillmore employs in his book *Mysteries of Genesis*. One of the reasons is that he understood the great importance of becoming acquainted with our twelve spiritual faculties, and he viewed the creation allegory as the earliest example we have of man's dawning awareness of these powers. Hence, his painstaking interpretation of the seven days of Creation as found in Genesis.

Fifth Step: Discrimination

> *In the fifth day's creation ideas of discrimination and judgment are developed. The fishes and fowls represent ideas of life working in mind, but they must be properly related to the unformed (seas) and the formed (earth) worlds of mind. When an individual is well balanced in mind and body, there is an equalizing force flowing in the consciousness, and harmony is in evidence.*[107]

> *Human judgment is the mental act of evaluation through comparison or contrast... Divine judgment is of spiritual consciousness... This faculty may be exercised in two ways: from sense perception or spiritual understanding. If its action is based on sense, its conclusions are fallible and often*

---

[107] Ibid, p. 23

> condemnatory; if on spiritual understanding they are safe.[108]

Charles Fillmore sees the fifth day of the Creation allegory as symbolizing the judgment faculty in us and all the ideas that are connected with the right use of judgment. Judgment is our ability to discern, evaluate, and come to decisions.

Sixth Step: Wisdom and Love:

> The sixth step in creation is the bringing forth of ideas after their kind... Wisdom and Love are the two qualities of Being that, communing together, declare, 'Let us make man in our image, after our likeness.'[109] [110]
>
> Wisdom is the 'male' or expressive side of Being, while love is the 'female' or receptive side of Being. Wisdom is the father quality of God and love is the mother quality. In every idea there exist these two qualities of mind, which unite in order to increase and bring forth under divine law. Divine Mind blessed the union of wisdom and love and pronounced on them the increase of Spirit. When wisdom and love are unified in the individual consciousness, we are a master of ideas and we bring them forth under the original creative law.[111]

---

[108] Fillmore, Charles, *Keep a True Lent*, p. 182
[109] Genesis 1:26
[110] Fillmore, Charles *Mysteries of Genesis*, pp. 24-25
[111] Ibid, p. 27

The male and female resulting from the sixth step in the allegory are symbolic of wisdom and love in man's spiritual nature. Wisdom and love in a human being reflect the wisdom and love of the creative Principle which created us. "Let us make man in our image, after our likeness."[112] The Real person is male and female; that is, thinking and feeling, wisdom and love. Charles Fillmore's final sentence in the second paragraph is especially significant: "When wisdom and love are unified in the individual consciousness, we are a master of ideas brought forth under the original creative law.

Seventh Step: The Sabbath:

> *All is first finished in consciousness and mind then rests, in faith, from further mental activity. This 'rest' precedes manifestation. The seventh day refers to the mind's realization of fulfillment, its resting in the assurance that all that has been imaged in it will come forth in expression.*[113]

The Sabbath type of rest is a rest of the mind, not necessarily of the physical body. It sometimes lasts no longer than a moment, but it is necessary for the good of the whole person, as well as for the right outworking of the entire creative process. To maintain the supply of creative energy, we need to take time out from constant expenditure of that energy. The true Sabbath occurs when we become quiet and still within.

---

[112] Genesis 1:26
[113] Fillmore, Charles *Mysteries of Genesis*, p. 31

Creation as an Ongoing Process

> *God is thinking the universe into manifestation right now. Even He cannot create without law. The law of the divine creation is the order and harmony of perfect thought.*[114]

> *It is therefore true, in logic and in inspiration that man and the universe are within God-Mind as living, acting thoughts. God-Mind is giving itself to its creations, and those creations thus are evolving an independence that has the power to co-operate with, or to oppose, the original God will. It is then of vital importance to study the mind and understand its laws, because the starting point of every form in the universe is an idea.*[115]

When we speak of creation as an ongoing process, it does not mean that each creative happening is a brand new creation. God's creation is finished in the sense that it is whole and complete with no parts missing. But within this creation of God a process is going on at all times. This process does not continue because of things being added to God's creation, but by means of what is already involved in God's creation. We have no idea how many energy levels and sources are yet to be tapped, just as we have no idea of the tremendous power lying dormant in our consciousness. Some of these things we are discovering, but we find that the more we discover, the more we realize still lies before us and above us. God's creation is finished, but it is living and because it is living, it

---

[114] Fillmore, Charles *Christian Healing*, p. 18
[115] Ibid, p. 19

is growing, unfolding, expanding. And so are we. Is there any limit to it? Will it ever end? Who can say? Most illumined minds say it is wrong to even use the words "limit" or "end" when speaking about the divine plan.

Process Theology

A modern theological student will encounter similar themes in process theology, is a type of theology developed from Alfred North Whitehead's (1861–1947) process philosophy, most notably by Charles Hartshorne (1897–2000) and John B. Cobb (b. 1925). Process theology and process philosophy are collectively referred to as "process thought." There is also extensive literature on Process New Thought. Process theology asserts:

- God is not omnipotent in the sense of being coercive. The divine has a power of persuasion rather than coercion. Process theologians interpret the classical doctrine of omnipotence as involving force, and suggest instead a forbearance in divine power. "Persuasion" in the causal sense means that God does not exert unilateral control.[116]
- Reality is not made up of material substances that endure through time, but serially-ordered events, which are experiential in nature. These events have both a physical and mental aspect. All experience (male, female, atomic, and botanical) is important and contributes to the ongoing and interrelated process of reality.
- The universe is characterized by process and change carried out by the agents of free will. Self-

---

[116] Hartshorne, Charles, *Omnipotence and Other Theological Mistakes* (Albany: State University of New York, 1984), 20-26

determination characterizes everything in the universe, not just human beings. God cannot totally control any series of events or any individual, but God influences the creaturely exercise of this universal free will by offering possibilities. To say it another way, God has a will in everything, but not everything that occurs is God's will.[117]

- God contains the universe but is not identical with it (panentheism, not pantheism or pandeism). Some also call this "theocosmocentrism" to emphasize that God has always been related to some world or another.
- Because God interacts with the changing universe, God is changeable (that is to say, God is affected by the actions that take place in the universe) over the course of time. However, the abstract elements of God (goodness, wisdom, etc.) remain eternally solid.
- Charles Hartshorne believes that people do not experience *subjective* (or personal) immortality, but they do have *objective* immortality because their experiences live on forever in God, who contains all that was. Some process theologians believe that people do have subjective experience after bodily death.[118]

---

[117] Cobb, John and David Griffin, *Process Theology: An Introductory Exposition* (Philadelphia: Westminster Press, 1976), 14-16, chapter 1
[118] Hartshorne, 32-36

Part II – The Nature of Humankind

Supplementary Reading:
- Cady, H. Emilie *Lessons in Truth*, Chapters 3 and 7
- Fillmore, Charles *Christian Healing*, Chapter 2
- Fillmore, Charles *Keep a True Lent* Chapters 8 and 12
- Lynch, Richard *Know Thyself*, Chapter 3
- Shanklin, Imelda *What Are You?*, Chapters 1 and 3

Part II takes us from a discussion of God to the nature of self, self-knowledge. It includes consciousness, our three-fold nature, mind, personality, individuality, spiritual evolution and our co-creative nature.

We have also included a separate chapter on faith; one of the twelve powers. There is chapter on salvation, a primary concern of some Christian traditions which answers the question: How could God, which is love, condemn millions to a hell of fire and brimstone? Of course, few really believe this, including Rob Bell, an evangelical minister who makes his case in a book: *Love Wins*.[119] Finally, we discuss a key: Denials and Affirmations.

As we continue in our study, we affirm:

I am a student of my own soul and search deeply for my real Truths.

---

[119] Bell, Rob Love Wins: *A Book About Heaven, Hell, and the Fate of Every Person Who Ever Lived*, HarperOne, 2011

Chapter 8 - Self Knowledge

Questions from the Text
1. Give a brief definition of I AM.
2. If God is omnipresence, then why do we speak of finding Him?
3. What are Divine Ideas?
4. What is the metaphysical meaning of "people?"

Questions for Advanced Discussion
1. When one is quickened to spiritual understanding and knows the Father or Christ (the Son, or I AM) within, what will be the result?
2. Explain the difference between the ideal human and the manifest human.
3. How do we lose our consciousness of divine harmony?
4. How are we restored to divine harmony?
5. What is the object of our existence?
6. Explain why we should be wise in the use of the term I AM.

Lesson Text:
Know Thyself

> *Our most important study is our own mind, not only the intellectual mind but the spiritual mind. 'Know thyself' was inscribed on the temple of Apollo at Delphi; and it must be inscribed on our own temple, 'over' the door of our mind.*[120]

---

[120] Fillmore, Charles *Keep a True Lent*, p. 38

> *'Know thyself'; know who and what you are, where you came from, what you are doing here, and where you are going. If you want to know all this, meditate upon the I AM.[121]*

Self-knowledge is the true prelude to Christ consciousness. Without genuine self-knowledge other knowledge often becomes a kind of clutter in the mind. With correct knowledge of self, however, other knowledge reveals its meaning and ripens into wisdom. One of the most effective ways to gain greater knowledge of self is to realize that you have a dimension of your mind that is even greater than your "thinking self." This greater level of your mind can actually observe your thinking self. It can evaluate what it observes. It can make decisions about what it observes. If it chooses it can control, change, and adjust what the thinking self is doing. It is from this higher level of your mind that true self knowledge is attained.

I AM

> *When your voice says 'I AM,' does it do so on its own responsibility, or is it moved by an invisible One? Who is the invisible One, and what is His relation to the voice through which He speaks? These are the most important questions that were ever put to any school on earth. When we begin to consider them, in even the most primary way, we are entering the realm of the gods.[122]*

---

[121] Fillmore, Charles *Talks on Truth*, p. 76
[122] Fillmore, Charles *Talks on Truth*, p. 76

When you say, "I AM," what do you really mean? If you mean only that you exist, that is not enough. If you mean you are a body, it is not enough. If you mean you are a soul, it is not enough. Even if you mean you are a spirit, it is not enough, for this I AM of you is that which has an existence. It has a body, a soul, even a spirit. If this real I of you is one that has these things, then it must be something which is even greater than these things it has. The highest concept of I AM possible to a human mind at present is that of Spirit.

Living in Two Worlds

> *The conscious I can look in two directions—to the outer world where the thoughts that rise within it give sensation and feeling, which ultimate in a moving panorama of visibility; or to the world within, whence all of its life, power, and intelligence are derived.*[123]

We should not make the mistake of thinking that by being conscious of living in two worlds we are making of ourselves "a house divided." Not at all. We actually then become a "house doubly strengthened." Our pivotal consciousness gives us a wonderful advantage in life. We are able to view both realities and to evaluate them correctly. We see our validity and interrelationship. But we see that the inner life should have priority, for it is the realm of causes and of spiritual resources. In the symbolism of the story of Jesus, Martha, and Mary, the lesson of the relative value of our two worlds is brought out in symbolism. Martha stands for our concerned

---

[123] Fillmore, Charles *Talks on Truth*, p. 10

feelings for the outer life. Mary stands for our serene contemplation of our inner life. Jesus valued both women, meaning that both aspects of our life are good. But Jesus indicates that "Mary hath chosen the better part, which will never be taken from her."[124]

Unexplored Consciousness

> *This Spirit of wisdom is right now a part of the consciousness of everyone. It is in you and about you, and you will come into conscious relations with it when you believe in it and its powers. If you ignore it and thereby deny that it exists in you and for you, you remain in the darkness of ignorance. It is exactly as if a man lived in the basement of a large house and refused to go upstairs, declaring that because the upper rooms did not come down to him they were not there.*[125]

Charles Fillmore is talking about the superconscious phase of our own minds. For those brief and rare moments when we make contact with it, the experience is unforgettable. We have new knowledge but do not know exactly how we learned it. Fillmore says that we need simply to "believe on it and its powers" in order to receive its illumination into the conscious level of our minds. He also often said that the prayer for illumination was the one most swiftly and surely answered. What causes this to be so is the existence of the superconscious phase of our minds, which is our direct connection with Divine Mind.

---

[124] Luke 10:42
[125] Fillmore, Charles *Keep a True Lent*, p. 57

Finding God

> *A key to God-Mind is with everyone—it is the action of the individual mind. Man is created in the 'image and likeness' of God; man is therefore a phase of God-Mind, and his mind must act like the original Mind. Study your own mind, and through it you will find God-Mind. In no other way can you get a complete understanding of yourself, of the universe, and of the law under which it is being brought forth.*[126]

One might ask the question: "If God is Omnipresence, then why do we speak of 'finding' Him?" The answer is that we do not actually find God, since Omnipresence is never absent. But what we must find is our point of contact with His Presence, and that can only be within our own consciousness. Mr. Fillmore advises us, "Study your own mind." Only we can do such a thing. We are actually more than our own mind. There is a level of us which can STUDY our own mind. Can we see the tremendous implications of this fact? If we were ONLY our own mind, then we could not rise to a dimension above it in order to observe it or "study it."

Divine Ideas

> *Divine ideas are our inheritance; they are pregnant with all possibility, because ideas are the foundation and cause of all that man desires... All the ideas contained in the one Father Mind are at the mental command of its offspring. Get behind a*

---
[126] Fillmore, Charles *Christian Healing*, p. 19

> *thing into the mental realm where it exists as an inexhaustible idea, and you can draw upon it perpetually and never deplete the source.[127]*

Too much cannot be said about the supreme importance of divine ideas. The most powerful thing in our universe are Divine ideas. The second most powerful thing is our consciousness of those ideas.

Our Many Selves

> *We have no independent mind-there is only universal Mind—but we have consciousness in that Mind, and we have control over our own thoughts, and our thoughts fill our consciousness. By analyzing ourselves we find that we unconsciously separate our self into different personalities.[128]*

It is true as Charles Fillmore states it that we do not have an independent mind, in the sense that we have created it and it belongs to us exclusively. We each partake of the one Mind, each to the degree of his or her current capacity. But we do have something called a "sense of I am." We have freedom of choice as to what we shall do with our sense of I am. We can connect our sense of I am with anything we choose, and it is because of our use of this freedom of choice that we create so many different "selves," or aspects of personality. In most of us, our sense of I am is not really unified or totally coherent. It is usually fragmented and a bit chaotic. Thus, most of us are functioning as "many selves."

---

[127] Fillmore, Charles *Christian Healing*, p. 13
[128] Fillmore, Charles *Teach Us to Pray*, p. 138

"Thought People"

> *Every thought we loose in our mind carries with it a certain substance, life, and intelligence. So we might call our thoughts our 'thought people.*[129]

This paragraph contains a key to the understanding of metaphysical Bible interpretation. In the system of symbols used in our Bible, "people" stand for thoughts and feelings within an individual consciousness. Male people represent thoughts and female people represent feelings. Wicked people stand for negative thoughts and feelings, and righteous people stand for true and positive thoughts and feelings. Marriage symbolizes the harmonious unifying of thought and feeling.

Life is Consciousness

> *You are mind. Your consciousness is formed of thoughts. Thoughts form barriers about the thinker, and when contended for as true they are impregnable to other thoughts. So you are compassed about with thought barriers, the result of your heredity, your education, and your own thinking. Likewise your degree of health is determined by your thoughts, past and present.*[130]

In addition to being a fact, the statement that "Life is consciousness" provides the key to changing one's life.

---

[129] Fillmore, Charles *Jesus Christ Heals*, p. 138
[130] Fillmore, Charles *Jesus Christ Heals*, p. 33

Self-Observation

> "We must learn to watch our consciousness, its impulses and desires, as the chemist watches his solutions. Man forms his own consciousness from the elements of God, and he alone is responsible for the results."[131]

When we observe ourselves, we become more than just the limits of our own mind. We momentarily transcend our "thinking self." The great importance of honest self-observation was emphasized by Jesus when He said, "Watch, and pray." Watch what? Watch how you are thinking and what your current attitudes are. Observe yourself, especially your inner states. In order for a person to know what to change within his consciousness he must take time to observe what is going on within himself.

The Great Work

> All things are in the consciousness and you have to learn to separate the erroneous from the true, darkness from light. The I AM must separate the sheep from the goats. This sifting begins right now and goes on until the perfect child of God is manifest and you are fully rounded out in all your Godlike attributes.[132]

What Charles Fillmore is describing in this paragraph is the main assignment for us on this planet of physical existence. Our purpose is to become masters of existence.

---

[131] Fillmore, Charles, *The Twelve Powers*, p. 163
[132] Fillmore, Charles *Atom-Smashing Power of Mind*

The first step in fulfilling this assignment was learning how to survive. Next was "how to be good." But the purpose for true religion on our current evolutionary level is no longer just physical survival and "how to be good." It now has to do with perfection of consciousness through individual evolution. This is the "seed" planted in collective consciousness by Jesus Christ. This is the purpose of metaphysical Christianity.

Chapter 9 - Consciousness

Questions from the Text
1. What is balanced four-sided consciousness? What are the aspects?
2. What did Charles Fillmore mean by "race" consciousness?

Lesson Text:
Evolution of Consciousness

> *When we evolve spiritually to a certain degree, we open up inner faculties that connect with cosmic Mind, and attain results that are sometimes so startling that we seem to be miracle workers. What seems miraculous is the action of forces on planes of consciousness not previously understood. When a man releases the powers of his soul, he does marvels in the sight of the material-minded, but he has not departed from the law. He is merely functioning in a consciousness that has been sporadically manifested by great men in all ages.*[133]

Evolution of consciousness is individual, not collective. Although the whole of humanity may benefit from certain changes brought about by evolution of others, evolution itself is experienced only through individual effort. All of the Unity teachings are about making those right efforts. In regard to miracles, it is good to remember that there will always be a level of consciousness above whatever level we are on at any

---
[133] Fillmore, Charles *Prosperity*, p. 64

given moment. The higher levels of consciousness generate higher types of energies. These higher types of energies can accomplish things on lower levels which can only be described as miraculous.

The "I AM"

> *The I AM is the polar star around which all the thoughts of man revolve. Even the little, narrow concept of the personal "I am" may be led out into the consciousness of the great and only I AM by filling its thought sphere with ideas of infinite wisdom, life, and love.*[134]

What Charles Fillmore here designates as the "little, personal I am" is actually our human sense of I am. You and I cannot do anything with our true I AM. We cannot change it, add to it, or take from it. But the case is different with our sense of I am. We can do practically anything with it. And it is what we choose to do with our sense of I am which determines the type of existence we have.

Balanced (Four-Sided) Consciousness

> *The fleeing of Moses to the wilderness represents the discipline that we must undergo when we seek the exalted One. Horeb means 'solitude;' that is, we have to go into the solitude of the within and lead our flock of thoughts to the 'back of the wilderness,' where dwells the exalted One, the I AM, whose kingdom is good judgment. There we are in training*

---

[134] Fillmore, Charles *Talks on Truth*, p. 25

> *forty years, or until we arrive at a four-sided or balanced state of mind.*[135]

This "four-sided or balanced state of mind" can be understood metaphysically as an evolutionary prerequisite to the development of Christ Consciousness. It would indicate a consciousness in which all four functions (sensation, intuition, thinking and feeling) are at least somewhat developed and functioning. Numbers are often used as important symbols in the Bible. The number forty is one of these. Four is the symbol of balance and sufficiency. Zero always symbolizes "unlimited or unspecified." So the symbol forty would stand for "a sufficient, but unspecified" period of time or state of consciousness.

Sensation

> *To be born into the Spirit is to come into an entirely new and different state of consciousness. This has a mighty meaning back of it. What makes up your present consciousness? Is it not largely the things of sense?*[136]

> *The ten virgins represent the senses. The senses are five in number but have a twofold action—five in the inner realm and five in the outer world... Each (outer) sense has an inner counterpart, which is connected with the one life, from which it draws its 'oil' or life current. There is a soul eye and a soul ear, and these on their inner side are in direct*

---
[135] Fillmore, Charles *The Twelve Powers*, p. 121
[136] Fillmore, Charles *Talks on Truth*, p. 80

> *contact with Spirit. But their outer side is in touch with the intellect and through the intellect with the formed organ of sense in the body.*[137]

Everything that exists has its counterpart on all discernable levels of being. As Charles Fillmore points out, this is also true of our senses. Each of our five outer senses has a corresponding dimension in our inner world and it is through these "inner senses" (intuition) that inspiration and insight can come into consciousness.

Intuition

> *Intuition—the natural knowing capacity. Inner knowing; the immediate apprehension of spiritual Truth without resort to intellectual means. The wisdom of the heart. It is very much surer in guidance than the head. When one trusts Spirit and looks to it for understanding, a certain confidence in the invisible good develops. This faith awakens the so-called sixth sense, intuition, or divine knowing. Through the power of intuition, man has direct access to all knowledge and the wisdom of God.*[138]

Intuition is the name of the very highest function of human consciousness. It is not Divine Mind, but it is our connection with Divine Mind. Intuition receives directly from Divine Mind, but such knowledge is not in the form of words. It comes in the language of Spirit, which is not words, but pure knowing and feeling.

---

[137] Fillmore, Charles *The Revealing Word*, Virgina
[138] Fillmore, Charles *The Revealing Word*, Intuition, p. 108

Thinking

> *Thinking—the formulating process of mind ... The thinking faculty is the inlet and the outlet of all your ideas. It is active, zealous, impulsive, but not always wise... The thinking faculty in you makes you a free agent, because it is your creative center; in and through this one power you establish your consciousness—you build your world.*[139]

> *Some persons confound the realm of knowledge about things formulated through the intellect with pure knowledge. Intellect and its plane of activity are not pure mind as the realm of matter is not Spirit. The same essences of being enter into both, but wisdom is sadly lacking in the intellectual realm. Intellect has formulated its conclusions from the sense side of existence instead of from the spiritual side, and these two sides are divergent.*[140]

Thinking should not be equated with such terms as "knowing," "wisdom," or "divine ideas." Divine ideas just ARE and have no dependency on thinking. Knowing (understanding) is a divine idea, and thinking does not change it. Wisdom is the ability to discern the meaning of any knowledge. Thinking is a process which occurs mainly in the area of the mind called intellect. The intellect can observe, express, and remember thoughts. Thoughts can be based upon divine ideas or on outer sense impressions. Divine idea thoughts are always true. Thoughts based on

---

[139] Fillmore, Charles *The Revealing Word*, Thinking, p. 192
[140] Fillmore, Charles *Atom-Smashing Power of Mind*, p. 89

sense impressions are always risky; they can be true or false.

Feeling

> *Feeling is external to thought; behind every feeling or emotion there lies thought, which is its direct cause. To erase a feeling, a change of thought is required.*[141]
>
> *Words and sounds are attempts to convey a description of emotions and feelings, while by the language of mind emotions and feelings are conveyed direct. But again you must transcend what you understand as emotion and feeling in order to interpret the language of God. This is not hard. It is your natural language, and you need only return to your pristine state of purity to achieve it entirely.*[142]

Metaphysical teachings pretty much agree that feelings and emotions are mostly subjective. They are generated by thoughts. They follow the trend of our thinking and, with sufficient practice, they can be brought under control by right thinking. In Bible symbolism the male (thought) appears first. Female (feeling) is called a "help mate" to thought. This is not to say that feelings and emotions are not vitally important to a human being. They are. "And God said, it is not good that man (thought) should be alone. I will make a help mate (feeling) for

---

[141] Fillmore, Charles *The Revealing Word*, Feeling, p. 73
[142] Fillmore, Charles *Jesus Christ Heals*, p. 33

him."[143] We are wise to always try to maintain some conscious control over feelings and emotions within ourselves. Right thinking is the safe way.

Collective[144] Consciousness

> *The beliefs that you and your ancestors have held in mind have become thought currents so strong that their course in you can be changed only by your resolute decision to entertain them no longer. They will not be turned out unless the ego through whose domain they run decides positively to adopt means of casting them out of his consciousness, and at the same time erects gates that will prevent their inflow from external sources. This is done by denial and affirmation; the denial always comes first.*[145]

Charles Fillmore is referring here only to the undesirable content of collective consciousness which needs to be detected and rejected. Not all of collective consciousness is negative or undesirable. There is also much good in it. Spiritual discrimination and good judgment enables us to discern the difference between true and false, positive and negative. And our illumined will enables us to make the right choices. Our consciousness can say "no" to the unwanted elements in collective consciousness. Our faith can affirm "yes" to the true and useful. Collective consciousness poses no real

---

[143] Genesis 2:18
[144] Charles Fillmore called this "Race Consciousness."
[145] Fillmore, Charles *The Twelve Powers*, p. 154

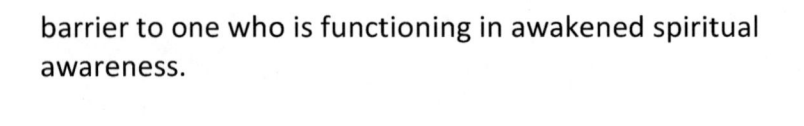

barrier to one who is functioning in awakened spiritual awareness.

Chapter 10 – The Trinity in Us

Questions from the Text
1. What are the three phases of Trinity in us?
2. How do we activate the Trinity in us?

Questions for Advanced Discussion
1. Are we limited by time, or in knowledge and power? How can we overcome belief in these limitations?
2. Explain how the Father can be in the Son, and the Son in the Father.
3. How are we begotten by the Word?
4. How do we manifest Christ?
5. How do we abide in Christ?
6. Give in your own words five affirmations for the realization of the indwelling Christ.
7. Give our phases as a threefold being, and explain the result if we fail to recognize this unity of our being.
8. What is the result if we fail to recognize the unity of being, as spirit, soul, body?
9. How do we identify self with the Absolute? How and what is it to acknowledge the Son?
10. What is the object of our existence?

Lesson Text:

We may understand the relation and office of the Father, the Son, and the Holy Spirit by analyzing our own mind and its apparent subdivisions during thought action, because each person is a perfect image and likeness first cause: God, the Father.[146]

---

[146] Fillmore, Charles *Keep a True Lent*, p. 17

> *The mind of God is Spirit, soul, body; that is, mind, idea, expression. The mind of man is Spirit, soul, body—not separate from God-Mind, but existing in it and making it manifest in an identity peculiar to the individual. Every man is building into his consciousness the three departments of God-Mind, and his success in the process is evidenced by the harmony, in his consciousness, of Spirit, soul, and body. If he is all body, he is but one-third expressed. If to body he has added soul, he is two-thirds man, and if to these two he is adding Spirit, he is on the way to the perfect manhood that God designed.[147]*

We are a Trinity of spirit, soul, and body, not in the abstract but in recognizable, concrete terms. We are a manifestation of the Trinity. As Charles Fillmore writes, the Trinity[148] within each person "... manifests in an identity peculiar to the individual."

Mind/Idea/Manifestation

> *The movement of every mind in bringing forth the simplest thought is a key to the great creative process of universal Mind. In every act is involved mind, idea, and manifestation. The mind is neither seen nor felt; the idea is not seen, but it is felt; and the manifestation appears.[149]*

---

[147] Fillmore, Charles *Christian Healing*, p. 22
[148] Not to be confused with the Trinity defined by Trinitarian Christians. The Trinity of some Christian groups is not found in the Bible, but was defined at the Council of Nicea to define Jesus as part of the Godhead.
[149] Fillmore, Charles *Jesus Christ Heals*, p. 54

In this paragraph Charles Fillmore reduces the creative process of the Trinity to what may well be its clearest and most simple presentation. We can see that he views the individual mind of a person as a "small scale model" of the Mind that created our universe. This illustrates an aspect of the law of correspondence: "as the macrocosm, so the microcosm." In a sense we, in our highest meaning, are the scaled-down image and likeness of our creator.

Spirit (Mind)

> *In its higher functioning the mind of man deals with spiritual ideas, and we can truthfully say that man is a spiritual being. This fact explains the almost universal worship of God by men and makes possible the conjunction of the heaven and the earth by those who understand the underlying laws of prayer. Jesus stated this emphatically in: 'God is Spirit; and they that worship him must worship in spirit and truth.'*[150] [151]

We are spiritual beings in the sense that we have a spiritual nature and a spiritual identity. In understanding the Trinity in us it is helpful to relate our threefold nature (spirit, soul and body) to the metaphysical meaning of the Trinity (mind, ideas and expression).

---

[150] John 4:24
[151] Fillmore, Charles *Jesus Christ Heals*, p. 74

Soul (Idea)

> *Soul—Man's consciousness; the underlying idea back of any expression. In man, the soul is the many accumulated ideas back of his present expression. In its original and true sense, the soul of man is the expressed idea of man in Divine Mind.*[152]

> *The one and only object of man's existence is the development of his soul, and any attainment, whether mental or material, that cannot be associated with and counted as an aid toward that end will ultimately be refused.*[153]

Many Truth students find difficulty in understanding exactly what is meant by soul. One of the reasons for this confusion is that different schools of thought use different terms in defining the soul. In spite of these differences, there need not be difficulty in dealing with the word "soul" because in Unity terminology it is simply the name given to the entire area of awareness in us. We are not yet certain of its full potential, nor of its limitations, but any part of our being which includes any sort of awareness is referred to as our soul. Jesus declared that the most important thing about a person is the worth of his soul. He said that it is of no profit that a person "gain the whole world, but forfeit his soul."[154]

---

[152] Fillmore, Charles *The Revealing Word*, Soul, p. 182
[153] Fillmore, *Teach Us to Pray*, p. 130
[154] Mark 8:36

Body (Manifestation)

> *Body—the outer expression of consciousness; the precipitation of the thinking part of man. God created the IDEA of the body of man as a self-perpetuating, self-renewing organism, which man reconstructs into his personal body. God creates the body idea, or divine idea, and man, by his thinking, makes it manifest. As God created man, in His image and likeness by the power of His word, so man, as God's image and likeness, projects his body by the same power. All thoughts and ideas embody themselves according to their character. Material thoughts make a material body. Spiritual thoughts make a spiritual body.*[155]

One of the most helpful Unity teachings is that our real body is created by God as an Idea. There is a divine idea body within all persons. It is a spiritual pattern of a perfect body. Today we function in a physical form which is an out-picturing of our current level of consciousness. Regardless of what happens to the physical body, the perfect body idea is always there and more and more of its perfection can be brought forth and expressed. All healing is based on this principle.

Activating the Trinity in Us

> *We set into action any of the three realms of our being, spirit, soul and body, by concentrating our thought on them. If we think only of the body, the*

---
[155] Fillmore, Charles *The Revealing Word*, Body, p. 26

> *physical senses encompass all our existence. If mind and emotion are cultivated we add soul to our consciousness. If we rise to the Absolute and comprehends Spirit, we round out the God-person.*[156]

Previously Charles Fillmore only analyzed the Trinity in us. In this paragraph he speaks of how to activate the Trinity. We can increase our awareness of any or all aspects of the Trinity in ourselves. Charles Fillmore was always careful to point out to students that we should make effort to activate all three, body, soul, and spirit. The method he sets forth is amazingly simple:

1. Acknowledge
2. Concentrate
3. Affirm

Our Destination

> *The natural man in the physical world is merely the beginning formation of the man planned by creative Mind. When the natural man finishes his unfoldment he enters the next stage, that of the Christ man illustrated by Jesus. Jesus was the first man or 'fruit' of the earth's first age, that of the natural man. He opened the way for all who aspire to the attainment of immortality.*[157]

In many other places in his writings (particularly in *Mysteries of Genesis*) Charles Fillmore deals with our concept of self as we think we are today; as being in a

---

[156] Fillmore, *Jesus Christ Heals*, p. 71
[157] Fillmore, Charles Atom-Smashing Power, p. 130

"fallen" state. That is, we were once consciously divine, but through desire for sensations departed from that level of consciousness and became involved with our own thought creations. In this concept, we are now working to regain what we once had. In the passage above, Mr. Fillmore takes the alternative view. Here he says, "The natural man in the physical world is merely the beginning formation of the man planned by creative Mind." In this concept we have always been moving in a forward direction toward new goals, not regaining what we have lost, but progressing into that which we have not yet experienced. Many students ask, "Which one is correct?" The answer would seem to be that either one might be correct. But whichever is correct, it does not change our destiny in any way. We must all continue to work on consciousness.

Chapter 11 – Mind - The Crucible

Questions from the Text
1. Give a brief definition for each of the following terms:
   - Conscious Mind
   - Subconscious Mind
   - Superconscious Mind

Questions for Advanced Discussion
1. What is thinking? What is a structure, and what builds all structures?
2. What is the Superconscious phase of mind?
3. What is the conscious phase of mind? What other names are given to this phase of mind?
4. What is the subconscious phase of mind? What other names are given to this phase of mind?
5. How are the conscious and subconscious phases of mind related?
6. Name some of the functions of the body carried on by the subconscious phase of mind.
7. How may one take conscious control of the involuntary functions?
8. From what source have many of the subconscious thought currents come?
9. Why do we sometimes think one thing and manifest another?
10. Why is it so important to think the Truth about life?
11. What line of thinking will overcome the belief in materiality?
12. Why should we hold ourselves and others, in the one all-knowing Mind?

13. How may all thought be brought into harmony with divine law?
14. What place has order in Divine Mind and in man's consciousness?

Lesson Text:
> *It is well said that the mind is the crucible in which the ideal is transmuted into the real. This process of transformation is the spiritual chemistry we must learn before we are ready to work intelligently in the great laboratory of the Father's substance. There is no lack of material there to form what we will, and we can all draw on it as a resource according to our purpose. Wealth of consciousness will express itself in wealth of manifestation.[158]*

The mind is truly a mystery. Here Charles Fillmore calls it a crucible. He also saw mind as the connecting link between God and us. The highest purpose of our mind is to transform divine ideas into experiences and manifestations.

Consciousness

> *Consciousness—the sense of awareness, of knowing. The knowledge or realization of any idea, object, or condition. The sum total of all ideas accumulated in, and affecting man's present being. The composite of ideas, thoughts, emotions, sensation, and knowledge that makes up the*

---
[158] Fillmore, Charles, *Prosperity*, p. 56

> *conscious phases of mind. It includes all that man is aware of—spirit, soul, and body.*[159]

This paragraph constitutes what many readers consider to be Unity's most concise and comprehensive definition of consciousness. Unity gives the word "consciousness" a far more expansive definition than do most sciences or philosophies. Our teachings seek to aim the direction of consciousness always in a forward or God-ward direction. Hence, Unity's usage of the word "consciousness" almost always has religious or spiritual overtones.

The One Mind

> *In Truth there is but one Mind; in it all things exist. Accurately speaking, man does not have three minds, nor does he have even one mind; but he expresses the one Mind in a multitude of ways.*[160]

> *When we seek the super consciousness and make conscious connection with it we harmonize all the forces of mind and body; we lift up the subconscious until a complete, conscious unification of the three phases of mind is affected and we become established in 'singleness of heart.'*[161]

When we speak of the one Mind, we are referring to the divine source of all intelligence, the universal source of all individual minds. There are many minds, but there is

---

[159] Fillmore, Charles *The Revealing Word*, Consciousness, p. 41
[160] Fillmore, Charles, *Christian Healing*, p. 97
[161] Fillmore, Charles *Keep a True Lent*, p. 92

only one Mind. Where did you get your mind, and how did you receive your intelligence? Jesus said it comes from the Father. Unity agrees, but we also identify that aspect of the Father as Divine Mind. Divine Mind is the true source of individual minds and is always connected with its "children."

Conscious Mind

> *Conscious mind—the mind that makes one know of one's mental operations and states of consciousness; that phase of mind in which one is actively aware of one's thoughts. The mind through which man establishes his identity.*[162]

Most persons automatically mean conscious self-awareness, and awareness of one's thoughts when they use the word "mind." Our sense of I am is usually centered on this level of our mind. It takes little or no effort to maintain this. But it does take effort to become aware of the other levels of mind. And it often takes great effort to raise our sense of I am to higher levels of mind. The conscious level of mind is the most familiar to us and generally it is where we feel most normal and "at home."

Subconscious Mind

> *The subconscious mind is the vast, silent realm that lies back of the conscious mind and between it and the superconscious. To one who does not understand its nature and its office, it is the 'great*

---

[162] Fillmore, Charles, *The Revealing Word*, Conscious, p. 41

> *gulf fixed' between our present state and the attainment of our highest desire, our good.*[163]
>
> *The subconscious realm of mind is the realm that contains all past thoughts. First, we think consciously and this thought becomes subconscious, carrying on its work of building up or tearing down, according to its character. The subconscious mind cannot take the initiative, but depends on the conscious mind for direction. When one is quickened of Spirit, one's true thoughts are set to work and the subconscious states of error are broken up and dissolved. In one's daily silence and communion with God, thoughts from the sub-consciousness come into the conscious realm of mind to be forgiven and redeemed.*[164]

These two paragraphs contain many of Charles Fillmore's clearest insights into the nature of the subconscious mind in general. It is important to remember that the specific contents of the subconscious mind in an individual are largely unknown. Much of our work in consciousness consists of bringing these contents into the light of conscious awareness.

Superconscious Mind

> *Super consciousness is the goal toward which humanity is working. Regardless of appearances there is an upward trend continually active throughout all creation. The super consciousness is*

---

[163] Fillmore, Charles *Keep a True Lent*, p. 87
[164] Fillmore, Charles *Atom-Smashing Power of Mind*, p. 76

> the realm of divine ideas. Its character is impersonal. It therefore has no personal ambitions; knows no condemnation; but is always pure, innocent, loving, and obedient to the call of God.[165]
>
> The superconscious mind lifts up, or regenerates, both the subconscious and the conscious, transforming them into the true image and likeness of God. The conscious mind must be faithful during this transformation. It must look ever to the superconscious for all direction and instruction. It can of itself do nothing with assurance, because the Spirit of Wisdom rests in the superconscious.[166]

In his book *Christian Healing*, Charles Fillmore refers to "that vast mysterious realm called super consciousness." In these paragraphs he helps solve some of that mystery by adding insight to his other explanations. For example: the super consciousness "has no personal ambitions," "knows no condemnation," and "is always pure, innocent, loving and obedient to the will of God."

Subconscious Impressions

> The subconscious may be called the sensitive plate of mind. Its true office is to receive impressions from the superconscious and to reproduce them upon the canvas of the conscious mind. Man, however, having lost the consciousness of the indwelling Father as an ever present reality, has reversed the process and impresses the

---

[165] Ibid, p 36
[166] Fillmore, Charles *Keep a True Lent*, p. 89

> *subconscious from the conscious mind. In this way the former is made to register impressions of both good and evil, according to the thoughts held in conscious mind the time the impression is made.*[167]

Most people do not allow evil impressions to enter their subconscious because they really want to. It is something which may happen without our being fully aware of it. Life makes impressions on us constantly. We don't make these impressions on ourselves. Life does. But we determine how we take those impressions, how we judge them, and how we react to them. All this goes into the subconscious. If we react negatively, selfishly, violently, then we have sent those impressions into the subconscious. It creates a sort of vicious circle. But when we remember the Truth we have learned, we can break the vicious circle. Forgiveness goes into the subconscious. Denial goes into the subconscious. New affirmations go into the subconscious. All can be made well again, for the Holy Spirit works on all levels of our being.

Externalization of the Superconscious

> *The super consciousness has been perceived by the spiritually wise in every age, but they have not known how to externalize it and make it an abiding state of consciousness. Jesus accomplished this, and His method is worthy of our adoption, because as far as we know, it is the only method that has been successful. It is set forth in the New Testament, and whoever adopts the life of purity*

---
[167] Ibid, p. 87

> *and love and power there exemplified in the experiences of Jesus of Nazareth will in due course attain the place that He attained.*[168]
>
> *This is all accomplished through the externalization of the super consciousness, which is omnipresent and ever ready to manifest itself through us as it did through Jesus. 'Let Christ be formed in you.*[169]

Charles Fillmore accepts Jesus as the only known example of one who was able to abide in the superconscious, and he calls our attention to the fact that we may attain that same ability if we follow the teachings given to us by Jesus. Jesus himself states the same things when he says, "If you abide in my word..."[170] It is hard to imagine what life would be like if we were producing manifestations directly from the superconscious. As we are now, almost all our manifestation comes from the subconscious. Subconscious may contain much error. Superconscious contains no error. Can we imagine a life in which no error is manifesting through us? Jesus tells us it can be done. Only the right effort is required on our part. All Truth teachings are for the purpose of helping us make those efforts.

---

[168] Fillmore, Charles *Atom-Smashing Power of Mind*, p. 36
[169] Ibid, p. 40
[170] John 15:7

Chapter 12 – Personality and Individuality

Questions from the Text
1. Give a brief definition for each of the following terms:
- Individuality
- Personality
- The Devil
- The Second Birth

Lesson Text
Two Individuals

> There are always two individuals in each of us. The individuals without is the picture that the man within paints with his mind. This mind is the open door to the unlimited principle of Being. When Jesus prayed He was setting into action the various powers of His individuality in order to bring about certain results. Within His identity was of God; without He was human personality.[171]

It is important to understand that the "two" Charles Fillmore speaks of here are not two distinct entities, but the two sides of a single entity: the inner and outer self. Our Bible is filled with character symbols who represent these two aspects of an individual life. Adam and Eve (this is one person), Cain and Abel (this is one person), Jacob and Esau (this is one person), Abraham and Sarah, Martha and Mary all are symbolic of the "two men" Mr. Fillmore speaks about. It is only in the character of Jesus that we

---
[171] Fillmore, Charles *Jesus Christ Heals*, p. 69

have a Bible symbol who is the same within and without. Jesus was not "two men." Perhaps this was one of His meanings when He said, "The Father and I are one."

Individuality

> *Individuality-The true self; that which is undivided from God; our spiritual identity... That which characterizes one as a distinct entity or particular manifestation of divine Principle. Individuality is eternal; it can never be destroyed.*[172]

Individuality is a word that has sometimes been misunderstood in our Unity terminology. Originally it simply meant each person's individual uniqueness. You are you, and you will always be you. You will change, day after day, but it will still be you. You may even reincarnate in many more lifetimes, but it will be you who reincarnates. This you who will always be you is your individuality. Christ is something even greater than individuality, but Christ has generated individuality. Christ is whole, complete, changeless, perfect, and divine. Individuality is unfinished, constantly evolving toward perfection and divinity.

Personality

> *Personality—the sum total of characteristics that man has personalized as distinct of himself, independent of others or of divine principle. The word personality as used by metaphysicians is contrasted with the word individuality. Individuality is the real; personality is the unreal, the mortal, the*

---

[172] Fillmore, Charles *The Revealing Word*, Individuality, p. 106

> *part of us that is governed by the selfish motives of the natural man...Personality is what man seems to be when he thinks in his three-dimensional consciousness; individuality is what he really is when he thinks in his unlimited spiritual consciousness. As the true Christ self emerges, personality decreases. The real self, the individuality, begins to express. 'He must increase, but I must decrease.'[173] [174]*

One might say that individuality is myself, and personality is the sum total of all my changing opinions about myself. This gives much insight to John the Baptizer's highly symbolic statement quoted here: "He must increase (individuality), but I must decrease (personality, opinions about myself)." Similar insight may come to us from Jesus' teaching that we must "... deny himself ... and follow me."[175] Who is this "himself" which Jesus asks us to deny? It may be that he meant something which needs to be released in regard to one's sense of self. It may well be that he meant the sense of self which claims to be the whole thing, or the self that believes there is nothing higher than itself. This is called selfishness or exaggerated self-centeredness. Surely this must be denied if one is to become aware of higher levels of being.

The Devil

> *The devil is the personal ego which has in his freedom formed a state of consciousness peculiarly*

---

[173] John 3:30
[174] Fillmore, Charles *The Revealing Word*, Personality, p. 148
[175] Luke 9:23

> *his own. When man lives wholly in the consciousness that personality has built up, he is ruled by the carnal mind, which is the adversary, or Satan.*[176]

The paragraph states that "The devil is the personal ego..." This can be expanded quite a bit. The devil is a biblical symbol. It is not the name of a creature that has an existence of its own. It is a part of human nature. He stands for more than just one thing; he stands for a combination of things, but generally we can say that the devil stands for the tendency toward negativity in human nature. Jesus also classifies him as the tendency to lie. ("He is a liar, and the father of lies.") He stands for selfishness and for all the offspring of selfishness. Still, his meaning is not entirely negative. He also stands for the adversary and the tempter. As tempter, he symbolizes opportunity for choice. We are always being "'tempted," which simply means constantly being given opportunities for choice. So we see that the devil has both positive and negative meaning in metaphysical symbolism.

The Second Birth

> *'... Ye must be born anew,'*[177] *was the proclamation of Jesus. The first birth is the human—the self-consciousness of man as an intellectual and physical being; the second birth, the being 'born anew,' is the transformation and translation of the human to a higher plane of consciousness as the son of God. The second birth is that in which we*

---

[176] Fillmore, Charles *The Twelve Powers*, p. 69
[177] John 3:7

> *'put on Christ.' It is a process of mental adjustment and body transmutation that takes place right here on earth. 'Have this mind in you, which was also in Christ Jesus,' is an epitome of mental and physical change that may require years to work out. But all men must go through this change before they can enter into eternal life and be as Jesus Christ is.*[178]

There are many ways of interpreting the new birth which Jesus says is necessary in order to "see the kingdom of God." Especially significant is this insight by Charles Fillmore: "It is a process of mental adjustment and body transmutation." The new birth occurs when a person makes a certain commitment to Spirit. It can be in many different forms, but basically it is a commitment to make the effort to change the level of one's religious thinking. For Truth students it is the effort to let go of inadequate God concepts and enter into worship of God as Spirit and as Truth. This brings about the beginning of new "mental adjustment and body transmutation" which Mr. Fillmore writes about.

Christ/Man

> *"The cry goes up: 'This is foolish, sacrilegious, to put man beside Jesus Christ and claim that they are equals.' The claim is not that mortals, in their present consciousness, are equal with Jesus, but that they must be equal with Him before they will emerge from the sense of delusion in which they now wander."*[179]

---

[178] Fillmore, Charles *Christian Healing*, p. 26
[179] Fillmore, Charles *Talks on Truth*, p. 143

This paragraph clarifies a common misunderstanding concerning Unity's views on Jesus. The important thing is what Jesus taught and demonstrated, and the important thing for modern Truth students is whether or not Jesus' teachings really work. However, to put them to the test requires that they first be understood, and this is where metaphysical interpretation comes in.

Christ in You

> *Paul urged that we let Christ be formed in us. That means that through the study of the life of Jesus and the discipline He gave His mind we shall put into our mind the same ideas that He had. These ideas will form in our mind a new kind of man, which is God's man.*[180]

If Christ already is within us, then why does Paul tell us to let Christ be formed in us? The answer lies in the difference between that which IS and that which we are aware of. The Truth always IS. But the field of our awareness always expands or contracts, according to our thoughts.

Your True Self

> *This perfect-idea-of-God man is your true self. God-Mind is, under the law of thought, constantly seeking to release its perfection in you. It is your Spirit, and when you ask for its guidance and place yourself, by prayer and affirmation, in mental touch*

---
[180] Fillmore, Charles Teach Us to Pray, p. 85

with it, there is a great increase of its manifestation in your life. It has back of it all the powers of Being, and there is nothing you cannot do if you give it full sway and make your thought strong enough to express the great forces that it is seeking to express through you.[181]

If you would bring forth the very best that is in you, study the methods of Jesus. Study them in all their details, get at the spirit of everything that is written about this wonderful man, and you will find the key to the true development of your soul and your body. If you will carry out His system, there will be revealed to you a new man, a man of whom you never dreamed, existing in the hidden realms of your own subconsciousness.[182]

The desire to become a new person is universal in the hearts of mankind. No matter how good we are, how many advantages we may enjoy, how much satisfaction we feel in our lives, the desire for newness of being is always there. This desire would not be implanted in us if it were not possible for successful fulfillment. The new person exists in every one of us in embryo form. It is the seed of regeneration, the spark of divinity. It is growing; it is unfolding. Charles Fillmore sees in the teachings of Jesus the right pattern to follow in helping this growth continue.

---

[181] Fillmore, Charles *Christian Healing*, p. 23
[182] Fillmore, Charles *The Twelve Powers*, p. 40

Chapter 13 – Spiritual Evolution

Questions from Text
1. What did Jesus do?
2. Give a brief definition for each of the following terms.
   - Reincarnation
   - Regeneration
   - Resurrection

Lesson Text

> *In every person the Christ, or Word of God is infolded; it is an idea that contains all ideas. Evolution is the result of the development of ideas in mind. What we are is the result of the evolution of our consciousness, and our consciousness is the result of the seed ideas sown in our mind. Therefore spiritual evolution is the unfolding of the Spirit of God into expression. It is the development achieved by man working under spiritual law. Humanity is the garden of God, of which the soil is the omnipresent thought substance. The Christ, or Word (Son) of God evolution of man is plainly taught in the New Testament as the supreme attainment of every man.*[183]

Charles Fillmore points out in the first sentence of this paragraph that Christ is "infolded" in us. Often there is the misconception that Christ is in "full bloom" in us. There is need for a great deal more spiritual evolution, as this paragraph points out. Sometimes Truth students make the

---
[183] Fillmore, Charles *Keep a True Lent*, p. 165

mistake of thinking that what is true in potential is the same as whatever is being manifested at any given moment. This is not what Jesus taught and it is not what Unity teaches. Charles Fillmore says in many different ways that manifest man is an unfinished product who has much work to do, much learning, much growing. And he can do all this very successfully because of the Christ or Word of God implanted (infolded) within him.

Life of Jesus

> *By thought, speech, and deed this Christ Mind is brought into manifestation. The new birth is symbolically described in the history of Jesus.*[184]
>
> *... Jesus was Himself a parable. His life was an allegory of the experiences that man passes through in developing from natural to spiritual consciousness.*[185]

Charles Fillmore had deep insight into the meaning of the life of Jesus. To persons without spiritual understanding statements such as "Jesus was himself a parable; His life was an allegory" might sound audacious. But to one with even a bit of metaphysical understanding, these statements ring true and provide a practical frame of reference for our work on spiritual evolution.

---

[184] Fillmore, Charles *Christian Healing*, p. 28
[185] Ibid, p. 74

God's Objective

> *One of the fundamental principles in the study of Christianity is that God's great objective is the making of a perfect man. Man is the apex of creation, made in God's image and likeness, and endowed with full authority and dominion over his elemental thoughts.*[186]

As we constantly progress in demonstrating dominion and mastery over conditions and situations in the relative world, more and more persons are coming into the realization that in the universe in which we now exist our consciousness is the "apex of creation."

What Jesus Did

> *Every thinker who studies the life and teachings of Jesus readily admits that He attained an understanding of spiritual things far beyond that of any other man that ever lived. His mind touched heights far beyond those of other advanced searchers for Truth. As we unfold spiritually we see more and more that Jesus understood the finer shades of metaphysical reasoning and related His mind and body to both ideas and their manifestation.*[187]

Something not ordinarily noticed about Jesus is the remarkable fact that He consciously saw Himself as a living symbol—that of spiritual awareness active in us. He

---

[186] Fillmore, Charles Prosperity, p. 160
[187] Fillmore, Charles *Jesus Christ Heals*

patterned His whole life on that symbolic role. Also, He conducted two ministries simultaneously: a ministry of works and a ministry of words. After His ascension His words began to take on a new light and have new meaning in the minds of His followers. We are the beneficiaries of that dawning, and we today are the congregation of His ministry of words. This is one aspect of the second coming of Jesus Christ.

Reincarnation

> *When a soul leaves the body, it rests for a season. Then innate desire for material expression asserts itself, and the ego seeks the primal cell and builds another body. This is reincarnation. Reincarnation will continue until the ego awakens to the Christ Mind and through it builds an imperishable body... But reincarnation is not a part of the divine plan and does not lift man out of mortal limitations. It is not an aid to spiritual growth, but merely a makeshift until full Truth is discerned.*[188]

> *A new soul is not created with every physical birth. A physical birth simply means that a soul is taking on another body. Every man inhabiting this earth and the psychic realms immediately surrounding it has gone through this process of dying and being reincarnated many times.*[189]

Little needs to be added to the clear and logical statements concerning reincarnation in these paragraphs

---
[188] Fillmore, Charles *The Revealing Word*, Reincarnation, p. 166
[189] Fillmore, Charles *The Twelve Powers*, p. 138

except to comment on one point. In light of the current findings in the relatively new science of genetics, Charles Fillmore's statement that "the ego seeks the primal cell and builds another body" sounds very similar to the DNA "programming" that goes into the primal fertilized cell prima; fertilized cell of the soon-to-be-formed embryo. This scientific discovery came long after he wrote these words.

Crucifixion and Resurrection

> *Having once seen Truth, having once had the illumination, you find that the next step is to demonstrate it and not be cast down or discouraged by the opposite. When the crucifixion comes and you are suffering the pangs of dying error, you may cry out, 'My God, my God, why hast thou forsaken me?' forgetting for the time the promises in the mount of transfiguration. This is when you need to realize that you are passing through a transforming process that will be followed by a resurrection of all that is worth saving.*[190]

Charles Fillmore always dealt with the crucifixion in connection with the resurrection. This gives his metaphysical interpretations of it a very positive and uplifting tone. The life of Jesus is really a representation of every person's life and destiny, but presented to our world on a larger-than-life scale.

---

[190] Fillmore, Charles *Atom-Smashing Power of Mind*, p. 155

Resurrection

> *The restoring of mind and body to their original, undying state. This is accomplished by the realization that God is Spirit and that God created man with power like that which He himself possesses. When man realizes this, his mind and body automatically become immortal. The resurrection takes place in us every time we rise to Jesus' realization of the perpetual indwelling life that is connecting us with the Father. A new flood of life comes to all who open their minds and their bodies to the living word of God.*[191]

As in so many of the important Bible symbols, Charles Fillmore sees resurrection as an ongoing process, not a once-and-for-all accomplishment. The resurrection experience can be a daily one for any person who is seriously committed to Spirit. Each effort with the attention directed forward (Godward) produces a new resurrection experience, new energies, higher vibratory rate, better molecular connections, truer thoughts, purer emotions, happier attitudes. These are all symptoms of the resurrection experience which any person may have who is willing to follow the Truth.

Regeneration

> *A change in which abundant spiritual life, even eternal life, is incorporated into the body. The transformation that takes place through bringing all the forces of mind and body to the support of*

---

[191] Fillmore, Charles *The Revealing Word*, Resurrection, p. 169

> *the Christ ideal. The unification of Spirit, soul, and body in spiritual oneness. Regeneration begins its work in the conscious mind and completes it in the subconsciousness. The first step is cleansing or denial in which all error thoughts are renounced. This includes forgiveness for sins committed and a general clearing of the whole consciousness. After the way has been prepared, the second step takes place. This is the outpouring of the Holy Spirit.*[192]

What is regeneration? We cannot exactly describe it because we have not as yet experienced it. But we find that most metaphysicians generally agree that it entails a connection in mind with a higher and finer type of energy to be utilized by the body. This is followed by a purifying and refining of the fluids, cells, and tissues of the body. Atomic vibratory rate and molecular connections are changed, and the result is a dramatic change in the nature and performing ability of the body. Mr. Fillmore often refers to this as "a body of light" or "the Lord's body."

New Age

> *Humankind is changing its vibrations to a higher rate, and the higher types of humankind must keep the equipoise by unfolding spiritually or they will lose their hold. Cases of loss of mental poise are now getting so numerous as to attract the attention of the medical world, and these cases will increase in frequency in the future, unless there is a*

---

[192] Fillmore, Charles *The Revealing Word*, Regeneration, p. 165

stronger development of the spiritual nature of men. Old things are passing away![193]

In the language of the zodiac we could say that the Piscean age is drawing to a close and the Aquarian age is beginning. Mankind is developing rapidly into this new age of awareness. Jesus said, "Follow me."[194]

---

[193] Fillmore, Charles *Atom-Smashing Power of Mind*, p. 165
[194] Matthew 16:24

Chapter 14 - Salvation

Questions from the Text
1. Give a brief definition for each of the following terms.
   - Christ Consciousness
   - The Christ Mind
   - Soul Unfoldment
   - Spiritual Illumination

Questions for Advanced Discussion
1. Explain how our bodies are transformed.
2. What is meant by believing on Christ unto salvation?
3. What is the way to build a consciousness of eternal life?
4. What is Christ? Explain fully how Christ is our salvation.[195]
5. How is Jesus, the Christ the Savior of humankind?

Lesson Text
Those who think they saved when they have been 'converted' will find that salvation has just begun. Conversion and 'change of heart' are real experiences, as anyone who has passed through them will testify, but they are merely introductory to the new life in Christ. When a person arrives at a certain exalted consciousness through the exercise of mind in thinking about God and God's laws, is lifted above the thoughts of the world into a heavenly realm. This is the beginning of entry into the Kingdom of the Heavens, which was the text of many of Jesus' discourses.[196]

---
[195] Colossians 1:27
[196] Fillmore, Charles *Teach Us to Pray*, p. 163

Just as Unity views resurrection as an ongoing process, it also sees salvation as a process, rather than a state of "having it made." Unity does not use the word salvation much, mainly because it carries a connotation that is not compatible with metaphysical thinking. But in another sense, salvation is a valid concern of metaphysical Christianity. The old statement that "Jesus saves" is correct on the metaphysical level. "Jesus saves us from hell" is also correct. Jesus is the living symbol of awakened spiritual awareness. The words of Jesus constitute what we call Truth. Hell is the biblical symbol for useless, unnecessary suffering. Spiritual awareness (Jesus) guides us into Truth, and following the Truth saves us from repeated useless, unnecessary suffering (hell).

Christ Consciousness

> *'God so loved the world that He gave His only begotten Son, that whosoever believeth on Him should not perish, but have eternal life.'[197] This does not mean that a personal man, named Jesus of Nazareth, was sent forth as a special propitiation for the sins of the world, or that the only available route into the Father's presence lies through him. It simply means that God has provided a way by which all may come consciously into God's presence in their own souls. That way is through the only begotten Son of God, the Christ consciousness, which Jesus demonstrated. This consciousness is the always present Son of the Father, dwelling as a*

---

[197] John 3:16

spiritual seed in each of us and ready to germinate and grow at our will.[198]

Christ consciousness is the name of the evolutionary goal for the present human family on earth. The term itself is hard to define or explain, and we often end up repeating words like Christ, divine, and perfect. So rather than attempt an intellectually satisfying explanation of it, we urge Truth students to let their intuition give them a "feel" for this term. Charles Fillmore helpfully reminds us that in our present state of consciousness, the only begotten Son (Christ) is still in the seed stage in most of us. We are still working to germinate that seed. Most of us are still far from being able to express the Christ to any degree of fullness. But right now our direction is the most important thing. Greater wonders will come later!

The Christ Mind

The mind of each individual may be consciously unified with Divine Mind through the indwelling Christ. By affirming at-one-ment with God-Mind, we eventually realize the perfect mind which was in Christ Jesus.[199]

One of the laws of mind is that man becomes like that with which he identifies himself. Christ is the one perfect pattern... Each should, therefore, be wise and identify himself with the Christ.[200]

---

[198] Fillmore, Charles *Twelve Powers*, p. 118
[199] Fillmore, Charles *Keep a True Lent*, p. 178
[200] Ibid, p. 180

"Christ Mind" and "Divine Mind" are the same in essence, but there is a difference as to how the terms are used. We speak of Divine Mind to describe God and the universe and all that is in the universe. That portion of Divine Mind that indwells us is Christ Mind. Identifying with the Christ simply means that we connect our sense of I AM with the great composite of all divine ideas—the Christ.

Spiritual Evolution:

> *Evolution is the result of the development of ideas in mind. What we are now is the result of the evolution of our consciousness, and our consciousness is the result of the seed ideas sown in our mind. Therefore spiritual evolution is the unfoldment of the spirit of God into expression. It is the development achieved by man working under spiritual law.*[201]

> *In plain, everyday language, we would say that Being, the original fount, is an impersonal principle; but in its work of creation it puts forth the idea that contains all ideas: The Logos, the Christ, the Son of God, spiritual man. This idea is the creative power, the concrete consciousness formulated by universal principle.*[202]

The second paragraph above contains what is perhaps Charles Fillmore's clearest definition of the Christ. He states, "Being (God) puts forth the idea that contains all

---

[201] Fillmore, Charles *Keep a True Lent*, p. 165
[202] Fillmore, Charles *Teach Us to Pray*, p. 168

ideas: the Logos, the Christ, the Son of God, spiritual man. This Idea is the creative power..." The phrase "idea that contains all ideas" is an important key to understanding the meaning of Christ.

Soul Unfoldment

> *When it dawns upon man that he has within him the primal spiritual spark of God, the living Word or Logos, and that through the Word he is identified with the original Mind, he has the key to infinite soul unfoldment. Even though a person does not at first have this higher revelation of his sonship and unity with creative Mind, the assumption helps him to bring it to realization.*[203]

As he does in so many other spiritual matters, Charles Fillmore sees soul unfoldment as an ongoing process. In this paragraph he goes so far as to refer to "infinite soul unfoldment." We cannot be certain whether or not the soul will unfold "infinitely," but for the time being we can feel safe in saying that our soul will continue to unfold indefinitely.

Spiritual Illumination

> *The relation of head and heart is illustrated in the lives of John the Baptizer and Jesus. They were cousins; the understanding of the head bears a close relation to the wisdom of the heart. They both received the baptism of Spirit, John preceding Jesus and baptizing Him. Here the natural order of*

---

[203] Fillmore, Charles *Jesus Christ Heals*, p. 144

> *spiritual illumination is illustrated. We receive first an intellectual understanding of Truth which we transmit to our heart, where love is awakened.*[204]
>
> *This is the first and the second coming of Christ, spoken of in the Scriptures. The first coming is the receiving of Truth into the conscious mind, and the second coming is the awakening and the regeneration of the subconscious mind through the superconscious of the Christ Mind.*[205]

In his very accurate interpretation of the metaphysical significance of the relationship between John the Baptizer and Jesus, Charles Fillmore is careful to point out the importance of observing the proper sequence of orderly progress. He places intellectual understanding (John) as a prerequisite to spiritual illumination and power (Jesus). Under divine order certain preliminary things must be taken care of before the greater inflow of power occurs. This is the symbolism of John the Baptizer being the "forerunner" of Jesus, but always acknowledging Jesus as being greater than himself.

The New Person

> *Step by step, thought added to thought, spiritual emotion added to spiritual emotion—eventually the transformation is complete. It does not come in a day, but every high impulse, every pure thought, every upward desire adds to the exaltation and gradual personification of the divine in man and to*

---

[204] Fillmore, *The Twelve Powers*, p. 90
[205] Ibid, p. 15

> *the transformation of the human. The 'old man' is constantly brought into subjection, and his deeds forever put off, as the 'new man' appears arrayed in the vestments of divine consciousness.*[206]

This paragraph is a further elaboration by Charles Fillmore on the ideas concerning the "New Man." The process he describes is depicted metaphysically in the Bible as the journey through spiritual evolution from Adam to Christ.

The Christ Life

> *It is no idle experiment, this keeping in mind the words of Jesus. It is a very momentous undertaking, and may mark the most important period in the life of an individual. There must be sincerity and earnestness and right motive, and withal a determination to understand the spiritual import. This requires attention, time, and patience in the application of the mind to solving the deeper meanings of the sayings that we are urged to keep.*[207]

> *This means mental discipline day after day and night after night, until the inertia of the mind is overcome and the way is opened for the descent of Spirit.*[208]

---

[206] Fillmore, Charles *Atom-Smashing Power of Mind*, p. 124
[207] Fillmore, Charles *Talks on Truth*, p. 174
[208] Ibid, p. 177

The Christ Life is a way of referring to a human being who has somehow made a serious commitment to Spirit. More specifically, it describes a commitment to things spiritual contained within the teachings of Jesus. Such a commitment is indeed a very serious thing and must be taken seriously. But if we are sincere in making such a commitment, and if we are faithful in our efforts to maintain it, great and wonderful things will result. One of the most beautiful and wonderful things that happens is that our lives immediately come under new and higher aspects of the law of mind action. Two of the main aspects of this law which become apparent are God's divine guidance and God's divine protection. These two aspects become the overseeing factor in every part of our existence.

Chapter 15 - Denials and Affirmations

Questions from the Text
1. Taking a life situation, write a denial and affirmation for it. Make sure it identifies you with The Christ.
2. Give a simple definition for the Law of Cause and Effect

Questions for Advanced Discussion
1. How may we bring our thoughts under conscious control?
2. What is an affirmation?
3. How are we helped by affirming Truth?
4. Give three affirmations that help one to realize unity with God.

Lesson Text
Thoughts are Things

Thoughts are things; they occupy space in the mental field. A healthy state of mind is attained and continued when the thinker willingly lets go the old thoughts and takes on the new. This is illustrated by the inlet and the outlet of a pool of water. Stop the inlet, and the pool goes dry. Close the natural outlet, and the pool stagnates, or, like the Dead Sea, it crystallizes its salts until they preserve everything that they touch.[209]

---

[209] Fillmore, Charles *The Twelve Powers*, p. 144

It is because thoughts are "things" that we can observe and talk about the law of mind action and the formative power of thought. The relationship of a human being to "things" holds true for the realm of thoughts. Things come and things go. Some things belong to us and some do not. Some things cause harm, others are blessings. All these observations about things are also true about thoughts, for they are things. All thoughts that come to us do not belong to us. We may have taken hold of certain thoughts that came to us and are calling them our own. If they are negative they will do us harm. But we can let go of these, and further harm will cease. We can then attract new and better thoughts to us. But best of all, we can begin doing our own thinking. This is quite a high attainment, much rarer than we may realize. When we are really doing our own thinking we receive much new inspiration and guidance, because we are then generating an energy that will let more light into our minds.

Keys to the Kingdom

> *Whatever we bind or limit in earth, in the conscious mind, shall be bound or limited in the ideal or heavenly realm, and whatever we loose and set free in the conscious mind (earth) shall be loosed and set free in the ideal, the heavenly. In other words, whatever you affirm or deny in your conscious mind determines the character of the super-mind activities. All power is given unto you both in heaven and in earth through your thought.*[210]

---

[210] Fillmore, Charles Prosperity, p. 177

Here Charles Fillmore emphasizes the great importance of the work done on the conscious level of the mind. It really and truly does have the keys to the kingdom. Actually, the keys to two kingdoms: heaven and hell. The conscious level of mind has two significant abilities not found on other levels of the mind. It can consent and it can refuse. It cannot create and it cannot destroy, but it can consent or refuse. This is where all trouble starts, but it is also where all improvement starts. The first step is to begin to pay more attention to what is going on in the conscious level of mind and make some decisions about what is going on, rather than just automatically accepting whatever is going on. The old Greek word for this control is "metanoia" inadequately translated into English as "repentance."

Denials and Affirmations

> *It is just as necessary that one should let go of old thoughts and conditions after they have served their purpose as it is that one should lay hold of new ideas and create new conditions to meet one's requirements. In fact we cannot lay hold of the new ideas and make the new conditions until we have made room for them by eliminating the old.*[211]

> *It is found that, by the use of these mind forces, man can dissolve things by denying their existence, and that he can build them up by affirming their presence. This is a simple statement, but when it is applied in all the intricate thought forms of the universe it becomes complex. The law of mental*

---
[211] Fillmore, Charles *Prosperity*, p. 175

> *denial and affirmation will prove its truth to all those who persistently make use of it.*[212]

Denial and affirmation are the two great expressions of polarized energy in the life. Both are essential. Both serve us in our efforts to evolve consciousness in obedience to spiritual law. Denial is the ability to let go of the old, the outworn, the negative attitude, the incorrect belief. It is also the ability to refuse, to reject. It is the great "nay, nay" saying power of mind. Affirmation is the ability to accept the newer, the truer, the higher, the more correct attitude and belief. It is also the ability to say yes and accept better concepts of divine ideas. It is the great "yea, yea" power of mind.

Cause and Effect

> There is a chain of mind action connecting cause and effect in all the activities of life. This chain is forged by man, and its links are thoughts and words.[213]

Cause and effect is a law of life which operates on many levels. A simple definition of this law is: "like attracts like," or "thoughts held in mind produce after their kind." On higher levels, the law of cause and effect is seen to have other dimensions and aspects. Feeling becomes involved. Cause does not have to lie only in the past. This is the gaining of insight into the God thought revealed by Jesus that is called Spirit, Father, or Absolute Good. Paul speaks of this higher, finer, more conscious level of the law

---

[212] Fillmore, Charles *Christian Healing*, p. 51
[213] Fillmore, Charles *Jesus Christ Heals*, p. 132

as "grace and truth." In Unity the terms, "law of cause and effect" and "law of mind action" are used synonymously.

Good and Evil

> *We should not assume that all manifestation is good because the originating idea came from Divine Mind. All ideas have their foundation in Divine Mind, but man has put the limitation of his negative thought upon them, and sees them 'in a mirror, darkly'.*[214]

> *What we form that is evil we must unform before we can take the coveted step up the mountain of the ideal. Here enters the factor that dissolves the structures that are no longer useful; this factor in metaphysics is known as denial. Denial is not, strictly speaking, an attribute of Being as principle, but it is simply the absence of the impulse that constructs and sustains.*[215]

Sin and evil are not self-existent things in and of themselves. They are words which describe certain human expressions or lacks. Primarily these words refer to any human attempt to negate any divine idea. This can take many forms. Mr. Fillmore calls denial an "absence of the impulse that constructs and sustains." This, of course, is the opposite of affirmation. But just as affirmation requires that a decision be made, followed by a certain effort of the mind, so it is with denial. A true denial is not just an "absence" of something. It is an effort made in

---

[214] Fillmore, Charles *Christian Healing*, p. 45
[215] Fillmore, Charles *The Twelve Powers*, p. 150

mind to bring about an "absence." It is the effort required to say "no," to let go, to refuse or reject.

How Denials Work

> *In all actual transformation of mind and body a dissolving, breaking-up process necessarily takes place, because thought force and substance have been built into the errors that appear. In each individual these errors have the power that man has given to them by his thought concerning them. These thought structures must be broken up and eliminated from consciousness. The simplest, most direct, and most effective method is to withdraw from them the life and substance that have been going to feed them, and to let them shrivel away into their own nothingness. This withdrawal is best accomplished by denial of the power and reality of evil and affirmation of the allness of Spirit. Nothing is destroyed, because 'nothing' can't be destroyed. The change that takes place is merely a transference of power from an error belief to faith in the Truth, through the recognition that God is good and is all that in reality exists.*[216]

In this paragraph Charles Fillmore urges us to confine the use of denial to errors found within our own consciousness. He does not suggest the use of denial on things already existing in the outer, nor on personalities that are already expressing. We do not deny the existence of things. We deny their power over us.

---

[216] Fillmore, Charles *Jesus Christ Heals*, p. 63

How Affirmations Work

> *One who knows Principle has a certain inner security given him by the understanding of God-Mind. Our affirmations are for the purpose of establishing in our consciousness a broad understanding of the principles on which all life and existence depend.*[217]

> *In order to demonstrate Principle we must keep establishing ourselves in certain statements of the law. The more often you present to your mind a proposition that is logical and true, the stronger becomes that inner feeling of security to you.*[218]

Affirmation works because of the faculty which is most directly involved in affirmation—faith. Affirmation plays an important part in the process of divine ideas becoming facts and experiences in man's existence on earth. More about this will be said in the next section on faith.

Conserving Creative Energy

> *Jesus said, 'Let your speech be, Yes, yes; No, no.'*[219] *Talking is a waste of energy—a dissipater of power. If you want the greatest success, do not talk too much about your plans. Keep a reserve force of new*

---

[217] Fillmore, Charles, *Prosperity*, p. 56
[218] Ibid, p. 57
[219] Matthew 5:37

> *ideas always on hand as a generative center. Let your work speak for itself.*[220]
>
> *Make your denials as if you were gently sweeping away cobwebs, and make your affirmations in a strong, bold, vehement, positive attitude of mind.*[221]

Although creative energy is limitless in the Absolute, it is limited through our capacity to receive it. Therefore it is important that we learn not to waste or misuse our creative energy. Too much mechanical talking wastes energy used in affirmation. Violence or too much force wastes energy used in denial. Rightly used creative energy generates more creative energy. This is why times of inner silence and stillness are so valuable. This is why continuous forgiveness of sins is so important. The alternative is squandering of energy, followed by disappointment and fatigue.

Absolute vs. Relative

> *Christian metaphysicians have discovered that we can greatly accelerate the formation of the Christ Mind in ourselves by using affirmations that identify us with the Christ. These affirmations often are so far beyond the present attainment of the novice as to seem ridiculous, but when it is understood that the statements are grouped about*

---

[220] Fillmore, Charles *Keep a True Lent*, p. 47
[221] Fillmore, Charles *Teach Us to Pray*, p. 183

> *an ideal to be attained, they seem fair and reasonable.*[222]

Affirmations are, of course, based upon acknowledgment of the Absolute, but they occupy a very special category in the vocabulary of Unity. Affirmations are verbalized divine ideas, and the language of absolutism is proper for them. Statement of facts and description of existing things are another matter. Here, the language of absolutism is out of place. Here is where accuracy of language, right names for things, and relative terms constitute the correct vocabulary.

---

[222] Fillmore, Charles *Keep a True Lent*, p. 71

Chapter 16 - Understanding Faith

Questions from the Text
1. What is faith?
2. What is the difference between true faith and blind bath?
3. What is the difference between faith thinking and intellectual thinking?
4. What is understanding faith?

Questions for Advanced Discussion:
1. What is the difference between spiritual understanding and intellectual understanding?

Lesson Text

> *Faith is the perceiving power of the mind linked with a power to shape substance. It is spiritual assurance, the power to do the seemingly impossible. It is a force that draws to us our heart's desire right out of the invisible spiritual substance. It is a deep inner knowing that that which is sought is already ours for the taking, the 'assurance of things hoped for.'*[223]

> *The office of faith is to take abstract ideas and give them definite form in substance. Ideas are abstract and formless to us until they become substance, the substance of faith.*[224]

---

[223] Fillmore, Charles *Keep a True Lent*, p. 148
[224] Fillmore, Charles Prosperity, p. 43

As we read these passages by Charles Fillmore regarding faith, we might be struck by the many resemblances these explanations have to what he also says in regard to imagination. We read that faith is "the perceiving power of the mind linked with a power to shape substance." When he explains imagination he states that the imagination has the power to perceive ideas and form mental energy into thoughts and concepts. This may, at first, sound as though faith and imagination both do the same things. But there is a distinction. Imagination shapes mental energy only into thought forms. It creates only the mental patterns, it does not actually produce the finished form. Faith actually brings substance into manifested form. The work of faith has a more definite and much wider range than imagination.

Blind Faith

> *Mighty things have been wrought in the past by those who had mere blind faith to guide them. To faith we now add understanding of the law, and our achievements will be a fulfillment of the promise of Jesus, 'He that believeth on me, the works that I do shall he do also; and greater works than these shall he do'*[225].[226]
>
> *The man who is grounded in faith does not measure his thoughts or his acts by the world's standard of facts. 'Faith is blind,' say people who are not acquainted with the real thing; but those who are in spiritual understanding know that faith*

---

[225] John 14:12
[226] Fillmore, Charles *Jesus Christ Heals*, p. 72

> *has open eyes, that certain things do exist in Spirit and become substantial and real to the one who dwells and thinks and lives in faith. Such a one knows.*[227]

At one time blind faith served a useful purpose, because it represented a step forward from older types of religious superstition. Blind faith simply refers to the exercise of faith without the understanding of spiritual law. There is nothing wrong with this if that is where a person is in his development of consciousness. When faith is based on understanding, however, one's thoughts, words and efforts become truly creative.

Understanding Faith

> *The careful modern metaphysician does not arrive at his conclusions through speculation; he analyzes and experiments with the operations of his own mind until he discovers laws that govern mind action universally.*[228]

> *Everyone coming into conscious recognition of the mind of Spirit knows that he knows, without having learned through any of the avenues recognized by the intellectual man as necessary. It is not a system of reasoning from premise to conclusion, but a direct summing up of the whole case in omnipresent knowing.*[229]

---

[227] Ibid, p. 106
[228] Fillmore, Charles *The Twelve Powers*, p. 143
[229] Fillmore, Charles *Talks on Truth*, p. 72

Charles Fillmore taught that anyone who seeks can find the principle of "omnipresent knowing" and tune in to it. The academic method of gaining knowledge is certainly one way of getting it, but Charles Fillmore knew it is not the only way. This is especially true concerning knowledge of spiritual things. Divine Mind is omnipresent. We have a unique connection with that Mind through Christ and our own super-consciousness. When the connection is open from the conscious level of mind, pure knowing is gained by the individual. This is understanding, and when it is working with faith, a mighty power for good is in operation.

Faith Thinking

> *We all have the thinking faculty located in the head, from which we send forth thoughts, good, bad, and indifferent. If we are educated and molded after the ordinary pattern of the human family, we may live an average lifetime and never have an original thought. The thinking faculty in the head is supplied with the secondhand ideas of our ancestors, the dominant beliefs of humankind, or the threadbare stock of the ordinary social whirl. This is not faith-thinking. Faith-thinking is done only by one who has caught sight of the inner truths of Being, and who feeds his thinking faculty on images generated in the heart, or love center.*[230]

In this paragraph Charles Fillmore describes the weak character of the ordinary stream of thought which passes through our minds with little or no effort on our

---

[230] Fillmore, Charles *Keep a True Lent*, p. 113

part. This process can also be seen as "collective consciousness running its course" through the channels of human minds. In the latter part of the paragraph he approaches the process of "faith-thinking," which he defines as thinking that is mostly generated in the love center.

Faith Thinking and Intellectual Thinking

> *Faith-thinking is not merely an intellectual process, based on reasoning. The faith-thinker does not compare, analyze, or draw conclusions from known premises. He does not take appearances into consideration; he is not biased by precedent. His thinking gives form, without cavil or question, to ideas that come straight from the eternal fount of wisdom. His perception impinges on the spiritual and he knows.* [231]

In contrasting faith-thinking to intellectual thinking, Charles Fillmore is not criticizing intellectual thinking, but rather revealing insights about faith-thinking. Only one who has experienced faith-thinking can really appreciate its validity and its beautiful results. We would do well to pay special attention to Mr. Fillmore's reference to "ideas that come straight from the eternal fount of wisdom." We are all connected to that eternal fount, and we can open our connection only from the conscious level of our own mind.

---

[231] Fillmore, Charles *Keep a True Lent*, p. 113

Developing Understanding Faith

> *Spiritual understanding is developed in a multitude of ways; no two persons have exactly the same experience. One may be a Saul, to whom the light comes in a blinding flash, while to another the light may come gently and harmoniously. The sudden breaking forth of light indicates the existence of stored-up reservoirs of spiritual experience, gained from previous lives.*[232]
>
> *It is possible to have a reality and yet neither touch it nor smell it nor see it nor in any way come into consciousness of it in the outer realm. That is what faith is. It is the consciousness in us of the realities of the attributes of mind. Before we can have the substance of faith we must realize that the mind creates realities.*[233]
>
> *Now this faith that we are all cultivating and striving for is built up through continuous affirmations of its loyalty to the divine idea, the higher self. You must have faith in your spiritual capacity.*[234]

We are told here that spiritual understanding may break forth in our mind in a manner similar to a sunrise, in a sudden breakthrough of light which was not there before. But, as Mr. Fillmore indicates, this does not come from "out of the blue." It comes as a result of previous

---

[232] Fillmore, Charles *The Twelve Powers*, p. 93
[233] Fillmore, Charles *Jesus Christ Heals*, p. 103
[234] Ibid

effort, in some cases from efforts in previous lives. There is always a reality greater than the present existence of physical forms. Charles Fillmore calls this "the realities of the attributes of mind." He is referring to Divine Ideas. Faith that works with divine ideas is the most powerful expression possible.

Basis for Understanding Faith

> *The Truth is, then:*
> - *That God is Principle, Law, Being, Mind, Spirit, All-Good, Omniscient, Omnipresent, Omnipotent, unchangeable, Creator, Father, Cause, and Source of all that is;*
> - *That God is individually formed in consciousness in each of us, and is known to us as 'Father' when we recognize Him within us as our Creator, as our mind, as our life, as our very being;*
> - *That mind has ideas and that ideas have expression; that all manifestation in our world is the result of the ideas that we are holding in mind and are expressing;*
> - *That to bring forth or to manifest the harmony of Divine Mind, or the 'kingdom of heaven,' all our ideas must be one with divine ideas, and must be expressed in the divine order of Divine Mind.*[235]

This is one of the most famous passages in Unity publications. It may be pointed out here that this is an example of a listing of what we might call the "technicalities of metaphysical Truth." This is not all there is to Truth. In addition to the technicalities we also have

---
[235] Fillmore, Charles *Christian Healing*, p. 16

the "essences of Truth" which are the feelings, the nuances, and the dimension beyond the printed word. The essences of Truth seldom are expressed on a printed page, but are mostly conveyed through a spoken message, lesson, or meditation.

Chapter 17 – Co-Creation

Questions from the Text
1. Give a brief definition for each of the following terms:
   - Involution
   - Evolution
2. What are the steps in creation?

Questions for Advanced Discussion
1. What will aid us in understanding how the one Mind creates?
2. Through whom are the divine attributes, or ideas, brought into expression and manifestation?

Lesson Text
Creation

> *God idealized two universal planes of consciousness, the heaven and the earth, or more properly, 'the heavens and the earth.' One is the realm of pure ideals; the other, of thought forms. God does not create the visible universe directly, as man makes a cement pavement, but He creates the ideas that are used by His intelligent 'image and likeness' to make the universe.*[236]

Again and again Charles Fillmore returns to the theme of the distinction between what we call the original creation of God, and the secondary creation in which we are continually involved. In the original creation there is no

---
[236] Fillmore, Charles *Keep a True Lent*, p. 176

co-creator. There is only God expressing as creative principle. It is sometimes difficult to comprehend the metaphysical insight that "God does not create the visible universe directly, as man makes a cement pavement." God's original creation, for us, is the omnipresent realm of divine ideas, out of which all possible forms may be brought forth. This "bringing forth" process is what we shall comment on in the next section of this course.

Co-Creation

> *Some metaphysicians teach that man makes himself, others teach that God makes him, and still others hold that the creative process is a cooperation between God and man. The latter is proved true by those who have had the deepest spiritual experiences. Jesus recognized this dual creative process, as is shown in many statements relative to His work and the Father's work. 'My Father works even until now, and I work.'[237] God creates in the ideal, and man carries out in the manifest what God has idealized.[238]*

We are endowed with a creative talent which our souls always long to express. However, our creativity has a narrower range than that of the original creator. Our creativity occurs within the realm called "existence" and finds its fulfillment in what is called "manifestation."

---

[237] John 5:17
[238] Fillmore, Charles *Christian Healing*, p. 42

Divine Ideas

> *The ideas of Divine Mind are whole and complete in their capacity to unfold perpetually greater and more beautiful forms according to the thinking capacity in man. Man catches mental sight of an idea in Divine Mind and proceeds to put it in terms comprehensible to him on his plane of consciousness. All ideas have their origin in Divine Mind, but their character as unfolded by man depends entirely upon his acquaintance with God.*[239]

Divine ideas are the most important and most powerful things in the universe. All that God has created for us is involved in those ideas. All possibilities for us are infolded in those ideas. We have only to accept those ideas and give them whatever expression we are capable of at our current level of consciousness. If we need additional help, we can always receive it from levels within ourselves above our current conscious level. We experience this as "divine help," even though it did not come from outside our being. "The kingdom of God is within you."[240]

Our Role

> *The ideas of God are potential forces waiting to be set in motion through proper formative vehicles. The thinking faculty in man is such a vehicle, and it is through this that the visible universe has*

---

[239] Fillmore, Charles *Atom-Smashing Power of Mind*, p. 94
[240] Luke 17:21

> *existence. Man does not 'create' anything if by this term is meant the producing of something from nothing; but he does make the formless up into form; or rather it is through his conscious cooperation that the one Mind forms its universe.*[241]

> *Get behind a thing into the mental realm where it exists as an inexhaustible idea, and you can draw upon it perpetually and never deplete the source.*[242]

Our role, at one time in the history of religious thinking on this planet was, first: survival and next: being good. But metaphysical Christianity has greatly expanded this role. We know how to survive and how to be good. We now need a religion which helps us become spiritually aware and truly creative. Our role now is to be co-creators in our Father's world. Stated quite simply: we are to be the conscious transformer of divine ideas into facts of life. All valid metaphysical Truth teachings help us learn how to do this.

Involution and Evolution

> *Involution always precedes evolution. That which is involved in mind evolves through matter.*[243]

> *The architect plans a house and sees it finished in his mind before a single stone is laid or a pound of earth excavated. He can change his plan many*

---

[241] Fillmore, Charles *Atom-Smashing Power of Mind*, p. 93
[242] Fillmore, Charles *Christian Healing*, p. 13
[243] Fillmore, Charles *The Twelve Powers*, p. 121

> *times before the construction commences. He can destroy it entirely if he so desires. So man builds the house of his consciousness. If he has been planning to build a home for himself alone, in which there is but one room, he created in mind just such a plan, and it is complete and awaits its coming into visibility. If he has made a plan of a larger structure, in which are many rooms, this plan will also come into visibility.*[244]

Involution is the existence of everything in an invisible or potential form. Evolution is the process of the transformation from the invisible, intangible potential into expression and greater manifestation. This is especially true of the evolution of man, which is the subject of our study in metaphysical Christianity. It is also true concerning all of our efforts to create. Involution always precedes evolution.

Our Executive Power

> *The Spirit of Truth is the mind of God in its executive capacity; it carries out the divine plan of the originating Spirit. It proceeds from the Father and bears witness of the Son. We have in the operation of our own mind an illustration of how Divine Mind works. When an idea is fully formulated in our mind and we decide to carry it out, our thoughts change their character from contemplative to executive. We no longer plan, but proceed to execute what we have already planned.*

---

[244] Fillmore, Charles *Keep a True Lent*, p. 46

> *So God-Mind sends forth its Spirit to carry out in man the divine idea imaged in the Son.*[245]

Charles Fillmore strongly believed (and demonstrated in his own life) that a sincere commitment to Spirit will cause an inner relationship with the very Spirit of Truth just as Jesus had said in the Gospels. In this relationship with the Spirit of Truth "thoughts change their character from contemplative to executive." Persons today have the option of using the great power of consciousness in one of two ways: as a recording and repeating device or as a transmitter of creative energy. The old duplicating type of consciousness still insists: "seeing is believing." So it repeats copy after copy of only the old patterns. It can be efficient. It works. But it is not part of creative evolution. The true follower of the metaphysical Truth teaching of Jesus seeks to have the same creative consciousness demonstrated by Jesus. Unity teachings are for the purpose of helping all who are interested in accomplishing this.

The Trinity in Creation

> *Substance is first given form in the mind, and as it becomes manifest it goes through a threefold activity. In laying hold of substance in the mind and bringing it into manifestation, we play a most important part.*[246]

> *All creative processes involve a realm of ideas and a realm of patterns or expressions of those ideas. The*

---

[245] Fillmore, Charles *Teach Us to Pray*, p. 124
[246] Fillmore, Charles *Prosperity*, p. 15

patterns arrest or 'bottle up' the free electric units that sustain the visible thing. Thus creation is in its processes a trinity, and back of the visible universe are both the original creative idea and the cosmic rays that crystallize into earthly things. When we understand this trinity in its various activities we shall be able to reconcile the discoveries of modern science with the fundamentals of religion.[247]

The Trinity permeates all things—the creative process itself and all things created by this process. This includes man and all his creations (manifestations). The benefits of acknowledging and making effort to understand the Trinity may not be apparent in the initial stages, but later on they will be experienced, perhaps in ways that cannot even be imagined now. The Trinity is basic to our existence. To understand it is to add new power to consciousness which will someday prove of utmost usefulness.

Steps in Creation

It is found that the mind establishes a permanent consciousness through seven steps or stages, called in Genesis 'days.' First, the mind perceives and affirms Truth to be a universal principle. Secondly, faith in the working power of Truth is born in consciousness. Thirdly, Truth takes definite form in mind. Fourthly, the will carries Truth into acts. Fifthly, discrimination is quickened and the difference between Truth and error is discerned. Sixthly, every thought and word is expressed in

---

[247] Ibid, p. 4

> *harmony with Truth. The seventh 'day' represents a peaceful confidence and rest in the fulfillment of the divine law.*[248]

In this paragraph Charles Fillmore gives us something not to be found anywhere else in the Unity literature: a clear, concise, highly condensed overview of the metaphysical meaning of the seven days of the creation allegory. He has placed the overview on a purely individual level of meaning. Each of us is that individual!

Theory vs. Practice

> *But the possession of this key is not all. A key is for use. We may know all about the way in which mind formulates states of consciousness and all about our relation to God, but unless we have made a change in our consciousness and realized, in a measure at least, the presence of God in our mind, we are not using the key. Theory is one thing; practice is another.*[249]

The idea presented by Mr. Fillmore in this paragraph is directly related to the difference between the technicalities of metaphysics and the essences of metaphysics. Study of theory and technicalities is necessary. But it is not the full education. It is only when the technicalities and essences are combined that real education in Truth has occurred. It is not an attainment, but a process. Theory must be transformed in practice.

---

[248] Fillmore, Charles *Teach Us to Pray*, p. 182
[249] Fillmore, Charles *Talks on Truth*, p. 125

Part III – The Relationship between Us and God

Supplementary Reading:
- Cady, H. Emilie *Lessons In Truth*, Chapters 3, 4, 5 and 6
- Fillmore, Charles *Christian Healing*, Chapter 3, 4 and 8
- Fillmore, Charles *Talks on Truth*, Chapter 14, Jesus Christ's Atonement
- Fillmore, Charles *Keep a True Lent*, Fillmore, Chapters 4, 10, 11 and 15
- Hausmann, Winifred, *Your God-Given Potential*, Chapters 1 and 2, "From Primordial Cell to Christ Oriented Man," "Discover a New World Within."
- Fillmore, Charles, *The Twelve Powers of Man*, Chapter 1
- Fillmore, Cora, *Christ Enthroned in Man*, Chapter 14

We continue our studies as Truth students. In this third part, we explore the meaning and message of Jesus, prayer, meditations and the twelve powers or abilities of God that reside in us. In addition to the Unity books listed above, you may want to read a contemporary book on prayer and refer to one or two on Jesus and one on the Twelve Powers:

- Marsella-Whitsett *How to Pray Without Talking to God: Moment by Moment, Choice by Choice* Hampton Roads Publishers, 2011

- Hasselbeck, Paul and Holton, Cher *PowerUp: The Twelve Powers Revisited as Accelerated Abilities* Prosperity Publishing House, 2009
- Searcy, Felica Blanco *Do Greater Things, Following in Jesus' Footsteps*, Unity House, 2009
- Shepherd, Thomas W. *Jesus 2.1* Unity Books, 2010
- Spong, John Shelby *Jesus for the Non-Religious* Harper San Francisco, 2007

Prayer

To God who is love unbounded
I come with a voiceless plea,
Knowing God's perfect wisdom
Has an open door for me.

I have but to trust God's goodness
And to listen and obey.
My soul doth wait in the silence
To hear what the God will say.

Chapter 18 – Jesus, the Christ

Questions from the Text
1. Explain the meaning of the names Christ, Jesus, and Jesus Christ from the historical and metaphysical standpoint.
2. What was Jesus' realization of oneness with God?
3. What was Jesus' custom in the matter of self-identification?
4. Why did many of the Jews not recognize Jesus as the Son of God?
5. Describe briefly your understanding of "Christ in you."

Questions for Advanced Discussion
1. Explain the meaning of the names Christ, Jesus, and Jesus Christ from the historical and metaphysical standpoint.
2. What was Jesus' realization of oneness with God?
3. What was Jesus' custom in the matter of self-identification?
4. Why did many of the Jews not recognize Jesus as the Son of God?
5. What is atonement?

Lesson Text
Jesus – the Man of Nazareth

> *Jesus was keenly conscious of the character of God and his own relationship to God. He knew God as unlimited love and as ever-present, abundant life; He knew God as wisdom and supply. He knew God*

as Father, who is ever ready and willing to supply every need of the human heart.[250]

He (Jesus) was a man on the quest, a man making the great discovery of his divinity, a man breaking through the psychological barrier between us and God, a man proving the Christ in us and his inherent potential for overcoming, for eternal life.[251]

Jesus is the name of the historical personal identity of the man from Nazareth who became the way-shower.

Christ

Christ abides in each person as his potential perfection. Each of us has within ourselves the Christ idea, just as Jesus had. We must look to the indwelling Christ in order to recognize our divine origin and birth.[252]

Christ is not a person. It is not Jesus. Christ is a degree of potential stature that dwells in every person.[253]

Christ in you is your hope of glory,[254] *for it is that of you that is of God and is God being projected into visibility as you. Christ in you is your own spiritual*

---

[250] Fillmore, Charles *The Revealing Word*, p. 111
[251] Butterworth, Eric *Discover the Power Within*, p. 20
[252] Fillmore, Charles *The Revealing Word*, p. 34
[253] Butterworth, Eric *Discover the Power Within*, p. 12
[254] Colossians 1:27

> *unity with the Infinite, the key of your heath and success.*[255]

Christ is a divine idea. It is the name of the perfect pattern of wholeness which is present in all of us. The Christ within is our true essence and our divine nature. It is the presence of God within us.

Jesus Christ

> *Jesus Christ is the union of the two, the idea and the expression, or in other words, he is the perfect person demonstrated.*[256]

> *The way would be more difficult for us without the way-shower, for in him we find the embodiment of what all of us truly are and are to be.*[257]

> *To say that we are as Jesus was is not exactly true because he dropped that personal consciousness by which we separate ourselves from our true God self. He proved in his resurrection and ascension that he had no consciousness separate from that of Being, therefore he really was Being for all intents and purposes.*[258]

Jesus Christ is the name which identifies the individual who perfectly understood the divine nature, who fully demonstrated his divine potential, and who completely fulfilled his divine purpose on this earth. The spirit of God within him expressed in its fullness. We, in

---

[255] Butterworth, *Eric Discover the Power Within*, p. 45
[256] Fillmore, Charles *The Revealing Word*, p. 112
[257] Wilson, Ernest, *The Emerging Self* p. 56
[258] Fillmore, Charles *Atom-Smashing Power of Mind*, p. 40

Unity, refer to Jesus Christ as our elder brother, teacher and way-shower who by his works and words, teaches us that we, too, have the ability to manifest our own Christ potential. We in Unity refer to Jesus the Christ, intentionally acknowledging that Christ is the name of Jesus' spiritual identity, not his earthly name.

Atonement

> *The mind of each individual may be consciously unified with Divine Mind through the indwelling Christ. By affirming at-one-ment with God-Mind, we eventually realize the perfect mind which is Christ Jesus."*[259]

Atonement is the spiritual experience in which we as individuals participate in conscious oneness with God. Though Jesus Christ did not accomplish this for us, by his life and teachings he showed us exactly the steps we must take to enter this state of consciousness as he did.

First and Second Coming

> *This is the first and second coming of Christ, spoken of in the Scriptures. The first coming is the receiving of Truth into the conscious mind, and the Second Coming is the awakening and regeneration of the subconscious mind through the superconscious or the Christ mind.*[260]

In Unity we interpret the concept of the first and second coming metaphysically. We do not expect the

---

[259] Fillmore, Charles *Keep a True Lent*, p. 178
[260] Fillmore, Charles *The Twelve Powers*, p. 15

physical re-entry of Jesus onto the earth plane. Rather we interpret the Scripture to mean that our divine nature, must come from the full realization in consciousness of the Christ mind within us.

Salvation

> *Our salvation is in living by the Christ pattern – not only by the teachings of the man Jesus Christ but by the Christ Mind with us.*[261]
>
> *Our salvation from sin, sickness, pain and death comes by our understanding and conforming to the orderly Mind back of all existence.*[262]
>
> *"God so loved the world that He gave His only begotten son, that whoever believes on him should not perish, but have eternal life."*[263] *This does not mean a personal man, named Jesus of Nazareth, was sent as a special propitiation*[264] *for the sins of the world, or that the only available route to God's presence lies through such a person. It simply means that God has provided a way by which all may consciously come into the Presence in their own souls. That way is through the only Begotten*

---

[261] Fillmore, Myrtle *Healing Letters*, p. 56
[262] Fillmore, Charles *Christian Healing*, p. 42
[263] John 3:16
[264] Propitiation (from Latin *propitiāre*, "to appease;" from *propitius*, "gracious")[1] is the act of appeasing or making well-disposed a deity, thus incurring divine favor or avoiding divine retribution

> *Son of God, the Christ, which Jesus demonstrated.*[265]

Salvation is a process that takes place within our own consciousness, not through the person named Jesus. We as individuals must cooperate with God in our own spiritual transformation, just as Jesus did. Salvation results in our being made free from ignorance, lack and limitation, and in being made free for wholeness, abundance, peace and fulfillment.

Following Jesus

> *It is no idle experiment, this keeping in mind the words of Jesus. It is a very momentous undertaking, and may mark the most important period in the life of an individual. There must be sincerity and earnestness and right motive, and with a determination to understand the spiritual importance. This requires attention, time, and patience in the application of the mind to solving the deeper meanings of the sayings that we are urged to keep.*[266]

In order to follow Jesus, we are to proceed on the path of spiritual enlightenment in the ways that he taught us. It is not worshipping the man, walking the way of mastery as he did that fulfills our responsibility to follow him.

---

[265] Fillmore, Charles *The Twelve Powers*, p. 118
[266] Fillmore, Charles *Talks in Truth*, p. 174

Christ Mind and Christ Consciousness

> *One of the laws of mind is that we become like that which we identify ourselves. Christ is the one perfect pattern. Each of us should, therefore, identify self with the Christ.*[267]

> *Christ consciousness... consciousness built in accordance with the Christ ideal, or in absolute relationship to God. The perfect mind that was in Christ Jesus.*[268]

> *This merging with God does not mean the total obliteration of our consciousness, but its glorification or expansion into that of the divine.*[269]

Christ mind is the real, innate possession of every individual. The Christ consciousness is the level of enlightenment we achieve through the process of self-mastery and spiritual unfoldment which is guided by the Christ mind. The attainment of Christ consciousness is the result of this process; it is not an instant achievement.

---

[267] Fillmore, Charles *Keep a True Lent*, p. 180
[268] Fillmore, Charles *The Revealing Word*, p. 42
[269] Fillmore, Charles *Mysteries of John*, p. 151

Chapter 19 – Prayer and Meditation

Questions from the Text
1. What is Prayer?
2. What is our link to God?
3. What is our prayer method called?
4. What is our inheritance from God?
5. What do we pray for?
6. As we engage in prayer it is important that we become…
7. What do denials and affirmations do?
8. What is the purpose of a daily meditation?
9. What is the silence?
10. What is realization?
11. What is prayer without ceasing?

Questions for Advanced Discussion
1. What is meant by asking in "His" name?
2. What is true prayer?
3. What is the "secret place of the most high?"
4. What is the meaning of the expression "going into the silence"?
5. What is meant by "Entering into your inner chamber… and shutting the door?
6. What is meant by "Hallowing" the name of God?
7. What is "our daily bread"?[270]
8. Explain why it is necessary to pray believing that we have received.
9. What is meant by "holding a thought "as used in connection with prayer

---

[270] Matthew 6:11

10. Name and explain the eight necessary conditions of true prayer.
11. Why is it necessary to be still in order to come into a realization of Truth?

Definitions

Prayer - the spiritual activity in which we enter into conscious oneness with God.

Affirmative Prayer - our prayer method in Unity

Divine Ideas - our inheritance from God. Therefore we pray for ideas and not things.

Denials and affirmations – they cleanse our consciousness of error beliefs so that we are able to claim the truth we know.

Meditation - the time when we take the opportunity to rest from all activity and listen for guidance and inspiration from the center of our being.

The Silence - the name for that inner place of stillness where we feel and know our oneness with God.

Realization - our sense of assurance and deep inner knowing that our prayers have been answered.

Pray without ceasing - to put God first in every area of our lives.

Lesson Text
Introduction

Prayer is the act of communicating with God. It is the most important spiritual activity in which we can participate. The more we understand about the activity of prayer, the more we come to realize that the time we spend in prayer is an investment in our process of attaining spiritual mastery and enlightenment.

In this chapter we will explore Unity's concept of affirmative prayer as we learn to celebrate the presence of God in ourselves and in our world.

Mind: Our Link to God

Mind is the common meeting ground between us and God, and it is only through the most highly accelerated mind action as in prayer that we can consciously make union with God, the one and only Creator. Prayer is the language of spirituality and improves the quality of our being. Prayer makes us master in the realm of creative Ideas. The inner silence of prayer is a great source of spiritual power.[271]

God is a great mind reservoir that has to be tapped by our mind and poured into visibility through our thought or word.[272]

In Unity, we place much emphasis on the power of the mind, and understand that true prayer requires much more than the repetition of memorized words.

---
[271] Fillmore, Charles *Keep a True Lent*, p. 10
[272] Fillmore, Charles *Jesus Christ Heals*

Prayer Defined

> *Prayer is both invocation and affirmation. Meditation, concentration, denial, and affirmation in the silence are all forms of what is loosely called prayer.*[273]
>
> *Prayer is not supplication or begging but a simple asking for that which we know is waiting for us at the hands of our Father and an affirmation of its existence.*[274]
>
> *Praying to God is actually a 'practice of the absence of God. The need is to return to the principle, 'the one.' and then pray from the consciousness of God... It is the celebration of the I AMness of you, giving focus to the creative process within ... that it may flow forth through you.*[275]

Prayer is the spiritual activity in which we enter into conscious oneness with God. Our prayer method in Unity is called "affirmative prayer" because we celebrate our awareness of God within us. We may wish to approach our time of affirmative prayer by acknowledging the presence and power of God and relaxing ourselves both physically and mentally. We may then allow ourselves to gently release our error beliefs as we begin to affirm the activity of God in our lives. As we continue to focus on Truth ideas we find our former cares and concerns

---

[273] Fillmore, Charles *Jesus Christ Heals*, p. 67
[274] Fillmore, Charles *Jesus Christ Heals*, p. 67
[275] *Metaphysical Bible Dictionary*, p. 13

transformed into feelings of peace and well-being. Then with a sense of joy and gratitude we give thanks that all is truly well. Continuing to set aside portions of our day for prayer gives us the opportunity to experience the most deeply satisfying and fully healing experiences in our lives.

Divine Ideas

> *True prayer is not asking for things, not even the best things. Prayer is the lifting of the consciousness to the place where these things are.*[276]

> *We often hear the remark that God gives us answers to our prayers, but we need to realize that these answers come to us in the form of ideas. These ideas may flash into our minds in answer to prayer, or they may be conveyed to us through the words of other people, or through books, magazines or newspapers.*[277]

It is important to keep in mind that when we pray we must pray for ideas and not just things. Our inheritance as children of God is divine ideas, and it is through our awareness of these ideas that all our needs are met. We, in Unity, believe that prayer is the most effective way in which we fulfill our creative potential.

---

[276] Sikking, Sue *A Letter to Adam*, p. 13
[277] Tait, Verna Dawson, *Take Command*, p. 55

Relaxation

> *The Mind of Spirit is harmonious and peaceful, and it must have a like manner of expression in our consciousness. When a body of water is choppy with fitful currents of air, it cannot reflect objects clearly. Neither can we reflect the steady strong glow of Omnipotence when our mind is disturbed by anxious thoughts, fearful thoughts, or angry thoughts.*[278]

In order for us to physically and mentally prepare for the experience of communing with God, we need to consciously relax ourselves and release all inner tension. The most conducive environment in which to attain relaxation and receptivity is one which is comfortable and peaceful and in which we are free from distractions.

Denials and Affirmations

> *Denial - the mental process of erasing from consciousness the false beliefs of the sense mind. Denial clears away belief in evil as reality and thus makes room for the establishing of Truth.*[279]

> *Affirmation, purpose of ¬ to establish in consciousness a broad understanding of the divine principles on which all life and existence depend. By affirming Truth we are lifted out of false thinking into the consciousness of Spirit.*[280]

---

[278] Fillmore, Charles *Jesus Christ Heals*, p. 176
[279] Fillmore, Charles *The Revealing Word*, p. 53
[280] Fillmore, Charles *The Revealing Word*, p. 11

> *Concentration on one kind of thoughts, error thoughts, has built up a consciousness of error, and these error thoughts have been reproduced in the life as error conditions. Emptying ourselves of these and concentrating on higher thoughts will lift our mind into the Christ consciousness, and this in turn will be reproduced as harmony in body and affairs.*[281]

One of the ways in which we establish peace in our minds is by the use of denials and affirmations. We let go of thoughts which clutter our minds with false beliefs and affirm that which clarifies and claims the truth we intuitively know.

Meditation

> *To open yourself to the inspiration of your indwelling Lord and then to listen for His inspiration, this is meditation.*[282]

> *Through the practice of meditation we can establish a center of peace and quietness within. We can turn to this center and gain great strength to help us meet all of life's experiences.*[283]

Meditation is the aspect of our conscious communion with God in which we are silently inspired with divine ideas. It is most important to take time each

---

[281] Foulks, Frances, Effectual Prayer, p. 59
[282] Rowland, May, *The Magic of the Word*, p. 143
[283] Ibid, p. 149

day to rest from all activity and focus our complete attention on God.

The Silence

> By quieting the mental, by passing through the discipline of intellectual silence, we arrive at the very threshold of Being. As we pass into the inner chamber, we find that we are entering the holy of holies, where noiselessly, silently a mighty work is always going on.[284]

> The silence is not something mysterious. It is that inner place of stillness where you feel and know your oneness with God".[285]

> The purpose of the silence is to still the activity of the individual thought so that the still small voice of God may be heard. For in the silence Spirit speaks Truth to us and just that Truth of which we stand in need.[286]

> God is mind. 'We have the mind of Christ, and it is for us to make conscious union in the silence with the all-providing Mind, lifting our thoughts to its standard of Truth and holding them in this Truth as we .go about our own particular duties of living.[287]

---

[284] Fillmore, Charles *The Twelve Powers of Man*, p. 24
[285] Rowland, May. *The Magic of the Word*, p. 144
[286] Fillmore, Charles, *The Twelve Powers of Man*, p. 17
[287] Fillmore, Myrtle, *Myrtle Fillmore's Healing Letters*, p. 51

> *The more we practice the silence the more readily will we receive inspiration.*[288]

All divine ideas have their origin in the silence. Silence and stillness are the matrix out of which come all of our guidance and inspiration. It becomes clear, then, that we must be persistent in our practice of daily meditation so that we will be able to recognize true guidance and act upon it.

Realization

> *To a meta physician realization is the conviction that a person gets when he has persistently concentrated his attention on an ideal until he feels assured of the fulfillment of that ideal".*[289].

> *Somewhere in all effectual prayer and in every quiet prayer, a point of release can be discovered, a point of time where the one who is praying can experience a sense of assurance.*[290]

As we dwell in the silence, specific aspects of universal Truth become real to us. Realization makes truth a permanent possession of our minds.

Thanksgiving

> *As you come out of the silence, count your blessings and give thanks for them. Realize that only the*

---

[288] Fillmore, Charles, p. 143
[289] Fillmore, Charles, *Jesus Christ Heals*, p. 45
[290] Wilson, Ernest C., *Soul Power*, p. 117

good exists in you and in your world, that the power you contacted in the silence may have opportunity to magnify and increase your blessings. Give thanks that you have already received the good for which you looked to God in the silence, feeling the assurance: 'Before they call I will answer; and while they are yet speaking, I will hear'.[291] [292]

"Praise and thanksgiving impart the quickening spiritual power that produces growth and increase in all things.[293]

In response to the blessings we receive in our prayer experience, we joyously offer our love and our praise to God, the source of our good. Giving thanks before our answer appears in the manifest realm is a powerful expression of our faith. Thanksgiving is a prayerful and joy-filled attitude of mind.

Pray Without Ceasing

We pray without ceasing when we habitually meet whatever comes to us with faith and with love, with a mind to draw from the event all that it has to give, with a willingness to do whatever has to be done to make the most and best of it.[294]

---

[291]

[292] Fillmore, Myrtle *Myrtle Fillmore's Healing Letters*, p. 49
[293] Fillmore, Charles *Prosperity*, p. 105
[294] Freeman, James Dilet *Prayer, the Master Key*, p. 41

To pray without ceasing is to put God in charge of your life. It is to look for direction. It is to expect Inspiration.[295]

Prayer is not a duty or a habit, but a pouring forth of the heart in gratitude - for every breath, every moment of life, every experience.[296]

If prayer is to be truly effective in our lives, it must be a perpetual activity. As we continue to commit ourselves to a life of prayer, we learn to put God first in our every thought, word and deed. This is what it truly means to pray without ceasing.

Meditation

God is the all-surrounding, all-penetrating Spirit-Mind, out of which all come. I live; that is, I am animated and inspired by and through Infinite Mind. I breathe into my lungs that which is necessary for the life of my physical body, and my mind is inspired with divine ideas, ideas of good which are in this Mind. I am ever in the presence of this Almighty One, and am being the qualities or attributes of God to the extent that; I know them.

I am God-life, God-intelligence, God-substance, to the degree of my understanding. A fish lives in the water, its natural element, and moves and has its being there. An animal lives and moves and has its being in the air, its natural element, that which is necessary for its well-being.

Spiritually, I am an idea in God-Mind, and I live and move and am the expression of God-Mind. I am sustained and eternally supplied with its substance through right

---

[295] Freeman, James Dillet *Prayer, the Master Key*, p. 42
[296] Sikking, Sue *A Letter to Adam*, p. 13

thinking and by not misapplying or misusing any of its ideas. I must learn to do this consciously; through choice I am to keep my thoughts on the good that is in and around all. In this way I consciously live and move and have my being in God.

Chapter 20 - The Twelve Powers

Questions from the Text
1. Describe briefly your understanding of "The Twelve Powers."
2. Name each of the twelve powers and describe their function,
3. Relate your understanding of the twelve powers to your current concept of regeneration.

Thoughts and Reflections

God, Supreme Being, is the source out of which all creation evolves. God-Mind is an omnipresent spiritual realm comprised of creative ideas. Through prayer and spiritual realization we may lay hold of these ideas . . . and create out of them the ideals of our hearts.[297]

Lesson Text
Introduction

Inherent within humankind are twelve fundamental spiritual faculties which reflect God's nature and which comprise our own divine nature. Through affirming their presence and by calling them forth into expression, we will quicken and develop them into real powers within us. In this chapter we will describe each of these attributes as it exists not only within consciousness but also within our bodies. We will discover how these twelve are to work together in the process of regeneration as we develop Christ consciousness.

---

[297] Fillmore, Charles *Christ Enthroned in Man*, p. 11

The Twelve Powers

> *Inherent in the fundamental Mind of Being are twelve fundamental ideas which in action appear as primal creative forces. It is possible for us to ally ourselves with and to use these original forces.*[298]

The twelve powers are the twelve fundamental aspect s of our divine nature, the twelve components of God's "image and likeness" in humankind, the twelve disciples of our Christ mind. They comprise the pattern for perfection within us. A t our present level of spiritual evolution these powers are incomplete in their development and expression. As we come t o a fuller realization of our true nature we become more able to fully demonstrate our divine potential.

Developing the Twelve Powers

> *Our work here and now is to awaken to the divine powers with which God has endowed us, to encourage and develop them under Go d direction and d to get about the business of becoming that which Jesus demonstrated in his life and told us we could become.*[299]

> *Within each person there is a new world awaiting discovery , a world in which there are capabilities of unlimited strength, perfect knowing , radiant life,*

---

[298] Fillmore, Charles *The Twelve Powers*, p. 52
[299] Hausmann, Winifred *Your God Given Potential*, p.23

> *and other latent abilities beyond our greatest present capacity to conceive.*[300]

Our increasing awareness of our twelve spiritual faculties will enable us to call them forth into dynamic expression within us. This process requires discipline, dedication, and a conscious recognition of ourselves as offspring of God.

Regeneration

> *Charles Fillmore's plan for the regeneration was based on the individual development of innate powers and abilities expressing through the human body. These centers are to be activated as the qualities are developed in mind, all under the supervision of the Christ or God-self of each person.*[301]

Once the transformation in consciousness begins to occur, as the twelve faculties are quickened within us, there are results in the manifestation of purity and wholeness within our bodies as well.

Threefold Nature of the Twelve

> *The following outline gives a list of the Twelve, the faculties that they represent, and the nerve centers at which they preside:*[302]

---

[300] Ibid, p. 24
[301] Ibid, p. 25
[302] Fillmore, Charles *The Twelve Powers*, p. 16

Faith	Peter	Center of Brain
Strength	Andrew	Loins
Discrimination or Judgment	James, son of Zebedee	Pit of Stomach
Love	John	Back of Heart
Power	Philip	Root of Tongue
Imagination	Bartholomew	Between the Eyes
Understanding	Thomas	Front of Brain
Will	Matthew	Center Front Brain
Order	James, son of Alpheus	Navel
Zeal	Simon, the Cananaean	Back Head, Medulla
Renunciation or Elimination	Thaddaeus	Abdominal Region
Life Conserver	Judas	Generative Function

The twelve faculties exist spiritually as realities in our mind and in God mind, symbolically as the twelve disciples of Jesus Christ, and literally as twelve centers of energy within the physical body of every individual.

Faith

Faith is the perceiving power of the mind. It is spiritual assurance, the power to do the seemingly impossible. It is a force that draws to us our heart's desire right out of the invisible spiritual substance. It is a deep inner knowing that that which is sought

> *is already ours for the taking, the 'assurance of things hoped for'.*[303]

> *"Faith is that quality in us which enables us to look past appearances of lack, limitation, or difficulty, to take hold of the divine idea and believe in it even though we do not see any evidence of it except in our mind. Through faith we know with an inner knowing the Truth that has not yet expressed in our manifest world."*[304]

Faith is our ability to perceive the reality of God's kingdom of good despite evidence to the contrary. It is the faculty of positive expectations and definite assurance that the power, presence, and promises of Go d are real here and now.

Strength

> *"In the Mind of God, Strength is an idea of enduring power, which to us means the continuous and d sustained energies with which Creation is projected and maintained".*[305]

> *"Strength . . . Freedom from weakness; stability of character; power to withstand temptation; capacity to accomplish".*[306]

---

[303] Fillmore, Charles *Keep a True Lent*, p. 148
[304] Hausmann, Winifred *Your God Given Potential*, p. 38
[305] Fillmore, Charles *Prosperity*, page 13
[306] Fillmore, Charles *The Revealing Word*, p. 186

Strength is the faculty of steadfastness, dependability, stability, capacity for endurance. It is not merely a physical endowment, but a degree of spiritual awareness". It is not force, manipulation, or defensiveness. It is spiritual courage and confidence. Nonresistance is the highest expression of strength. Nonresistance does not mean non-action; it is an effective, calm, single-minded God-centered attitude of mind.

Judgment

> *"Judgment . . . Mental ac t of evaluation through comparison or contras t . . . spiritual discernment".[307]*

Judgment is the faculty by which we appraise, evaluate, and discriminate in order to make correct decisions. It is our ability to maintain enlightened objectivity about our life and our world.

Love

> *"Love, in Divine Mind, is the idea of universal unity. I n expression, it is the power that joins and binds together the universe and everything in it. Love is a harmonizing, constructive power. When it is made active in consciousness, it conserves substance and reconstructs, rebuilds, and restores us and our world".[308]*

---

[307] Ibid, p. 113
[308] Fillmore, Charles *Keep a True Lent*. P. 151

"Divine love is impersonal... it loves for the sake of loving... Love is an inner quality that sees good everywhere and in everybody... Love is the great harmonizer and healer ".[309]

Love is that attracting, harmonizing, unifying faculty of mind; it is the constructive building force of Spirit. It is our power to comprehend oneness. Spiritual love is the total, unconditional acceptance of everyone and everything.

Power

From Divine Mind we inherit power over the forces of our mind--in truth, power over all ideas. A quickening from on high must precede our realization of our innate control of thought and feeling.[310]

The mind and the body of man have the power of transforming energy from one plane of consciousness to another. This is the power and dominion implanted in man from the beginning".[311]

Power, we must understand, is not an end in itself, not a goal to be sought. Rather, it is simply a means that enables us to attain the end of bringing forth God ideas on earth... It is to be exercised not for the purpose of controlling others, but for the purpose of taking dominion over our own thoughts and

---

[309] Fillmore, Charles *The Revealing Word*, p. 125
[310] Fillmore, Charles *The Twelve Powers*, p. 61
[311] Fillmore, Charles *The Twelve Powers*, p. 63

> *feelings in order to come into a greater God awareness".[312]*

Power is the faculty that enables us to have authority over our thoughts and feelings. Our greatest creative power is generated by our realization of the power of God within us. Our spoken words are vehicles through which this power is manifested in our lives.

Imagination

> *It will be found that every form and shape originated in the imagination. It is through the imagination that the formless takes form".[313]*
> *The idea is first projected into mind substance, and afterward formed in consciousness. The mind sees all things through thought forms made by the imagination".[314]*

Imagination is our conceiving, picturing faculty. It is the formative power of mind which shapes thoughts into mental images which have color, variety, and dimension. The highest use of imagination is to shape thoughts images which most fully reflect the nature of the original divine.

---

[312] Hausmann, Winifred *Your God Given Potential*, p. 95
[313] Fillmore, Charles *The Twelve Powers*, p. 71
[314] Fillmore, Charles *Christian Healing*, p. 103

Understanding

>Spiritual understanding is the ability of the mind to *apprehend and realize the laws of thought and the relation of ideas one to another".[315]*

>*So we find that there is in us a knowing capacity transcending intellectual knowledge".[316]*

Understanding is the faculty by which we receive enlightenment and insight. It is our capacity to gain direct perceptions of Truth. It is our faculty of spiritual intelligence.

Will

>*The will is the executive faculty of the mind, our determining factor.[317]*
>*The will moves into action all the other faculties of the mind...[318]*

Will is the decision making, directing, choosing faculty of the mind. It is our capacity to say "yes" or "no" to opportunities and options. The highest expression of will is willingness, conscious consent to the will.

---

[315] Fillmore, Charles *The Revealing Word*, p. 202
[316] Fillmore, Charles *The Twelve Powers*, p. 88
[317] Fillmore, Charles The Revealing Word, p. 309
[318] Fillmore, Charles *The Twelve Powers*, p. 97

Order

> *Order in the Mind of God is an idea of harmonious progress, evolution. Order in us is our ability to perceive and cooperate with the la w of growth.*[319]
>
> *The divine idea of order is the idea of adjustment, and as this is established in our thought, our mind and affairs will be at one with the universal harmony.*[320]
>
> *To develop divine order in our life, we must learn to cooperate with spiritual law.*[321]

Order is the faculty by which we establish harmony, balance, right adjustment, and right sequence of action in our lives. Order is the one underlying law of manifestation, and we must participate consciously in that process which enables growth without struggle.

Zeal

> *Zeal is the great universal force that impels us to spring forward in a field of endeavor and accomplish the seemingly miraculous".*[322]
>
> *To be without zeal is to be without the zest of living. Zeal and enthusiasm incite to glorious*

---

[319] Fillmore, Charles *Prosperity*, p. 138
[320] Fillmore, Charles The Revealing Word, p. 143
[321] Fillmore, Charles Hausmann, Winifred Your God Given Potential, p. 156
[322] Fillmore, Charles *Atom Smashing Power of Mind*, p. 26

achievement in every aim and ideal that the mind conceives. Zeal is the impulse to go forward, the urge behind all things".[323]

Zeal is the faculty of enthusiasm, intensity, and exuberance. It provides our inner urge to progress; it is our motivation to achieve. The highest expression of zeal is in an unflagging, fervent interest in knowing, speaking, and doing good.

Elimination and Renunciation

A letting go of old thoughts in order that new thoughts may find place in consciousness. A healthy state of mind is attained when the thinker willingly lets go the old thoughts and takes on the new. This is illustrated by the inlet and outlet of a pool of water.[324]

Thoughts are things; they occupy space in the mental field. A healthy state of mind is attained and continued when the thinker willingly lets go the old thoughts and takes on the new.[325]

Elimination is the faculty by which we release false beliefs and accomplish a mental cleansing. Elimination enables us to surrender to Spirit any thought that is not for our highest good so that transformation and purification of consciousness can take place.

---

[323] Fillmore, Charles *The Twelve Powers*, p. 130
[324] Fillmore, Charles *The Revealing Word*, p. 167
[325] Fillmore, Charles *The Twelve Powers*, p. 144

Life

> *In the phenomenal world, life is the energy that propels all forms to action.*[326]

> *Life in us is our increasing consciousness of the world, our inner activities, the forces and movements about us. It is our power to express the eternal activity of God.*[327]

Life is the faculty of movement, vitality, wholeness, and creativity. It is the expression of the pure, eternal life of God within us.

Our Work/Our Goals

> *Our work is to transmute the natural powers (starting where we are in consciousness and spiritual growth) into the spiritual powers we are designed to express for the fulfillment of our Christ potential. Each faculty is discovered first as an intellectual concept. This concept is explored and nurtured through prayer as it gradually grows into the spiritual idea from which it came. Finally we have no sense of separateness, but rather a realization of our oneness with the God-power itself, expressing through us entirely under the guidance and direction of the Christ.*[328]

---

[326] Ibid, p. 161
[327] Fillmore, Charles *Prosperity*, p. 144
[328] Fillmore, Charles *Your God-Given Potential*, p. 27

"Remember, each power functions in three ways - first, the perfect idea in Divine Mind; second, the growing concept in our consciousness; third, the expression through the physical center, and (indirectly) through our entire body. The long-range goal is to attain a complete and perfect expression of all twelve powers through all phases of our being. This would be the fulfilling realization of oneness with our Creator. We believe that Jesus reached and demonstrated this oneness.[329]

Our transformation into fully conscious and enlightened beings is achieved through the development of our twelve spiritual faculties. Our goal is to express our Christ potential unselfishly, lovingly, and powerfully.

---

[329] Ibid, p. 28

Part IV – Practical Application of Metaphysics

Supplementary Reading:
- Cady, H. Emilie *Lessons In Truth,* Chapters 3 through 6
- Fillmore, Charles *Christian Healing*, Chapters 3, 4 and 8
- *Fillmore, Charles Talks on Truth*, Chapter 14, Jesus Christ's Atonement
- Fillmore, Charles *Keep a True Lent*, Chapter 4, 10, 11 and 15

This section contains three chapters:
- Metaphysical Basis for Health and Healing
- Metaphysical Basis for Prosperity
- Keys to Demonstration

Although, by this point, the application of the spiritual principles have caused profound changes in your live, we will explore health and prosperity in depth.

As we explore heath and healing, we affirm:

> *The healing power of Spirit is flowing through all the cells of my body. I am made of the one universal God-substance.*

Thy perfect light is omnipresent in all my body. Wherever that healing light is manifest, there is perfection. I am well, for perfection is in me.

I am the Changeless, I am Infinite. I am not a little mortal being with bones to break, a body that will perish. I am the deathless, changeless Infinite.

Chapter 21 – Metaphysical Basis for Health and Healing

Questions from the Text
1. What is the sequence of the process of the Divine idea of manifestation?
2. What is practical Christianity?
3. What is the metaphysical vs. physical basis of heath?
4. Give a brief definition for each of the following terms.
   - Trinity of Healing
   - Realization
   - Receptivity
   - Miracles
   - Outlet and Inlet
   - Persistence
   - The Logos
   - Regeneration
   - The Harmonizer
   - Power of Thought
   - Secondary Power of Thought
5. In what two ways can energy be used?
6. What is the Silent Unity method?
7. What is the Power of the Word?
8. What was Jesus' healing method?
9. Briefly describe your understanding of the metaphysical basis for health
10. Be prepared to discuss Unity's method of Spiritual Healing.

Supplementary Reading

    Cady, Emilie *How I Used Truth*, Chapters 9 and 10
    Fillmore, Charles *Jesus Christ Heals*, Chapters 1, 4, 9 and 11
    Lynch, Richard *Know Thyself*, Chapters 9 and 10
    Shanklin, Imelda *What Are You?*, Chapter 9

Lesson Text
Creation

> *There are two steps in creation—mind ideates that which it later brings forth in the outer, just as a man works out in his mind his invention before he makes the model. God is the all-powerful mind. God creates first in thought, and God's idea of creation is perfect, and that idea exists as a perfect model upon which all manifestation rests. The body of man must rest upon a divine body idea in Divine Mind, and it logically follows that the inner life, substance, and intelligence of all flesh is perfect."*[330]

    Charles Fillmore strongly believed and taught that the attainment of permanent health is based upon belief in a God-created perfect body idea as the pattern for the human physical body. He said that this perfect body idea is established in mind, and then is worked out into body manifestation under the law of mind action. The God-created perfect pattern is the fundamental basis we should always return to in our human thinking, and upon which we rest As we do this, Charles Fillmore maintained, the results will take care of themselves.

---

[330] Fillmore, Charles *Keep a True Lent*, p. 19

Health

> *Health is our normal condition and for all creation. We find that there is an omnipresent principle of health pervading all living things. Health, real health, is from within and does not have to be manufactured in the without. Health is the very essence of Being. It is as universal and enduring as God.*[331]

Health as the normal condition is a new idea for some persons. There is a strong tendency in human consciousness to view health as the exception, a privilege for the lucky few. This view changes as a person begins to grasp the fact that health is essentially a divine idea. All divine ideas are "normal" in the truest sense of the word. Sickness is an abnormality in the sense that it is a departure from the perfect pattern of life and order—the components of good health.

Mind Idea Expression

> *Our consciousness is formed of mind and its ideas, and these determine whether we are healthy or sick. Thus to know the mysteries of our own being we must study mind and its laws."*[332]

> *So if we want to know the secrets of health and how right thinking forms the perfect body, we must go to the mind and trace step by step the movements that transform ideas of health into*

---
[331] Fillmore, Charles *Jesus Christ Heals*, p. 24
[332] Ibid, p. 31

light, electrons, atoms, molecules, cells, tissues, and finally into the perfect physical organism.[333]

Charles Fillmore has listed the sequence of the process of a divine idea becoming a manifested experience. In this case it is the divine idea (health) becoming the experience (becoming healed). The sequence traces the process of mind into matter:

1. Idea of health Into
2. light into
3. electrons into
4. atoms into
5. molecules into
6. cells into
7. tissues into
8. healed organism.[334]

Practical Christianity

If I can conceive a truth, it follows that there is a way by which I can make it manifest. If I can conceive of omnipresent life as existing in the omnipresent ethers, there is a way by which I can make that life appear in my body. When once the mind has accepted this as an axiomatic truth, it has arrived at the point where the question of procedure arises.[335]

---

[333] Ibid, p. 40
[334] One can take this sequence and read it backward, substituting the word "from" instead of "into." This practice helps give a real feel for this process and makes a deep impression on consciousness.
[335] Fillmore, Charles *Jesus Christ Heals*, p. 133

This paragraph illustrates what is meant in Unity by the term "practical Christianity." We are first given the theoretical and idealistic side of the presentation. Then the practical side is given in the final sentence: "Once the mind has accepted this as an axiomatic truth, it has arrived at the point where the question of procedure arises." It is this "question of procedure" that makes up the practical aspect of Unity's approach to Christianity.

Trinity in Healing

> *Concisely stated, three great factors enter into every consciousness—intelligence, life, substance. The harmonious combination of these factors requires the most careful attention of the ego, because it is here that all the discords of existence arise.*[336]

> *The one essential fact is that there can be no without Intelligence as factor or constituent to understand manifestation a fundamental part. Every form in the universe, every function, all action, all substance—all these have a thinking part that is receptive to and controllable by us. Material science has observed that every molecule has three things: intelligence, substance, and action. It knows where it wants to go, it has form, and it moves. This intelligent principle in all things is the key to the metaphysician's work.*[337]

---

[336] Fillmore, Charles *The Twelve Powers*, p. 164
[337] Fillmore, Charles *Christian Healing*, p. 50

The power of attention is of tremendous importance in the existence of humankind. The mind, through the power of attention, can make a connection with the innate intelligence of anything that is in existence, whether it be animal, vegetable, or mineral. And this is especially so with regard to the intelligence in the cells of our bodies.

Power of Thought

> *That the body is moved by thought is universally accepted, but that thought is also the builder of the body is not so widely admitted.*[338]

> *"The cells of the body are centers of force in a field of universal energy. There are no solids. That which appears solid is in reality the scene of constant activity. The eye is not keyed to the pulsations of this universal energy and is therefore deceived into believing that things are solid."*[339]

The idea that thought is the builder of the body takes on new significance in the light of new discoveries in the science of genetics. The discovery of the DNA programming in the genes, all contained within the single original fertilized cell, places Charles Fillmore's teaching in a new context. The building of the body is carried on by the DNA programming u p to a point. After that point is reached, the individual's own consciousness takes over. Intelligence is a divine idea. Therefore it is omnipresent in our world. Intelligence is alive and all living things can be

---

[338] Fillmore, Charles *Christian Healing*, p. 40
[339] Fillmore, Charles *Jesus Christ Heals*, p. 172

communicated with. Our intelligence can communicate with intelligence in all existing things, including the very cells, molecules, and atoms of our own bodies.

Metaphysical vs. Physical Basis for Health

> *The physician takes it for granted that disease germs exist as an integral part of the natural world; the metaphysician sees disease germs as the manifested results of anger, revenge, jealousy, fear, impurity, and many other mind activities. A change of mind will change the character of a germ. Love, courage, peace, strength, and good will form good character and build bodily structures of a nature like these qualities of mind.*[340]

> *The laborious methods of the medical profession are all for the purpose of stimulating the healing forces of nature.*[341]

The very nature of the physical basis for health makes it necessary for its practitioners to think in pathological terms. This is very useful for combatting existing diseases and malfunctions. But it is not the same as the creating and maintaining of stabilized perfect health. The whole direction of metaphysical thinking is creative. It does not fight or combat. It creates and sustains. This is not to criticize pathological knowledge, which is needed as long as there are accidents, diseases, malfunctions to be cured. But more importantly, we need

---

[340] Fillmore, Charles *Atom-Smashing Power of Mind*, p. 104
[341] Fillmore, Charles *The Twelve Powers of Man*, p. 152

metaphysical thinking to create and maintain the living patterns of stabilized good health.

Realization

> *The scientific metaphysician fixes attention powerfully on the consummation of a certain idea until there is a realization, which means that the idea has nucleated a certain amount of thought substance. When this realization is had the metaphysician rests 'from all work.' Through faith and work the metaphysician has fulfilled the law of mind and now rests in the conviction that ideal of health will appear in manifestation in due season.*[342]

In this paragraph Charles Fillmore has described the process in which metaphysical thinking causes the faith faculty to "clothe the divine idea with substance." At a certain point, the degree of attention is sufficient to cause a breakthrough from the invisible to the manifest. Charles Fillmore adds to this the idea of "keeping the Sabbath," symbolizing the observing of a time of rest from external effort, and even from thinking about the case.

Miracles

> *In reality miracles are events that take place as a result of the application of a higher law to certain conditions.*[343]

---

[342] Fillmore, Charles *Jesus Christ Heals*, p.45
[343] Fillmore, Charles *Keep a True Lent*, p. 178

> *The forces invisible are much closer than we think, and when we turn our attention in their direction the response is usually so pronounced and so swift that we cannot but feel that a miracle has been performed. A more intimate acquaintance with the divine law convinces us that under it all things are possible if we only believe, and if we at the same time conform our thoughts to its principles."*[344]

Yesterday's miracles can become today's normal procedures. Evolution continues for us, and our evolution consists of gaining new and higher levels of insight and spiritual awareness. The more spiritually aware we become the more we perceive higher levels of the laws of life. As we proceed to work from those higher levels, the results often appear spectacular to those not yet on those levels. This is the metaphysical background for the marvelous ministry of works performed by Jesus, which can be duplicated by all who follow him.

Developing a Healing Consciousness
Faith in the Possibility

> *The first move in all healing is a recognition on the part of the healer and the part of the patient that God is present as an all-powerful mind, equal to the healing of every disease, no matter how bad it may appear. 'With God all things are possible.'*[345] [346]

---

[344] Fillmore, Charles *Christian Healing*, p. 92
[345] Matthew 19:26
[346] Fillmore, Charles *The Twelve Powers of Man*, p. 177

Faith is our great affirmative power. In developing a healing consciousness faith work s by affirming the omnipresence of Go d and all divine ideas. The divine idea is always o f a greater dimension than any existing thing. In the case of a healing need, the divine idea of health is greater and more powerful than anything on the level of the existing sickness. Faith (affirmations) makes contact with that greater dimension of power and causes the needed adjustment which manifests as healing.

Faith and Receptivity

> *The first step in all is faith, and the next spiritual healing is receptivity."*[347]

> *Health, real health, is from within and does not have to be manufactured in the without. It is our normal condition, a condition true to the reality of being. The first step in all spiritual healing is the using of faith, and the next step is to become open and receptive to the stream of healing life.*[348]

Actually, receptivity can be understood as a part of faith. Faith is our great affirmative power. Receptivity is a result of using faith to affirm willingness. Jesus said to the man at the pool of Bethesda, "Wilt thou be made whole?"[349] In modern English this would be stated, "Are you willing to be healed?" If we affirm willingness toward health, we will become very receptive to the idea, and the

---

[347] Fillmore, Charles *The Twelve Powers of Man*, p. 152
[348] Fillmore, Charles *Keep a True Lent*, p. 173
[349] Matthew 19:26

idea will be transformed into an experience of being healed.

Our Inlet and Outlet

> *In our right relationship, we are the Inlet and the outlet of an everywhere present life, substance, and intelligence. When our "I AM" recognize this fact and adjusts to the invisible expressions of the one Mind, our mind becomes harmonious; our life, vigorous and perpetual; our body, healthy. It is imperative that the individual understand this in order to grow naturally.[350]*

One of the best health-producing exercises for our minds is realizing one's self as the inlet and the outlet for all divine ideas. Divine ideas generate energies which culminate as manifestations and experiences in us and for us. A human being is both a receiving station and a broadcasting station for divine ideas such as intelligence, love, substance, and life. We can use and share all of them. If we do so willingly and gratefully, our consciousness will continually improve, and so will the state of our health.

Thought Out-Picturing

> *The fruit of our thought is our body, and we can judge our thought by the character of our body. So also can we change our body by changing our thoughts. Then here is the key to the situation: To resurrect the body we must change our thoughts.*

---

[350] Fillmore, Charles *Christian Healing*, p. 22

> *Every thought must be in accordance with absolute Truth; there must be no adverse thought."*[351]

Many readers are disturbed by statements such as: "the fruit of your thought is your body," and "Every thought must be in accordance with absolute Truth." Statements such as these, however, should not turn a reader away from the generally helpful idea of the paragraph. The point is that our thinking does have a direct effect on our bodies, perhaps not as literally as is implied in this paragraph, but, to the extent that it does behoove us to pay attention to the general trend of our thinking.

Affirmations and Denials

> *A good healing drill is to deny the mental cause first, then the physical appearance. The mental condition should first be healed. Then the secondary state, which it has produced in the body, must be wiped out and the perfect state affirmed.*[352]

> *To demonstrate principle keep establishing yourself in certain statements (affirmations) of the law. The more often you present to your mind a logical and true proposition, the stronger becomes the inner feeling of realization.*[353]

---

[351] Fillmore, Charles *Talks on Truth*, p. 116
[352] Fillmore, Charles *Jesus Christ Heals*, p. 36
[353] Fillmore, Charles *Keep a True Lent*, p. 177

One of the questions which arise in many minds in regard to denials is: "Do I have to find out exactly what the error is in my consciousness before I can deny it?" In many cases the error will become apparent and one will know what it is. In such a case, the denial will probably be quite specific. Bu t even if one does not know exactly what the error is, denial can still be used effectively. One can deny whatever the cause is without having to identify the cause by naming it, just as a person can forgive sin without knowing the names of all the sins. Affirmations, however, are verbalized divine ideas, and it is helpful to know what divine ideas we wish to verbalize and to call them by their right names.

Overcoming Resistance

> *By experimentation modern metaphysical healers have discovered a large number of laws that rule in the realm of mind, and they agree that no two cases are exactly alike. Therefore one who prays for the health of another should understand that it is not the fault of the healing principle that his patient is not instantly restored. The fault may be in his own lack of persistency or understanding; or it may be due to the patient's dogged clinging to discordant thoughts. In any case the one who prays must persist in this prayer until the walls of resistance are broken down and the healing currents are tuned in. Metaphysicians often pray over a critical case all night."*[354]

---

[354] Fillmore, Charles *Jesus Christ Heals*, p. 85

Each need we encounter is unique. Even though the symptoms may appear to be identical to those of other cases, the case itself is not exactly like any other. Each healing need should be approached with the attitude that it is one of a kind. This prevents us from getting too literal and mechanical in our spiritual efforts. Another important point in this paragraph is the challenge of subconscious (or unconscious) resistance. Human resistance to divine help is a great mystery which necessitates much persistence in prayer in certain cases.[355]

Persistence

> *Every Christian healer has had experiences where persistent prayer saved his patient. If he had merely said one prayer, as if giving a prescription for the Lord to fill, he would have fallen far short of demonstrating the law. Elijah prayed persistently until the little cloud appeared or, as we would say, he had a 'realization;' then the manifestation followed.*[356]

In cases where persistence in prayer is needed we can think of it as a type of exercise. Just as physical exercise strengthens the body, mental exercise can strengthen consciousness. Prayer is the highest type of all exercises, and repetition of prayer strengthens the soul. A person who prays sincerely will receive personal inner

---

[355] In a case where a patient simply will not give up inner resistance; will not accept the divine idea of health, the person praying should not feel guilty about it. Each soul has its own freedom of choice, and each soul is entitled to its secret reasons for making choices.
[356] Fillmore, Charles *Atom-Smashing Power of Mind*, p. 127

guidance as to how much or how little repetition is necessary in each case.

The Foundation

> *In our silent meditations and prayers we must infuse into the inner mind realms the same energy that, used without, would make us notable in some worldly achievement. But unless we do this inner work and lay the foundation of strength and power in the subjective mind, we shall find ourselves in failing health when called upon for extra exertion in some great effort.*[357]

Charles Fillmore recognized that energy can be utilized in two ways:

1. In some outer aim to accomplish a good result, or,
2. As a "reserve pool" in the inner realms of the soul

Throughout his writings he urges us to do both, but to be particularly careful that we do not fail to do this "inner investing. He felt that this inner reserve was especially needed in times of unexpected events.

The Object

> *Remember that the object of all treatment is to raise the mind to the Christ consciousness, through which all true healing is accomplished."*[358]

---

[357] Fillmore, Charles *The Twelve Powers*, p. 123
[358] Fillmore, Charles *Teach Us to Pray*, p. 178

Be of good cheer.[359] *The intelligence that created your body knows how to repair it. Get still, relax, and turn your attention to the sustaining life forces within your organism.*[360]

Greater consciousness should be the primary aim of any spiritual effort we make. We may have other reasons also, but these should be secondary. Such things as health, prosperity and happiness are results, not causes. The cause of any worthwhile thing for us is our forward (Godward) direction of consciousness.

The Silent Unity Method
Peace

The first step in prayer for health is to get still. 'Be still and know that I AM God.' To get still the body must be relaxed and the mind quieted. Center the attention within. There is a quiet place within us all, and by silently saying over and over, 'Peace, be still,' we shall enter that quiet place and a great stillness will pervade our whole being.[361]

Jesus gave us the consciousness of peace. 'My peace I give unto you.[362] *The mind of peace precedes bodily healing. Cast out enmity and anger and affirm the peace of Jesus Christ, and your healing will be swift and sure.*[363]

---

[359] John 16:33
[360] Ibid, p. 105
[361] Fillmore, Charles *Jesus Christ Heals*, p. 80
[362] John 14:27
[363] Ibid, p. 21

These two paragraphs contain two very significant keys in regard to healing. They are: (1) The first step in prayer for health is "to get still". (2) The mind of peace precedes bodily healing." "To get still" is essential, for stillness is pure strength at its source. "The mind of peace" is also essential, for true peace is silence, and silence is pure power at its source. When we are established in stillness and silence we are connected to the inner source of pure strength and pure power. If we then use our faith in affirming the Truth of the divine idea of health, we will have the experience Charles Fillmore describes in this second paragraph: "Your healing will be swift and sure."

Receptivity

> *The reason that prayers and treatments for healing are not more successful is that the mind has not been put in a receptive state by affirmations of peace. The Mind of Spirit is harmonious and peaceful, and it must have a like manner of expression in man's consciousness. When a body of water is choppy with fitful currents of air it cannot reflect objects clearly. Neither can we reflect the steady strong glow of Omnipotence when our mind is disturbed by anxious thoughts, fearful thoughts, or angry thoughts.*[364]

Divine ideas require proper channels in order to express themselves, and the most important channel for purposes of healing is the mind. If a person's mind is in a turbulent, negative, violent state, then It Is not a proper

---

[364] Fillmore, Charles *Jesus Christ Heals*, p. 176

channel of expression for the divine idea of health. Through our sense of I AM, we can control our own states of mind. It takes practice, but it can be done. Denial and affirmation are good methods, as are any form of meditation and prayer which helps us realize oneness with God.

Realization

> *A spiritual realization is a realization of Truth. A spiritual realization of health is the result of holding in consciousness a statement of health until the logic of the mind is satisfied and we receive the assurance that the fulfillment in the physical must follow. In other words, by realizing a healing prayer we lay hold of the principle of health itself and the whole consciousness is illumined; we perceive principle working out health problems for us.*[365]

> *There is a partial unity with Spirit and there is a complete unity with Spirit. Whenever we wholly merge our mind with creative Mind we meet Christ in our consciousness, and it is when we are in this consciousness that our prayers are fulfilled.*[366]

In spiritual healing, the all-important realization occurs when the person really feels oneness with Principle. Such a realization does not perceive principle as a cold abstract formula or statistic, but as a living intelligent Presence, which is what spiritual principle really is. When a

---

[365] Fillmore, Charles *Jesus Christ Heals*, p. 39
[366] Fillmore, Charles *The Twelve Powers of Man*, p. 20

person has this realization, as Charles Fillmore says, "We perceive principle working out health problems for us."

Idea-Thought-Word

> *Ability to pick up the life current and through it perpetually to vitalize the body is based on the right relation of ideas, thoughts, and words. These mental impulses start currents of energy that form and also stimulate molecules and cells already formed, producing life, strength, and animation where inertia and impotence was the dominant appearance. This was and is the healing method of Jesus.*[367]

> *It is a metaphysical law that there are three steps in every demonstration; the recognition of Truth as it is in principle; holding the idea; and acknowledging fulfillment. Pray believing that you have received, and you shall receive.*[368] [369]

The metaphysical sequence of idea – thought - word is the law of Trinity in its most personal aspect where we are concerned. This has always been one aspect of the Silent Unity method of prayer. As Charles Fillmore often points out, we can involve ourselves directly in the Trinity and experience remarkable, even miraculous results. This formula is clear and easy to remember: Idea (the Divine Idea), thought (our thought), word (affirmation).

---

[367] Fillmore, Charles *Jesus Christ Heals*
[368] Mark 11:24
[369] Ibid, p. 109

No Effort Wasted

> *The law of spiritual healing involves full receptivity on the part of the one under treatment. God does not do things in us against our will, as will acts both in the conscious and subconscious realms of mind. However much it may appear that the word is thwarted in its original intent, this is never true; it goes on, and enters where reception is given. In this way we are quickened, whether we see the result with physical vision or not, the process is as sure as Godself.*[370]

What happens to the energy of prayer help when the one for is not willing to receive it? Was that effort wasted? Is help nullified? Charles Fillmore says no: "However much it may appear that the word (prayer help) is thwarted in its original intent, it goes on, and it enters where reception is given it." In the divine economy no spiritual effort is ever wasted.

True Spiritual Healing

> *In connection with the Holy Spirit, here is an important point for a healer to consider. Do not regard the Holy Spirit altogether as a restorative principle without feeling, sympathy, or love. This reduces your healing method to intellectual logic and the slow process of mental science. Under this method the patient must always be educated in Truth principles before he can be healed. No instantaneous healing ever takes place under this*

---

[370] Fillmore, Charles *Jesus Christ Heals*, p. 112

> method. The Holy Spirit is sympathetic, comforting, loving, forgiving, and instantly healing.[371]

> It is found by those who have faith in the power of God that prayer for health is the most quickly answered. The reason for this is that the natural laws that create and sustain the body are really divine laws, and when man silently asks for the intervention of God in restoring health, he is calling into action the natural forces of his being.[372]

In our efforts to understand the principles of spiritual healing it is good to remember that there is also such a thing as instantaneous healing through the grace of God. This can be a comforting thought for those beginning Truth students who have an immediate healing need. It is not always necessary to understand completely the principles of the healing process in order to be healed.

Seeing Perfection

> Some of the most miraculous cures ever made have been where the healer simply saw perfection in the patient. He saw with the eye of Spirit that which really exists, and the shadow conformed to his seeing just to the extent of his realization of that spiritual reality.[373]

> It is wonderful how quickly our body responds to a thought of life and health, how we can feel a flow

---

[371] Ibid, p. 183
[372] Ibid, p. 80
[373] Fillmore, Charles *Talks on Truth*, p. 93

of health instantly if we hold the right thought. Just closing our mind to outer things and holding the thought that we are the perfect manifestation of Divine Mind will often heal our body of its illnesses. Disease is not natural. We must let go of it, relax, and let Spirit carry on its perfect work in us; and all at once evil or sick conditions disappear, and we are whole. Those who have had divine healings tell us that their best work was done by simply letting go and realizing that there is but one universal Mind and that this Mind makes a perfect body for every person.[374]

There is quite often misunderstanding about Unity's teachings on "seeing perfection," or "seeing the good," or "beholding the Christ" in others. Unity uses the word "see" in a very special sense in these teachings. We do not mean to pretend or to hallucinate. We really do not even mean "to see" in the literal sense. We are speaking rather of inner acknowledgment regardless of whether or not the outer appearance matches the acknowledgment at the moment. This is also sometimes called "holding the thought" or "laying hold of the Truth."

The Word
Power of the Word

Perfect health is natural, and the work of the spiritual healer is to restore this perfect health, which is innate and can be spoken into expression. Our ills are the result of our sins or failure to adjust our minds to Divine Mind. "We have authority on

---

[374] Fillmore, Charles *Keep a True Lent*, p. 22

> *earth to forgive sins.' When the sinning state of mind and the right state of man is established, we are restored to our primal and natural wholeness. This is a mental process, and so all our conditions are the result of thinking. 'As we think in our heart so are we.'[375] [376]*

> *As we are quickened with spiritual faith, our words are endowed with power. It becomes so charged with spiritual energy that we are enabled to heal all manner of diseases, even at a distance.[377]*

The power of the word does not originate with the word itself. It comes from the divine idea which the word expresses, and it also comes from the sense of I AM of the person who speaks the word. A consciously spoken word which has good intentions behind it carries great power. A mechanically spoken word with not much intention behind it carries little or no power. If a word is consciously spoken with the sole Intention of expressing a divine idea, it is called affirmation, and it carries the greatest power of all.

The Word of God

> *The Word of God is immanent in us and all the universe. All creation is carried forward by and through our conscious recognition of this mighty One. We are the consummation of the Word. God's spirit has, within it, the concentration of all that is contained within the Word. God being perfect, His*

---

[375] Proverbs 23:7
[376] Fillmore, Charles *Jesus Christ Heals*
[377] Fillmore, Charles *The Revealing Word*, p. 213

> *idea, thought, and Word must be perfect. Jesus expresses this perfect Word of God as spiritual man. 'The Word became flesh, and dwelt among us.'*[378] [379]

> *The 'seed' is the creative idea inherent in the word, the nature that it inherits from its parent source-- God.*[380]

The Word of God is creative Principle in action. This idea is first presented in the book of Genesis. The symbolic imagery is that of a gigantic "person" who literally speaks words that instantly comes true. This makes an interesting story, but it raises a number of unanswerable questions on the strictly literal level. Taken as allegory, however, it illustrates the action of the creative Principle of God in the form of the Word (or Logos). This is the meaning of "And God said…"[381]

The Logos

> *The meaning of the word "Logos" is speech based upon reason. If the reasonable premise that God is the omnipresent God is well grounded in you, you cannot speak anything but healing and uplifting words. Your words must be for the healing of the nations, because they are true words flowing forth from a source which in Truth has no opposite.*[382]

---

[378] John 1:14
[379] Fillmore, Charles *The Revealing Word*, p. 213
[380] Fillmore, Charles *Christian Healing*, p. 65
[381] Genesis 1:3
[382] Fillmore, Charles *The Twelve Powers of Man*, p. 172

> *An understanding of the Logos reveals to us the law under which all are brought forth, the law of mind action. Divine Mind creates by thought through ideas.*[383]

Logos is a Greek word translated Into English as Word with a capital "W". There doesn't seem to be a clear definition nor interpretation of this Greek word. The definitions seem to point in a direction, but come to no real conclusion. This is probably not a defect, since the metaphysical meaning of Logos is not concrete, literal, and finished. The general consensus seems to be that Logos denotes creative Principle in action as it relates to the universe. Logos originates in God. Logos reaches its later stage in us, where it is expressed through us as conscious speech.

Jesus' Healing Method

> *Whatever these various theories of Jesus' remarkable healing power may be, no one disputes one point: He used words as the vehicle of the healing potency. He always spoke to the patient "as one having authority."*[384] *He had a certain assurance, an inner conviction, that he was speaking the truth when he said, 'Thou art made whole;'*[385] *and the result of his understanding carried conviction to the mind of the patient and*

---

[383] Fillmore, Charles The Revealing Word, p. 124
[384] Matthew 7:29
[385] John 5:15

> *opened the way for the 'virtue' that went forth from the speaker.*[386]

> *Jesus laid great stress on the power of the word. The word has two activities: One is that of the still small voice in the silence, and the other is that of the 'loud voice' that was used by Jesus when he raised Lazarus from the dead. In the beginning 'God said, let there be'... and there was. We are the offspring of God, and our words have power proportionate to our realization of our indwelling spiritual kingdom.*[387]

Jesus is the prime example of Logos reaching its final stage as conscious speech. Jesus exemplified this to such an extent that he is sometimes referred to as "the Word become flesh." We must not overlook the fact that the words of Jesus came from a consciousness which we probably cannot even as yet comprehend. It was this consciousness which went into his words and caused them to have the overwhelming power they had. Jesus himself constantly called attention to the importance of his words. His words are one form of his presence with us today. This is one meaning of the "second coming of Christ," and it is happening now.

What are Words?

> *Words—the vehicles through which ideas make themselves manifest. Words that have in them the realization of perfection, everywhere-present,*

---

[386] Fillmore, Charles *Teach Us to Pray*, p. 165
[387] Fillmore, Charles *Atom-Smashing Power of Mind*, p. 148

> *always present divine life, our oneness with this life, and are dominant in the restoration of life and health. When spiritual words abide in our consciousness, the word or thought formed in intellectual and sense mind must give way to the higher principles of Being. The whole consciousness is then raised to a more spiritual plane. Affirmations of words of Truth realized in consciousness bring the mind into just the right attitude to receive light, and power and guidance from Spirit.*[388]

Realization of the power of words will not come to one who thinks of them only as being sounds or as combinations of letters on a printed page. Words are really expressions of consciousness and in our world, consciousness is the ruling factor. Words carry the power and authority of their originating consciousness, just as certain ambassadors have the mandate to carry the power and authority of their government.

The Spoken Word

> *The spoken word carries vibrations through the universal ethers, and also moves the intelligence inherent in every form, animate or inanimate. It has been discovered that even rocks and minerals have life. This is proof of the omnipresence of the one animating substance. We, being the highest emanation of Divine Mind, have great directive*

---

[388] Fillmore, Charles The Revealing Word, p. 213

> *power and are really co-operators with God in forming the universe."*[389]

Again, when Charles Fillmore writes of the spoken word he means much more than just the audible sound of the word. He includes the consciousness of that person who speaks it. This means that what a person's consciousness is able to do, his words are able to do.

When words of Truth are consciously spoken, the Truth consciousness is in those words, and mighty things are accomplished. The most powerful of all spoken words are affirmations of Truth.

Speaking the Word

> *Every time we speak we cause the atoms of the body to tremble and change their places. Not only do we cause the atoms of our body to change their position, but we raise or lower the rate of vibration and otherwise affect the bodies of others with whom we come in contact.*[390]
>
> *Thus he who realizes most thoroughly that God is the supreme perfection and that in God can be no imperfection, and speaks forth that realization with conviction, will cause all things to arrange themselves in divine order."*[391]

Since words express states of consciousness there is a very close relationship between the words we speak

---

[389] Fillmore, Charles *Christian Healing*, p. 68
[390] Ibid, p. 65
[391] Fillmore, Charles *Teach Us to Pray*, p. 172

and our various physiological states. Charles Fillmore relates this idea to the atoms and vibratory rates of the human body. Our spoken words also have an effect on other persons' bodies, to the degree that a person makes himself subjective to the words of others. In the second paragraph Charles Fillmore carries this Idea one step further. He extends the influence of the spoken word into the arrangement of "things." This would probably include circumstances and events. It is helpful to remember that when Charles Fillmore makes these kinds of statements about the power of the spoken word, he is not referring to just any kind of spoken word. He means only the consciously spoken word that has spiritual motivation behind it. The other kind of spoken words are of little or no creative value. Jesus calls these "vain repetitions."[392] In metaphysics we call this "mechanical talking."

Regeneration

> *Regeneration follows generation in our development. Generation sustains and perpetuates the human; regeneration unfolds and glorifies the divine.*[393]

> *Regeneration—A change in which abundant spiritual life, even eternal life, is incorporated into the body. The transformation that takes place through bringing all the forces of mind and body to the support of the Christ ideal. The unification of Spirit, soul, and body in spiritual oneness."*[394]

---

[392] Matthew 6:7
[393] Fillmore, Charles *The Twelve Powers*, p. 3
[394] Fillmore, Charles *The Revealing Word*, p. 165

One of the difficulties in understanding the concept of regeneration is that we do not have any examples of it around to point to. At the present time it is a term for an ideal still to be attained. What is it? Basically it refers to a level of consciousness wherein a person is able to avoid the death experience. It is a level of control of the life expressions through the body which keeps the flow of vital energies constant and ever-renewing. It can be attained only by sufficient growth of spiritual consciousness.

True Church of Christ

> *Many have caught sight of the fact that the true church of Christ is a state of consciousness in man, but few have gone so far in the realization as to know that in the very body of each man and woman is a temple in which the Christ is present at all times : 'You are a temple of God.'[395] The appellation was not symbolical, but a statement of architectural truth. Under the direction of the Christ, a new body is constructed by the thinking faculty in us; the materials entering into this superior structure are the spiritualized organic substances, and the new creation is the temple or body of Spirit.[396]*

In this paragraph Charles Fillmore presents a concept that captured readers' imaginations from the very first: "In the very body of each man and woman is a temple in which the Christ is present at all times." These

---

[395] I Corinthians 3:16
[396] Fillmore, Charles Talks in Truth, p. 105

words have lifted the minds and hearts of many, many persons down through the years. This paragraph also contains one of the first mentions made by Charles Fillmore about the new body now in construction in all who are to any degree in awakened spiritual awareness. While this is Fillmore's first mention of it, he returns to this theme again and again in many of his later writings.

Denials and Affirmations

> *In every change of consciousness on the physical plane, there is a breaking down of some cells and building up of other cells to take their place. Mentally this is denial and affirmation, and this process in the body is the result of these two movements in the mind which have occurred at some previous period.*[397]

> *Regeneration begins its work in the conscious mind and completes it in the subconscious. The first step is cleansing or denial in which all error thoughts are renounced. This includes forgiveness for sins committed and a general clearing of the whole consciousness. After the way has been prepared, the second step takes place. This is the outpouring of the Holy Spirit."*[398]

The principles of denial and affirmation are involved in every important area in the Unity teachings. Charles Fillmore sees the energy needed for regeneration

---

[397] Fillmore, Charles *The Twelve Powers*, p. 128
[398] Fillmore, Charles The Revealing Word, p. 166

as starting with the correct expression of denial and affirmation in the human consciousness.

Reconstructing the Organism

> *So you will find in your experience with the work of the Holy Spirit in reconstructing your organism that the present structure must be literally torn down atom by atom. It is in its present state temporary and without the conscious life of the indwelling Spirit. You, with all humankind, have separated yourself from God in consciousness; that separation extends to the body, the most remote plane of consciousness.*[399]

> *Spirit is the dynamic force that releases the pent-up energies within us. The energies have been imprisoned in the cells, and when release d are again restored to action in the body by the chemistry of creative Hind. The perfection of this regeneration is in proportion to the understanding and industry of the individual.*[400]

Some resist the concept of regeneration because they think of it as eternal life in the body as it now is. Charles Fillmore assured readers that this would not be the case, that the present state of the body is not its true one. Prior to regeneration there would be the experience of "reconstruction" which would result in an entirely different "texture" of body. He often calls it a "body of light." It is in this reconstructed organism that we would

---

[399] Fillmore, Charles *Talks on Truth*, p. 108
[400] Fillmore, Charles *Jesus Christ Heals*, p. 138

begin a regeneration existence. And, as always, he emphasize d that this is to be attained only by sufficient development of spiritual awareness.

Life Substance - Intelligence

> *Life and substance are ideas in Divine Mind. Life is the acting principle; substance is the thing acted upon. In the phenomenal world, life is the energy that propels all forms to action. Life is not in itself intelligent; it requires the directive power of an entity that knows where and how to apply its force in order to get the best results."*[401]

Here again Charles Fillmore returns to the idea of the Trinity. In this case he applies it to the requirements for a healthy organism. Life is necessary for health. Substance is necessary for health. Intelligence is necessary for healthy coordination of life and substance. Charles Fillmore often instructed students to affirm that their bodies were "perfect life, substance, and intelligence."

Eternal Life

> *Life is divine, spiritual, and its source is God, Spirit. The river of life is within us in our spiritual consciousness. We comes into consciousness of the river of life through the quickening of Spirit. We can be truly quickened with new life and vitalized in mind and body only by consciously contacting*

---

[401] Fillmore, Charles *The Revealing Word*, p. 121

> *Spirit. This contact is made through prayer, meditation, and good works."*[402]
>
> *We all have life, and it is God's eternal life but it does not become ours in reality until we consciously realize it. The one who enters into eternal life, as did Jesus, must lay hold on that omnipresent life and make it one with his body. This is the secret of inheriting eternal life."*[403]

Life is a divine idea! All divine ideas are eternal. Thus, life is eternal. There is, however, a difference between eternal life and physical existence as it is now. If eternal life meant eternal physical existence as it now is, then it might not be desirable for all. But it does not mean that. It means to be an eternal expression of divine life.

Nourishing the Life Force

> *We may nourish a good thing by thinking how good it is— a beautiful face, a beautiful form, whatever it may be that is good ; but suppose we take the negative side, shall we then get results also? Yes, absolutely. We shall get just what we think about. The thought of nourishing is a very good thought because it shows us just what we do. Mind draws upon the vital forces, and according to physiological laws we alter our tissues. Either we tear down our bodies or we build them up.*[404]

---

[402] Fillmore, Charles *The Revealing Word*, p. 122
[403] Fillmore, Charles *Keep a True Lent*, p. 122
[404] Fillmore, Charles *Jesus Christ Heals*, p. 128

Ordinarily, we use the word "nourish" in connection with food and the physical body. In this paragraph we are using the word in another sense—in the sense of quickening and increasing the effectiveness of the life force in our bodies. Charles Fillmore often taught that praise and thanksgiving result in an increase of the good we experience. We can praise and give thanks for the life force within us, and thereby "nourish" it into greater effectiveness in our bodies. This is mostly a matter of thought and attitude.

Transformation through Mind

> *We can imagine that we have some evil condition in body or affairs, and through the imagination build it up until it becomes manifest. On the other hand, we can use the same power to make good appear on every side. The marks of old age can be erased from the body by one's mentally seeing the perfection in it. Transient patching up with lotions and external applications is foolish; the work must be an inner transformation. 'Be transformed by the renewing of your mind.'*[405][406]

Charles Fillmore believed strongly in the ever-present possibility of transformation through the expansion of consciousness. The process of transformation through mind consists of simply establishing a strong enough consciousness of something so that it results in a manifestation of good. Of course, the imagination would enter into this, but consciousness is much more than just

---

[405] Romans 12:2
[406] Fillmore, Charles *Christian Healing*, p. 105

imagining. Charles Fillmore often stated that the untapped powers in human consciousness were beyond belief—especially the power to transform patterns inherited from past belief systems.

Responsibility for Wholeness
Resurrection

> *The 'resurrection' of the body has nothing whatever to do with death, except that we may resurrect ourselves from every dead condition into which sense ignorance has plunged us. To be resurrected means to get out of the place that you are in and to get into another place. Resurrection is a rising into new vigor, new prosperity; a restoration to some higher state. It is absurd to suppose that it applies only to the resuscitation of a dead body.*[407]

> *The resurrection of the body is not dependent for its demonstration on time, evolution or any of the man-made means of growth. It is the result of the elevation of the spiritually emancipated mind of the individual.*[408]

Ordinarily the word "resurrection" means to regain that which one has lost. Charles Fillmore sees resurrection as something more. He sees it as not only regaining a state from which we may have fallen, but to actually rise to a state higher than ever before. He says, "Resurrection is a rising into new vigor, new prosperity, and a restoration to

---

[407] Fillmore, Charles The *Atom-Smashing Power of Mind*, p. 119
[408] Ibid, p. 123

some higher state." So we see that there is an element of "ascension" in Fillmore's definition of resurrection.

Mind

> *Above all other Bible writers Paul emphasizes the importance of the mind in the transformation of character and body. In this respect he struck a note in religion that had been mute up to this time; that is, that Spirit and Mind are akin and that we are related to God through God's thoughts. Paul sounds again and again in various forms this silent but very essential chord in the unity of God and man and his body.*[409]

> *Have faith in the power of your mind to penetrate and release the energy that is pent up in the atoms of your body, and you will be astounded at the response. Paralyzed functions anywhere in the body can be restored to action by one's speaking to the spiritual intelligence and life within them.*[410]

Again and again Charles Fillmore emphasized that the connecting link between God and us is Mind, and he uses Paul as a biblical resource for this teaching. It takes but little experimenting for us to realize that the teaching is absolutely true. How else can any of us become aware of divine ideas and relate our sense of I AM to them correctly? It can be only in the mind.

---

[409] Ibid, p. 29
[410] Fillmore, Charles *Atom-Smashing Power of Mind*, p. 11

Mental Causes

> *All things have their cause, and every cause is mental. Whoever comes in daily contact with a high order of thinking cannot help but take on some of it. Our mind takes it on unconsciously just as our lungs breathe the air of the room. Ideas are catching, and no one can live where true ideas of wholeness and abundance and peace are being held without becoming more or less infected with them.*[411]

The primal causes of all existing things are divine ideas. However, all things now in existence have not come directly from the primal causes, but from secondary causes. The secondary causes of existing things are the thoughts of mankind. We can pattern our thoughts from divine ideas to greater or lesser degrees. Primal (first) cause is divine, spiritual. Secondary (form producing) cause is human. Human thinking is capable of becoming more and more aligned with divine ideas, and the mind can produce results of greater and greater Truth and beauty.

Power of Thought

> *You cannot have consciousness without thinking. It is the nature of the mind to think; your every thought, no matter how trivial, causes vibrations in the universal ether that ultimate in the forms of visibility. You know that the working power of mind is thought and that through thought all the*

---

[411] Fillmore, Charles *Jesus Christ Heals*, p. 136

> conditions that seem to encompass you were formed.[412]

> "Thoughts are alive and are endowed by the thinker with a secondary thinking power; that is, the thought entity that the I A M forms assumes an ego and begins to think but only with the power you give to them.[413]

Most people take thoughts so much for granted that there is very little thinking about thought in our world today. Charles Fillmore was not only a great thinker, he was a profound observer of and thinker about thought. He beheld thoughts as actual "entities" on the mental plane which inherited a certain amount of creative power from their parent (the human thinker). He called this "the secondary power of thought.

Secondary Power of Thought

> Each thought of mind is an identity that has a central ego. By this we mean that every thought has a center around which all its elements revolve and to which it is obedient when no higher power is in evidence. Thoughts are capable of expressing themselves— they think. We think, and we think into our thoughts all that we are; hence our thoughts must be endowed with a secondary power of thought. There is, however, a difference between the original thinking and the secondary thought. We have an animating center in Spirit; the other, in

---

[412] Fillmore, Charles *Keep a True Lent*, p. 65
[413] Fillmore, Charles *Prosperity*, p. 118

> thought. One is the Son of God; the other is the son of man.[414]

This paragraph, which contains Charles Fillmore's first insight into the secondary power of thought, puzzles some readers, irritates some, and delights some. The irritant for some persons might be that this first formulation of the idea came before he began to clarify the distinction between divine ideas and human thoughts. He rather mixes them up in his earlier writings, and tends to call everything "thought." Divine ideas are primal causes. Our thoughts are secondary causes. Using Bible symbolism, Charles Fillmore says, "One is the Son of God (divine ideas); the other is the son of man (human thoughts).

Self-Control

> *The problem of self-control settled until all that man into touch with the divine will and understanding. You must understand all your forces before you can establish them in harmony. This overcoming is easy if you go about it in the right way. But if you try to take dominion through will force and suppression, you will find it hard and never accomplish any permanent results. Get your I AM centered in God, from that place of Truth speak true words. In this way you will real spiritual mastery and raise consciousness from the human to the divine.[415]*

---

[414] Fillmore, Charles *Christian Healing*, p. 50
[415] Ibid, p. 115

This paragraph contains an important key to understanding the difficulty we often have in living up to our own good intentions or in eliminating undesirable habits. The hard way to go about this is to try to attack the problem in the outer and effect change through human will. The easy way is to begin with the correct inner work. The difference between self-control and self-chaos depends for the most part on what our sense of I AM is connected with at any time. If it is connected with any negative emotions, then self-control becomes difficult (if not impossible).

Thinking and Eating

> *There is a relationship between thinking and eating, and as you grow spiritually the character of your food and all that pertains to eating may have to be changed in conformity with the new order of things. If you will leave meat and all animal products out of your food you will see a change for the better. But above all, keep your thought mastery and do not be controlled by appetite. Do not fear to eat. Eat with thanksgiving and bless your food.*[416]

Some readers feel that Charles Fillmore places too much emphasis on eating; others feel he did not place enough emphasis on it. When we study the Gospels to see what Jesus has to say about food and spirituality, we find that he says practically nothing other than, "Be not anxious."[417] In another place he says "Hear and

---

[416] Fillmore, Charles *Atom-Smashing Power of Mind*, p. 73
[417] Matthew 6:25

understand: not what goes into the mouth defiles a man, but what comes out of the mouth, this defiles a man."[418] In any case, Charles Fillmore does end his paragraph with these cheerful words, "Do not fear to eat. Eat with thanksgiving and bless your food."

Love, the Harmonizer

> *Among people who observe and think there is no question about love's being the greatest harmonizing principle known to us. The question is how to get people to use love in adjusting their discords.*[419]

> *Love, in Divine Mind, is the idea of universal unity. In expression, it is the power that joins and binds together the universe and everything in it. Love is a harmonizing, constructive power. When it is made active in consciousness, it conserves substance and reconstructs, rebuilds, and restores us and our world.*[420]

It is important to realize that love does more than just "join and bind together." It is possible for things to be joined and bound together that would be better separated and kept apart. The all-important thing about love is that it harmonizes and blesses what it causes to be unified. Discontent and inharmony in being "joined and bound together" occurs only when love is no longer doing the joining and binding. We should work to make love a

---

[418] Matthew 15:11
[419] Fillmore, Charles *Teach Us to Pray*, p. 107
[420] Fillmore, Charles *Keep a True Lent*, p. 152

permanent attitude in our outlook and in our nature. A loving attitude causes harmony to become the dominant factor in mind and body, and maintenance of good health becomes easy.

Chapter 22 – Metaphysical Basis for Prosperity

Questions from the Text
1. What is prosperity?
2. What does Charles Fillmore mean when he says that we are living in two worlds?
3. What is "the object"?
4. What is the essential factor in the metaphysical approach to prosperity?
5. What is a spiritual substance?
6. What is the two-step process?
7. Outline the essential steps in developing a spiritual prosperity consciousness.
8. What is the key?
9. Briefly define:
    - Law of Mind Action.
    - Law of Increase
    - Law of Giving and Receiving
    - Law of Love
    - Law of Tithing
10. What does money represent?
11. The practice of tithing can have a negative application. What is it?

Lesson Text

There is both a primary and a secondary law of increase. We pile up possessions by human effort, interest, and other ways of secondary increase, and grow into the thought that these are the real means of attaining prosperity. But possessions

> *gained in this way rest on a very insecure foundation and are often swept away in a day. Then we are in despair and often think that their means of existence is gone forever and life is not worth living. Such persons are really never happy in their wealth, because there is always a lurking fear that they may lose it. They are secretly troubled with the thought of lack, in the presence of worldly plenty.*[421]

The physical, or outer, approach to prosperity is a difficult and risky one. It involves competition, opportunism, and other practices which may coarsen consciousness and defeat the purpose of true prosperity.

Also, this approach carries with it the possibility of loss, which is terrifying to the material minded one. Yet the outer approach certainly does get results for some persons, even spectacular results in some cases. Why? Because, as Charles Fillmore explains, it is part of the "secondary law of increase."

Metaphysical Basis for Prosperity

> *Realize first of all that prosperity is not wholly a matter of capital or environment but a condition brought about by certain ideas that have been allowed to rule in the consciousness. When these ideas are changed the conditions are changed in spite of environment and all appearances, which must also change to conform to the new ideas.*[422]

---

[421] Fillmore, Charles *Keep a True Lent*, p. 101
[422] Fillmore, Charles *Prosperity*, p. 88

> *Every visible item of wealth can be traced to an invisible source. Food comes from grain, which was planted in the earth; but who sees or knows the quickening love that touches the seed and makes it bear a hundredfold? An unseen force from an invisible source acts on the tiny seeds, and supply for the multitude springs forth.*[423]

The metaphysical, or spiritual, approach to prosperity need not be difficult and is not risky. It involves no competition, opportunism, or any other practice which coarsens consciousness and defeats the purpose of true prosperity. Also, this approach carries with it the possibility of loss which is terrifying to the material-minded one. Yet the outer approach certainly does get results for some persons, even spectacular results in some cases. Why? Because as Charles Fillmore explains, it is part of the "secondary law of increase."

Living in Two Worlds

> *Apparently we live in two worlds: an invisible world of thoughts, and a visible world of things. The invisible world of thought substance is the real world, because it is the source of the world of things, and we stand between the two, handing out with thoughts the unlimited substance of Spirit. When we get understanding of the right relation between the visible and the invisible into our mind and active in our thoughts, all our needs will be met. This is what Jesus meant when he said, 'Seek*

---
[423] Ibid, p. 104

> first God's kingdom and righteousness; and all these things shall be added unto you.'[424] [425]

The two worlds spoken of in this paragraph are the inner invisible world and the outer visible world. Our consciousness is pivotal, so we live in both realms simultaneously. The thing which determines where we are at in any given moment is our attention, or our sense of I AM. As Charles Fillmore says, when a person gets a real understanding of the right relationship between these two realms a greater dimension of power is added to consciousness "and all needs will be met."

Faith

> In this lesson we are considering the subject of faith, as it applies to the demonstration of prosperity. In this study, as in all others, we must start in the one Mind. God had faith when God imaged man and the universe and through faith brought all things into being. Man, being like God, must also base his creations on faith as the only foundation. Here then is our starting point in building a prosperity consciousness and making our world as we would have it. We all have faith, for it is innate in everyone. Our question is how we put it to work in our affairs.[426]

Faith is an essential factor in the metaphysical approach to prosperity. It is the great affirmative power of

---

[424] Matthew 6:33
[425] Fillmore, Charles *Keep a True Lent*, P. 102
[426] Fillmore, Charles *Prosperity*, p. 42

the universe working in and through us. The affirmative attitude is constantly saying "yes" to Divine ideas. With such an attitude, a person cannot avoid being truly prosperous. Even if we do not care for material wealth, we will experience prosperity of the very highest order.

Ideas

> *By prayer we accumulate in our mind ideas of God as the substance of our supply and support. There is no lack of this substance in infinite Mind. Regardless of how much God gives, there is always an abundance left. God does not give us material things, but Mind substance—not money but ideas—ideas that set spiritual forces in motion so that things begin to come to us by the application of the law.*[427]

Divine ideas are the only true wealth, for they are the primary causes for all that is good in life. They are always fully available and cannot be depleted or annihilated. The mind causes the energies of divine ideas to project into the realm of form (manifestation) and such forms constitute our supply. The supply is our experience of prosperity, but the divine ideas behind the supply are the prosperity. Jesus called these inexhaustible divine ideas "the Father's Kingdom." He said, "It is your Father's good pleasure to give you the kingdom."[428]

---

[427] Ibid, p. 31
[428] Luke 12:32

Substance

> *The spiritual substance from which comes all visible wealth is never depleted. It is right with us all the time and responds to our faith in it and our demands on it. It is not affected by our talk of hard times, though we are affected because our thoughts and words govern our demonstration.*[429]

> *Just as the earth is the universal matrix in which all vegetation develops, so this invisible spirit substance is the universal matrix in which ideas of prosperity germinate and grow and bring forth according to our faith and trust.*[430]

Substance is the invisible "matrix" of all possible forms of supply. Substance is not matter, but it makes matter possible. Our senses experience the energies generated from substance as matter. Substance is a very simple and complicated thing at the same time, at least from our point of view and because of the limitations of human language and definition.

The Two-Step Process

> *It is not sufficient however to sit down and hold thoughts of abundance without further effort. That is limiting the law to thought alone, and we want it to be fulfilled in manifestation as well. Cultivating ideas of abundance is the first step in the process. The ideas that come must be used. Be alert in doing*

---

[429] Fillmore, Charles *Prosperity*, p. 13
[430] Fillmore, Charles *Keep a True Lent*, p. 184

whatever comes to you to do, cheerful and competent in the doing, sure of the results, for it is the second step in the fulfilling of the law.[431]

We should give equal emphasis to both steps in fulfillment of the law of prosperity. We must begin with the formative power of thought, but we must follow through with appropriate action. We are created to be thinkers and doers. If we attempt to function as just one or the other, we are fulfilling only half of the law, and our existence will be unsatisfactory in many ways. Prayer does not bring just things. Prayer often brings guidance, and guidance is to be followed. This is our part in fulfillment of the law.

New Economic Basis

Spiritual discernment reveals that we are now in the dawn of a new era, that the old methods of supply and support are fast passing away, and that new methods are waiting to be brought forth. In the coming economy we will not be a slave to money. Humanity's daily needs will be met in ways that are not now thought practical. We shall serve for the joy of serving, and prosperity will flow to us and through us in streams of plenty. The supply and support that love and zeal will set in motion are not as yet largely used by us, but those who have tested their providing power are loud in their praise.[432]

---

[431] Fillmore, Charles *Prosperity*, p. 92
[432] Ibid, p. 9

This paragraph gives Charles Fillmore's prophetic vision of what may be called "New-Age Economy." Material-minded readers may find this vision too idealistic. Skeptics may reject it because they see no evidence of it happening in the world today. But metaphysical thinkers have recognized the Truth in these words from the time they first appeared in print. These are the persons Charles Fillmore is alluding to in his closing words: "Those who have tested their providing power (love and zeal) are loud in their praise."

Prosperity Goal

> *Our work is to bring men and women to the place of true and lasting dominion where they are superior to both riches and poverty. We can do this by showing them that they are spiritual beings that they live in a spiritual world here and now, and that through the apprehension of the Truth of their being and their relationship to God this dominion is to be realized.*[433]

Prosperity is neither riches nor poverty, but a state of consciousness superior to both. Of course, it is natural to equate riches to prosperity rather than poverty. But riches can be dangerous in the wrong hands. Prosperity can never be dangerous in the wrong hands, because it cannot come to wrong hands. The true goal of prosperity is the attainment of a level of consciousness, not the attainment of an amount of riches.

---

[433] Ibid, p. 155

Developing a Prosperity Consciousness
First Principle of Demonstration

> *The secret of demonstration is to conceive what is true in Being and to carry out the concept in thought, word, and act. If I can conceive a truth, there must b e a way by which I can make that truth apparent. If I can conceive of an inexhaustible supply existing in the omnipresent ethers, then there is a way by which I can make that supply manifest. Once our mind accepts this as an axiomatic truth it has arrived at the place where the question of process begins to be considered.*[434]

In the opening sentence of this paragraph Charles Fillmore lists the first step in following the principle of demonstration as "to conceive what is true in Being and to carry out the concept in thought, word, and act." The question in some readers' minds is, what exactly does it mean to "conceive what is true in Being?" This is simply another way of referring to recognizing a divine idea. Divine ideas are what is true in Being. Then someone might ask, "But how can I recognize a divine idea?" And the answer is that a human mind always does recognize a divine idea, because divine ideas are the true components of what we see and respond to as good. Love, wisdom, health, order, etc. are divine ideas. Prosperity is a divine idea, and any divine idea that our minds conceive of can be brought into expression and manifestation.

---

[434] Ibid, p. 37

Overcoming Fear of Lack

There is no lack of anything anywhere in reality. The only lack is the fear of lack in the mind of man. We do not need to overcome any lack, but we must overcome the fear of lack.[435]

Most of us rush around trying to work out our problems for ourselves and in our own way, with one idea, one vision: the material thing we seek. We need to devote more time to silent meditation and, like the lilies of the field, simply be patient and grow into our demonstrations. We should remember always that these substance ideas with which we are working are eternal ideas that have always existed and will continue to exist, the same ideas that formed this planet in the first place and that sustain it now.[436]

Lack is not a divine idea, therefore it is not a reality in the true meaning of reality. Lack is a sort of mirage. People call it real because it appears. Lack appears. But is it real? The answer is the same as regarding a mirage in the desert. It appears. But is it real? You might say it is a "real mirage," but spiritual awareness will replace the mirage with the real thing. Lack can be replaced by supply through spiritual consciousness.

---

[435] Ibid, p. 52
[436] Ibid, p. 34

Attention: The Key

> *We do not have to wait until we have fully entered the kingdom or attained a complete understanding of Spirit before prosperity begins to be manifest, but we do have to see, to turn the attention in that direction.*[437]

> *Daily concentration of mind on Spirit and its attributes will reveal that the elemental forces that make all material things are here in the ether awaiting our recognition and appropriation. It is not necessary to know all the details of the scientific law in order to demonstrate prosperity. Go into the silence daily at a stated time and concentrate on the substance of Spirit... This opens up a current of thought that will bring prosperity into your affairs.*[438]

The power of attention within consciousness is a very great power indeed—far greater than most persons realize. When the direction of consciousness is forward, or Godward, mighty energies are being generated, and prosperity results. What Charles Fillmore says here about ease of success in demonstrating the prosperity law works the same in the laws of healing. This is dramatically symbolized in the Gospels in the incident of the woman who was healed after touching the hem of Jesus' garment. This symbolizes successful results under the healing law without having intricate understanding of all the workings of that law. Just touching its "garment" with faith can get

---

[437] Ibid, p. 38
[438] Ibid, p. 41

the needed results. The same idea holds true in regard to prosperity.

Thoughts are Seeds

> *Thoughts are seeds that, when dropped or planted in the subconscious mind, germinate, grow, and bring forth their fruit in due season. The more clearly we understand this truth the greater will be our ability to plant the seeds that bring forth desirable fruits. After sowing the plants must be tended. After using the law we must hold to its fulfillment. This is our part, but God gives the increase. You must work in divine order and not expect the harvest before the soil has been prepared or the seed sown. You have now the fruits of previous sowings. Change your thought seeds and reap what you desire. Some bring forth very quickly, others more slowly, but all in divine order.*[439]

In many of his parables Jesus used the illustration of seeds as representing thoughts and words of Truth. In this paragraph, Charles Fillmore reminds us that human beings can plant the seeds and can guard and tend the seeds, but that only God can give the increase. One of our most persistent enemies is impatience. Thoughts and words of Truth are seeds and must go through a process before becoming a harvested crop. It is during this time of process that impatience is most dangerous. The thing to remember is that the more patient we become during processing time, the shorter the time element becomes.

---

[439] Fillmore, Charles *Jesus Christ Heals*, p. 112

The chances are that if we could totally overcome impatience our demonstrations might become quick enough to be called instantaneous.

Concentration

> *Every thought that goes forth from the brain sends vibrations into the surrounding atmosphere and moves the realm of things to action. The effect is in proportion to the ability of the thinker to concentrate his mental forces. The average thought vibration produces but temporary results, but under intense mind activity conditions more or less permanent are impressed upon the sensitive plate of the universal ether, and through this activity they are brought into physical manifestation.*[440]

We should be careful not to confuse true concentration with strained attention. True concentration can be quite relaxed. It simply has to be genuine. True concentration means that we keep an idea or a goal secure in mind. Frivolous or erratic changes of mind can spoil concentration, but intelligent changes of mind can actually be part of real concentration. It only has to be genuine and it will bring about the good results described in this paragraph.

Law of Mind Action

> *You will become more prosperous and successful so gradually, simply, and naturally that you will not realize that it derives from a divine source and in*

---
[440] Fillmore, Charles *Christian Healing*, p. 63

> *answer to your prayers. We must realize all the while however that whatever we put as seeds into the subconscious soil will eventually bring forth after its kind and we must exercise the greatest caution so that we do not think or talk about insufficiency or allow others to talk to us about it. As we sow in mind, so shall we reap in manifestation.*[441]

As Charles Fillmore's opening sentences of this paragraph tells us, "You will become more prosperous and successful so gradually, simply, and naturally that you will not realize that it derives from a divine source and in answer to your prayers." This is so true. However, as Truth students we are so accustomed to hearing or reading about spectacular demonstrations of an amazing kind, especially in regard to prosperity, that we tend to feel inadequate when our own prosperity prayers are answered in a gradual but sensible way. This should not be. No one is inadequate who is trusting God and affirming Truth. Success will come just as surely as day follows night. Patience, trust, and inner gratitude will ease whatever waiting period there may be.

Thanksgiving

> *You should expect prosperity when you keep the prosperity law. Therefore, be thankful for every blessing that you gain and as deeply grateful for every demonstration as for an unexpected treasure dropped into your lap. This will keep your heart fresh; for true thanksgiving may be likened to rain*

---

[441] Fillmore, Charles *Prosperity*, p. 67

> *falling upon ready soil, refreshing it and increasing its productiveness.*[442]

This paragraph speaks of thanksgiving for blessings received. But even more potent is thanksgiving in advance of blessings received. To give thanks after a blessing does not usually require much of an effort. It is not hard to be polite when something nice has happened to us. But to give thanks before receiving may take some effort. All good effort is rewarded under spiritual law.

Secondary Effects of Prosperity Consciousness

> *All this is true not only of your own affairs. The effects extend also to those with whom you come in contact. They will become more prosperous and happy. They may not in any way connect their improvement with you or your thoughts, but that does not affect the truth about it. All causes are essentially mental, and whoever comes into daily contact with a high order of thinking must take on some of it. Ideas are catching, and no one can live in an atmosphere of true thinking, where high ideas are held, without becoming more or less inoculated with them.*[443]

It is a fact that other persons can be the beneficiaries of your work on your own prosperity consciousness. We are never truly happy with our blessings unless there is some way of sharing them with

---
[442] Fillmore, Charles *Prosperity*, p. 105
[443] Ibid, p. 40

others. In the case of being blessed with greater consciousness, we find great happiness by realizing that it sort of "spills over" from us and touches others. Charles Fillmore says, "Ideas are catching." And an increased consciousness radiates Truth ideas in every direction.

Balance

> *We are not studying prosperity to become rich but to bring out those characteristics that are fundamental to prosperity. We must learn to develop the faculty that will bring prosperity and the character that is not spoiled by prosperity.*[444]

> *Again, if we seek the kingdom of substance for the sake of the loaves and fishes we may get out of it will surely be disappointed in the end. We may get the loaves and fishes, that is quite possible; but if there remains in the soul any desire to use them for selfish ends, the ultimate result will be disastrous.*[445]

How to get supply is one thing. How to handle supply is another. The two must balance and complement each other. If not, there is no real prosperity. There can be a lot of "clutter," but not true prosperity. The danger involved in the fact that it is relatively easy to use mental ways of getting supply is the temptation toward selfishness or acquisitiveness. These quickly become an addiction. True metaphysical thinking will enable us to avoid this danger.

---

[444] Ibid, p. 161
[445] Ibid, p. 19

The Laws of Money: Seek the Kingdom

> *There is a kingdom of abundance of all things, and it ma y be found by those who seek it and are willing to comply with its laws. Jesus said that it is hard for a rich man to enter into the kingdom of heaven. This does not mean that it is hard because of his wealth, for the poor man gets in no faster and no easier. It is not money but the thoughts we hold about money, its source, its ownership, and its use, that keep us out of the kingdom. Our thoughts about money are like our thoughts about all possessions; they believe that things coming out of the earth are theirs to claim and control as individual property, and may be hoarded away and depended on, regardless of how much others may be in need of them. The same belief is prevalent among both rich and poor, and even if the two classes were suddenly to change places, the inequalities of wealth would not be remedied. Only a fundamental change in the thoughts of wealth could do that.*[446]

This paragraph is one of Charles Fillmore's most comprehensive essays on the errors of strictly materialistic thinking about supply. He sees this kind of thinking as futile, unpleasant, and unnecessary because there is a dimension of consciousness where abundance is always available. He calls this "the kingdom." It is the same kingdom Jesus often speaks about. Jesus did not advocate poverty. He only commented on the danger of riches. Likewise, the Fillmores certainly did not recommend

---
[446] Fillmore, Charles *Prosperity*, p. 16

poverty, but by their own lives were examples of what can be attained when one shuns avarice or acquisitiveness.

Law of Compensation

> *'Give, and it shall be given unto you'[447] is the statement of a law that operates in every thought and action. This law is the foundation of all barter and financial exchange. Men scheme to get something for nothing; but the law, in one of its many forms, overtakes them in the end. Even metaphysicians, who above all people should understand the law, often act as if they expected God to provide abundantly for them before they have earned abundance. It is an error to think that God gives anybody anything that has not been earned.[448]*

Most people think only of working as a way of earning. But Charles Fillmore saw that under spiritual law, giving is also a way of earning. There are countless ways of giving, and not all of them would be recognized by the world as such. Sometimes just deciding on an attitude is a way of giving. Sometimes just giving up an attitude is giving. There are so many ways to give and all of them are recognized and rewarded by Spirit.

What Money Represents

> *It is not money, but the love of money, that is the root of all evil. What we need to know is that*

---

[447] Luke 6:38
[448] Fillmore, Charles *The Twelve Powers*, p. 27

> *money represents a mind substance of unlimited abundance and accessibility; that this mind substance cannot safely be hoarded or selfishly used by anyone; that it is a living magnet attracting good of every kind to those who possess it; that those who train their thoughts to depend on this mind substance for supply of all kinds never lack.*[449]

The statement that "money represents a mind substance of unlimited abundance and accessibility" is worth pondering very seriously. When understood, it opens all sorts of new insights and realizations and can change one's basic attitude about money. The difficulty connected with this metaphysical insight is that mind substance is not visible and tangible; only its representative is. And so the tendency is to worship money rather than the divine source of the mind substance. When this attitude changes, and the divine source is worshipped, prosperity can be enjoyed to the fullest.

The Money Idea

> *The wise metaphysician deals with the money idea and masters it.*[450]

> *Watch your thoughts when you are handling your money, because your money is attached through your mind to the one Source of all and all money. When you think of your money, which is visible, as something directly attached to an invisible source*

---

[449] Fillmore, Charles *Keep a True Lent*, p. 106
[450] Fillmore, Charles *Christian Healing*, p. 136

> *that is giving or withholding according to your thought, you have the key to all riches and the reason for all lack.*[451]

Here Charles Fillmore expands the metaphysics of money and sees it as an "idea" as well as a "representation." In the second paragraph we detect what that idea might be. It is the idea that money, like everything else in existence, is connected to the invisible Source through our minds. This makes good metaphysical sense. Money itself is not the trap one may fall into, but erroneous attitudes about it can be a trap.

The Law of Increase

> *There is a universal law of increase. It is not confined to bank accounts but operates on every plane of manifestation. The conscious cooperation of man is necessary to the fullest results in the working of this law. You must use your talent, whatever it may be, in order to increase it. Have faith in the law. Do not reason too much but forge ahead in faith and boldness.*[452]

The Hebrew Scriptures is a record of religious thinking based upon belief in a law of even exchange. The Christian Scriptures is a record of religious thinking based on the law of increase. Jesus often tells his hearers, "You have heard that it was said… But I say unto you… "Such passages illustrate a rise in the level of religious thinking.

---
[451] Fillmore, Charles *Keep a True Lent*, p. 102
[452] Fillmore, Charles Prosperity, p. 81

This rise must occur in all who seek to attain a true prosperity consciousness.

The Law of Giving and Receiving

> *There is a law of giving and receiving and it requires careful study if we would use it in our prosperity demonstrations. It is a law of mind action, and it can be learned and applied the same as any other law.*[453]

> *Law of Giving and Receiving - The law of substance that equalizes all things. To realize and maintain divine order, substance must have both an inlet and an outlet in consciousness, and must be kept moving. To demonstrate substance as supply, the law governing it must be recognized and kept. Those who, from pride or ignorance, do not open themselves to the inflow of substance do not demonstrate supply, and all who by selfishness refuse it an outlet, also fail.*[454]

Giving and receiving is one more example of the necessity for polarity of energy expressions in order to have manifestation. Manifestation cannot occur without polarized energy expressions. This is a law of physics as well as metaphysics. Giving and receiving are the two poles of the same universal energy. This energy is experienced in most persons as feelings of generosity. This energy wants to be expressed, and so we feel the promptings from our hearts to give and receive. Giving and

---

[453] Ibid, p. 145
[454] Fillmore, Charles *The Revealing Word*, p. 119

receiving cause a flow of substance in soul and body which out-picture in a person's affairs.

Law of Love

> Many who have found the law of true thinking and its effect wonder why supply does not come to them after months and years of holding thoughts of bounty. It is because they have not developed love. They have formed the right image in mind, but the magnet that draws the substance from the storehouse of Being has not been set into action.[455]

The all-important presence of love is an essential in all spiritual demonstration. Without it, the possibility of failure is great. At the very least, disappointment comes even with success. Love should permeate all our human desires and efforts. Love should be part of all motivation and this must include the desire for prosperity. Selfishness tends to crowd out love, so it must be overcome. On the other hand, love crowds out nothing good, but simply "casts out all fear."[456]

Law of Tithing

> Tithing is giving a tenth of one's supply to God and God's work. Tithing is a tacit agreement that we are in partnership with God in the conduct of finances… Tithing, which is based on a law that cannot fail, establishes method in giving. It brings into the consciousness a sense of divine order that

---
[455] Fillmore, Charles *Talks on Truth*, p. 55
[456] I John 4:18

is manifested in one's outer life and affairs as increased efficiency and greater prosperity. It is the surest way ever found to demonstrate plenty, for it is God's own law and way of giving.[457]

By the act of tithing, we make God a partner in financial transactions and thus keep the channel open from the source in the ideal to the manifestation in the realm of things. Whoever thinks that we are helping to keep God's work going in the earth cannot help but believe that God will help. This virtually makes God not only a silent partner but also active in producing capital from unseen and unknown sources, in opening up avenues for commercial gain, and in various other ways making the individual prosperous.[458]

Tithing is a very special kind of giving. It is in a class by itself. It is giving with the thought of God uppermost in mind. This is why tithing is always connected with something religious, usually a church or a religious organization. It is not the church which causes it to be a tithe, but the thought of God in the mind of the giver. Charles Fillmore suggests that the thought of God as "partner" is a good one to adopt in tithing. Others may choose the thought of God as Source, or Increase, or unfailing Substance. But whatever form one may choose, it is the thought of God which constitutes the difference between tithing and just giving in general.

Tithing is a giving plan. It is not a spiritual law in the sense that there is a punishment by not practicing tithing.

---

[457] Fillmore, Charles *The Revealing Word*, p. 195
[458] Fillmore, Charles *Keep a True Lent*, p. 105

All giving is from the heart and is to be done without fear, compulsion or resentment. In fact Jesus said:[459]

> *Woe to you, teachers of the law and Pharisees, you hypocrites! You give a tenth of your spices--mint, dill and cumin. But you have neglected the more important matters of the law--justice, mercy and faithfulness. You should have practiced the latter, without neglecting the former.*

The Divine Economy and Balance

> *As we continue to grow in the consciousness of God as omnipresent life and substance we no longer have to put our trust in accumulations of money or other goods. We are sure that each day's need will be met, and we do not deprive ourselves of today's enjoyment and peace in order to provide for some future and wholly imaginary need. In this consciousness our life becomes divinely ordered, and there is a balance in supply and finances as in everything else. We do not deprive ourselves of what we need today; neither do we waste our substance in foolish ways nor deplete it uselessly.*[460]

Divine order is a factor necessary in every department of life in order for true enjoyment of existence to become possible. This is especially so in the areas of bodily health and prosperity. Regret about what we don't have can get in the way of appreciation of today's blessings. Charles Fillmore tells us that realization of God

---

[459] Matthew 23:23
[460] Fillmore, Charles Prosperity, p. 172

as omnipresent health and substance will help protect us from disrupting the order and balance needed in our thinking about health and prosperity.

Idea of Possession

> *Every thought of personal possession must be dropped out of mind before we can come into the realization of the invisible supply. They cannot possess money, houses, or land selfishly, because they cannot possess the universal ideas for which these symbols stand. We cannot possess any idea as our own permanently. We may possess its material symbol for a little time on the plane of phenomena, but it is such riches that 'moth and rust consume, and where thieves break through and steal.'*[461] [462]

Belief in exclusive possession is another error which can ruin one's enjoyment of prosperity. Even a person who is expert at getting supply can short circuit his enjoyment of it by believing in exclusive ownership. The Truth is not in ownership, but in stewardship. Nothing in all the world belongs to anyone exclusively. Everything that is belongs only to our Creator, God. But, by the same token (to paraphrase Jesus somewhat), "All that the Father has is mine. Not to have and to hold. But to receive, enjoy, and share forever."[463]

---

[461] Matthew 6:19
[462] Fillmore, Charles Prosperity, p. 17
[463] John 17:24

Hoarding Invites Disaster

> *Money saved as an 'opportunity fund' brings an increase of good, but money hoarded from fear as a motive or with any miserly thought in mind cannot possibly bring any blessing. Those who hold the thought of accumulation so dominant in the world today are inviting trouble and even disaster, because right along with this thought affirmation of the fear riches. Their actions and the loss they dread goes a strong of loss of bespeak fear, is certain or later." to be manifested sooner.[464]*

> *In our ignorance we are creating thought forces that will react upon us. 'With what judgment you judge, you shall be judged. With what measure you mete, it shall be measured unto you.'[465] Whatever thought you send out will come back to you. This is an unchangeable law of thought action.[466]*

The law of mind action is always in operation in the life of every person. "Like attracts like; like begets like." Belief in lack, fear of loss, and anticipation of insufficiency; all these things go to make up what Jesus termed a "hath not" consciousness. Jesus said that the "hath not" consciousness would manifest as the "hath not" experience. While the "hath" consciousness as the "hath" experience. He gives this teaching in the parable and that parable is just as true today as it ever was. Therefore it

---

[464] Fillmore, Charles Prosperity, p. 166
[465] Matthew 7:2
[466] Fillmore, Charles *Christian Healing*, p. 122

behooves us to be conscious about how we use of power of consciousness.

Illusion of Debt

> *Debt is a contradiction of the universal equilibrium, and there is no such thing as lack of equilibrium in all the universe. Therefore, in Spirit and in Truth, there is no debt... Debts exist in the mind, and in the mind is the proper place to begin liquidating them. These thought entities must be abolished in mind before their outer manifestations will pass away and stay away. Debt is a thought of lack with absence at both ends; the creditor thinks they lack what is owed and the debtor thinks they lack what is necessary to pay, else they would discharge the obligation rather than continue it. There is error at both ends of the proposition and nothing in the middle. This being true, it should be easy to dissolve the whole thought that anyone owes us or that we owe anyone anything... Thus we find that the way to pay our debts is by filling our mind with the substance of ideas that are the direct opposite of the thought of lack that caused the debts.*[467]

Debt is not necessarily a negative concept, although that is the context in which Charles Fillmore presents it in this paragraph. There is also a positive side to the concept of debt, which is not harmful to either side. This is when the concept of debt is a matter of gratitude, rather than of lack or obligation. In this concept, one does not feel that anyone owes me anything, but rather that I

---
[467] Fillmore, Charles Prosperity, pp. 120-21

owe much gratitude and thanks, and I am more than willing to pay.

Stewardship

> *See yourself as the steward of God handing out God's inexhaustible supplies. In this manner you are setting into action mental and spiritual forces that eventually bring large results into visibility. Be happy in your giving. God loves a cheerful giver because God's mind and heart are open to the flow of the pure substance of Being that balances all things.*[468]

Charles and Myrtle Fillmore took the concept of stewardship very much to heart and made it a cornerstone in the Unity organization. The same can be true in each individual life. If we see ourselves as stewards of all God's good, with exclusive ownership of nothing, we avoid trouble. Prosperity is the wages for good stewardship, and this form of prosperity can be permanent.

Giving Freely

> *A gift with reservations is not a gift; it is a bribe. There is no promise of increase unless we give freely, let go of the gift entirely, and recognize the universal scope of the law. Then the gift has a chance to go out and to come back multiplied. There is no telling how far the blessings may travel before it comes back, but it is a beautiful an d encouraging fact that the longer it is in returning,*

---

[468] Fillmore, Charles Prosperity, p. 152

> the more hands it is passing through and the more hearts it is blessing. All these hands and hearts add something to it in substance, and it is increased all the more when it does return.[469]

Giving freely is the only valid kind of giving. Any other kind is either a pretense, a loan, or a gesture of self-congratulating. Giving freely is full compliance with divine law, and it should be a beautiful experience. Generosity is more than a virtue, it really is a divine idea. It is part of divine love. When giving is purely an expression of love and generosity, then one has willingly cooperated with a divine idea. There is no higher or finer action possible to us than this. One who does this should not just stop with the pleasure of giving. We should make room in self for an additional experience: receiving. Do not be reluctant to receive. It is part of the same law that inspired you to give. Freely give. Gratefully receive.

Partnership

> There is an omnipresent financial Mind, and if we begin to deal with this financial Mind we will have a partner that has all resources a t His command. If you want to become rich, if you want to be possessed of every good thing in the world, take God as your partner, incorporate God's mind into your mind, in your daily living. Give of your substance with the thought that it is God's money you are handling. Realize that it is God's tenth that you are giving. With this thought in your mind you

---

[469] Ibid, p. 143

will begin to attract new spiritual resources, and things will begin to open up in your affairs.[470]

The idea of conducting your financial affairs with the thought of God always in mind as your partner is a valid one. It has worked wonderfully for many people. But, the thought of partnership with God can be extended into more than the financial affairs of life. It can be made part of all areas of life. We can think of ourselves as partners with God in expressing goo d health, in all human relationships, in our recreational enjoyments, in all things. This adds a dimension to our awareness that we may never have known before.

---

[470] Fillmore, Charles *Keep a True Lent*, p. 85

Chapter 23 - Keys to Demonstration

Questions from the Text
1. There are nine keys to demonstration. Define each one in your own words.
2. What is "the adversary"? What is the current adversary in your life?
3. How can we experience Divine ideas?

Lesson Text
Purpose

> *Purpose gives joy and zest to living. When our eye is on the goal we are not so easily perturbed. Purpose awakens new trains of thought; purpose directs these trains of thought into new fields of achievement. Really to succeed we must have some great purpose in mind, some goal toward which we are to work.*[471]

We might also consider the word "motivation" along with purpose. Both purpose and motivation are generated in consciousness through the faculty of zeal. As we become more aware of our twelve powers we should praise these powers and thank God constantly for them. This causes an increase in their functioning through us. Quickened zeal will work to make us more and more aware of spiritual motivation and good purposes in our life. Life then become s more interesting and enjoyable.

---
[471] Fillmore, Charles *The Twelve Powers of Man*, p.45

Meditation

> *By meditation we light up the inner mind, and we receive more than we can put into words. Only those who have strengthened their interior faculties can appreciate the wonderful undeveloped possibilities in us.[472]*

> *We get our most vivid revelations when in a meditative state of mind. This prove s that when we make the mind trustful and confident, we put it in harmony with creative Mind; then its force flows to us in accordance with the law of like attracting like.[473]*

Meditation becomes more enjoyable and beneficial as one practices it. Things can happen in a person's mind as a result of meditation which may not happen through any other means. Illuminations, insights, expanded viewpoints—all these and many other good things can be experienced in the mind of one who meditates.

Prayer

> *Do not supplicate or beg God to give you what you need, but get still and think about the inexhaustible resources of infinite Mind, its presence in all its fullness, and its constant readiness to manifest itself when its law s are complied with. This is what Jesus meant when He said, "But seek first the*

---

[472] Fillmore, Charles *Christian Healing*, p. 86
[473] Fillmore, Charles *Jesus Christ Heals*, p. 82

> *kingdom and righteousness, and all these things will be given to you as well."*[474]
>
> *Pray with persistence and pray with understanding. Be insistent in prayer; and never allow anything to keep you from having your daily quiet hour of communion with God, your own indwelling Father.*[475]

Jesus taught that God is always more willing to give than we are willing to receive. This is the real meaning of the statement that God's will is greater than ours. When we realize this, prayer becomes easy. Prayer is the method we can use to fulfill the Law of the Word. Three ways which we can use to fulfill the law of the Word (prayer) are: (1) asking (2) affirming (3) giving thanks in advance.

Demonstration

> *When Peter tried to walk on the water to meet Jesus, he went down in the sea of doubt. He saw too much wetness in the water. He saw the negative side of the proposition, and it weakened his demonstration. If you want to demonstrate, never consider the negative side.*[476]

In addition to Charles Fillmore's advice to "never consider the negative side," we might add: "never become fearful because of a negative side." Peter did not sink just because he "saw" the "wetness in the water." He began to

---

[474] Ibid, p. 77
[475] Fillmore, Charles *Atom-Smashing Power of Mind*, p. 32
[476] Fillmore, Charles *Jesus Crist Heals*, p. 106

sink because he became "afraid." It is not just admitting the existence of the negative aspect of anything which hurts us or spoils our demonstration. It is often either identifying with the negative, or letting the negative cause us to become fearful, which hurts our demonstration.

See the Good

> *If you will start right now with the idea of universal and eternal goodness uppermost in your mind, talk only about the good, and see with your mind's eye everything and everybody as good, then you will soon be demonstrating all kinds of good. Good thoughts will become a habit, and good will manifest itself to you. You will see it everywhere.*[477]
>
> *Pronounce every experience good, and of God, and by that mental attitude you will call forth only the good. What seemed error will disappear, and only the good will remain. This is the law, and no one can break it. The adversary always flees before the mind that is fixed on the pure, the just, and the upright. There is no error in all the universe that can stand for one moment in the presence of the innocent mind. Innocence is its own defense, and as we invoke God with pure motive and upright heart, we need not fear any experience.*[478]

There is a universal Principle of good that is omnipresent. We are connected to that Principle through our minds and may use our minds to affirm the presence

---

[477] Fillmore, Charles *Prosperity*, p. 60
[478] Fillmore, Charles *Talks on Truth*, p. 107

of the Principle at all times and under all circumstances. This does not mean that every "thing" or that every "event" is good or that every personality is always good. It does mean that the Principle of good is always present. There is some degree of innate good in anything that exists. There has to be some validity, some meaning, and some usefulness. Even if we cannot see any trace of it, the innate good is somehow, some way there. If we make an effort to perceive it, affirm its presence, and give thanks in advance for its revelation, we will experience good results.

Harmony

> *Resolve to become one with God through the Christ. Harmonize yourself with God and all your world will be in harmony. Be on the alert to see harmony everywhere. Do not magnify seeming differences. Do not keep up any petty divisions but continually declare the one universal harmony. This will insure perfect order and wholeness. The Christ Mind is here as the unifying principle of humankind, and we must believe in this Mind working in us and through us and know that through it we are joined to the Father-Mind.*[479]

Harmony is a divine idea, and all divine ideas can be assimilated into our experience. We can experience Divine ideas directly by (1) believing in the idea, and (2) becoming totally willing toward the idea and affirming it. If we will do these things, then the divine idea will do its part. It will become our experience.

---

[479] Fillmore, Charles *Jesus Christ Heals*, p. 131

Praise and Blessing

> *Let your words of praise and blessing be to Spirit and the increase will be even greater than it has been when addressed to others. The resources of Spirit are beyond our highest flights of imagination. You can praise a weak body into strength, a fearful heart into peace and trust; shattered nerves into poise and power; a failing business into prosperity and success; want and insufficiency into supply and support.*[480]

There is a statement in this paragraph to which we should pay very close attention and take to heart: "The resources of Spirit are beyond our highest flights of imagination." If we can remember this we will learn to trust Spirit more than we ever had before. We will rise above all doubt or mistrust where Spirit is concerned.

Love

> *Love does not seek its own--its own comes to it without being sought.*[481]

> *When love, the universal magnet, is brought into action in our consciousness, it will change all our methods of supplying human wants. It will harmonize all the forces of nature and will dissolve the discords that now infest earth and air. It will control the elements until they obey us and bring forth that which will supply all our needs, without*

---

[480] Fillmore, Charles *Teach Us to Pray*, p. 92
[481] Fillmore, Charles, *Christian Healing*, p. 135

> *the labor that is called the sweat of our face. The earth shall yet be made paradise by the power of love. That condition will begin to set in for each one just as soon as he develops the love nature in himself.*[482]

The kingdom of love on earth is something every person really wants in his heart of hearts. Even those who appear to disrupt the earth probably want this kingdom of love in the deeper levels of their souls. Bu t love, like peace, can only be established by individuals. As we become more loving, we are fulfilling our responsibility of individually. Only in this way can we ever become a part of the kingdom of love on earth.

Nonresistance

> *Jesus went back to the very source of all discord, and showed how all resistance and antagonism must cease. He did not stop to argue whether the cause was just or not, but he said, 'Agree with thine adversary quickly; 'If any man would go to law with thee, and take away thy coat, let him have thy cloak also.'*[483] *To the mortal mind this seems like foolishness, but Jesus spoke out of the inner wisdom that knows that it is dangerous to allow any kind of opposing thoughts to form in consciousness. He knew that the universal law of justice would adjust all matter, if we would trust it and cease fighting mentally for their rights.*[484]

---

[482] Fillmore, Charles *Talks on Truth*, p. 61
[483] Matthew 5:25
[484] Fillmore, Charles *Keep a True Lent*, p. 175

There is something in every life which Jesus calls "the adversary,"[485] and it is in dealing with this "adversary" that correct nonresistance is necessary. This "adversary" is a force that is a necessary part of human life. It comes in many forms, mostly as opposition, difficulties, delays, or "challenges" as we prefer to say in Unity. It must come for it is a necessary part of the creative process. Here is where nonresistance is important. Resisting, resenting, fighting the "adversary" only increases it. Finding a way to harmonize and blend our desire and our "adversary" is a full-time job on earth. When we do this correctly, good results appear. This is the pattern which Jesus revealed to us as the ongoing process of our evolution within God's creation.

---

[485] Hebrew: שטן *satan*, meaning "adversary"; Arabic: ش يطان *shaitan*, meaning; "astray", "distant", or sometimes "devil" is a word appearing in the texts of the Abrahamic religions that brings evil and temptation, and is known as the deceiver who leads humanity astray. The word is not meant to indicate a person, power or force. See:

- Numbers 22:22,32 "and the angel of the LORD stood in the way for an adversary against him."
- 32 "behold, I went out to withstand thee,"
- 1 Samuel 29:4 The Philistines say: "lest he [David] be an adversary against us"
- 2 Samuel 19:22 David says: "[you sons of Zeruaiah] should this day be adversaries (plural) unto me?"
- 1 Kings 5:4 Solomon writes to Hiram: "there is neither adversary nor evil occurrent."
- 1 Kings 11:14 "And the LORD stirred up an adversary unto Solomon, Hadad the Edomite"[12]
- 1 Kings 11:23 "And God stirred him up an adversary, Rezon the son of Eliadah"
- 25 "And he [Rezon] was an adversary to Israel all the days of Solomon"

Section V

Chapter 24 – Hebrew and Christian Scriptures

Advanced Questions for Discussion
1. Give reasons for considering the Scriptures allegorical.
2. What phase of creation is described in the first chapter of Genesis?
3. What evidence have we in the Bible that this is an ideal and not a manifest creation?
4. Who or what is Jehovah, the Lord God of the Scriptures?
5. What and where is the "tree of life" as spoken of in the Scriptures?
6. How should the Scriptures be "divided" in interpreting the use of the term man?
7. What does the "heart," as the term is used in the Scriptures, represent?
8. How do we demonstrate the mastery and dominion which are ours as mentioned in Genesis?[486]
9. What is meant by the statement, "I will put my law in their inward parts, and in their heart will I write it"?[487]

Although we give these discussion questions here as they apply to Unity Metaphysics, a discussion of the many aspects of the metaphysical basis of the Hebrew and Christian Scriptures are found in these Unity Spiritual Center publications:

---

[486] Genesis 1:26
[487] Jeremiah 31:33

- *Spiritual Interpretation of the Hebrew Scriptures*
- *Spiritual Interpretation of the Christian Scriptures: the Gospels*
- *Spiritual Interpretation of the Christian Scriptures: Acts – Revelation.*

Appendix - Answers to Advanced Discussion Questions

Chapter 2
1. What is God?

God is Spirit, Divine Mind, Father, Being, Truth, Creator, Principle and Law, Source and Cause of all that is; All Good, Absolute Good, omnipresence, omnipotence, omniscience.

The Sanskrit equivalent of the word God means "shining." This "shining" may take many forms according to the channel through which it pours. Therefore, it may appear to man as power, love, wisdom, goodness, law, abundance, Truth, strength, and so on.[488]

Behind the outpouring, the "shining," stands the immutable Source of all -- eternal, creative Divine Mind, the Principle of Absolute Good which upholds and in-forms the universe and is, therefore, Being, omnipotent, omnipresent, and omniscient.

> *Divine Mind -- God-Mind; ever-present, all-knowing Mind; the Absolute, the unlimited, omnipresent, all-wise, all-loving, all-powerful Spirit.*[489]

> *There is but one Mind, and that Mind cannot be separated or divided, because, like the principle of mathematics, it is indivisible. All that we can say of the one Mind is that it is absolute and that all its manifestations are in essence like itself.*[490]

---
[488] Fillmore, Charles *Christian Healing*, p. 16
[489] Fillmore, Charles *The Revealing Word*
[490] Ibid, p. 56

2. Is God a person? Explain fully.

God is not a person. The word person implies a human being with desires, passions, frailties, limitations. God is changeless, limitless, and passionless. When we consider God as Principle only, God appears too abstract, too far beyond the human conception to inspire the trusting love of the human heart which makes the relation a personal one.

However, God as immanent Spirit individuated in us takes on a personal character but has none of the limitations of human personality. As immanent Spirit, God seeks to reveal self in an infinite creative plan with us as a center of consciousness through which to express love for all creation. In this plan we are known as the child of God, the beloved of the Father/Mother.

God is the Absolute; we are the relative, learning to express God's nature in its fullness.

3. What is God as Principle? as Law?

God as Principle is the Genesis and Revelation of our Bible, while all that is contained in between is the working of the law. God as Principle is the absolute Truth that is back of all cause, all expression, and all manifestation. It is the passive, formless Mind substance in which all divine ideas inhere. Principle is the total of all the fundamental elements of Being, all the underlying truths that are classed as spiritual realities, all the qualities (ideas) that man attributes to the eternal, self-existent One. The character, the name that is given the ideas, designates the native elements that are inherent within them.

> *Principle -- Fundamental Truth. Divine Principle is fundamental Truth in a universal sense, or as pertaining to God, the Divine. It is the underlying*

> *plan by which Spirit (God) moves in expressing itself.*[491]

God as Law is the dynamic, intelligent, changeless rule of action of the underlying principles of Being (God). Law is the working power that produces results, for God as Law is the manner in which God as Principle expresses.

> *God as law -- Principle in action.*[492]

Law is invariable in its action, the same for everyone, in any place, at any time, under all circumstances and conditions. Principle is always universally in action through the law inhering within it but creation (including man) must avail itself of the law of good in order to produce perfect results.

4. What is meant by "God immanent in the universe"?
Immanent means indwelling. "God immanent in the universe" means the ideals of God-Mind reproducing mental forms and then manifesting themselves through these forms as shapes. Every manifestation is the embodiment of an idea.

"God immanent in the universe" is Spirit dwelling within the form as life, intelligence, and substance. God immanent is the perpetual urge within every form of life to perfect its form and fulfill the purpose for which it was created.

God immanent in man is the "only begotten Son"[493] that the Father gave to the world as the inspiration of

---

[491] Fillmore, Charles *The Revealing Word*, p. 156
[492] Ibid, p. 84
[493] John 3:16

every created thing. Cradled in substance, the creating ideas are fed by substance, and out of substance grow the forms in and through which the ideas are manifested. The knowledge that God dwells at the center of our being, that He is the life, substance, and intelligence in every cell of our body, gives us the key to all wisdom, eternal life, and unending power.

5. **Explain Omniscience**

The word omniscience comes from two Latin words: *omnis*, meaning all, and *scientia*, meaning infinite knowledge. Omniscience is therefore knowledge that is infinite, unbounded, and complete; intelligence that is orderly and related to unchanging principles. It is the one science out of which all sciences are produced.

Divine intelligence is Divine Mind in its passive, unrelated character; knowledge is intelligence expressing itself as related ideas in the human consciousness. Wisdom is knowledge that is shaped by divine order and judgment; it is the righteousness (right-use-ness) of the kingdom of God, the perfect activity and expression of the primal, passive, unrelated intelligence of God.

Omniscience is the unrelated, the related, and the expressed, all in one. It includes all stages of the birth, growth, relation and inter-relation, progress, expression, and manifestation of its offspring.

6. **Explain Omnipresence**

Omnipresence, like omniscience, applies to God as the universal Spirit of Good. It means all or everywhere present, and in its completeness includes both omniscience and omnipotence.

Omnipresence designates the infinite, eternal, immutable, all-pervading substance that is the source, cause, and sustenance of all being in its absolute wholeness (holiness). Omnipresence is the substance idea, the "body of God" (i.e., the embodiment of all good). Omnipresence is the passive phase, the Mother aspect of Spirit. It embraces all being in the Absolute and holds within it all intelligence, life, purity, power, love, and joy. It is stronger than any need, greater than any circumstance, more powerful than any personality. In it are order and judgment and all things in their right relation.

Omnipresence includes the activity of the Holy Spirit (third phase of the Godhead or Holy Trinity) ever seeking to have the righteousness of God-consciousness move through man as the expresser of divine ideas. It is the all-pervading Good in which "we live and move and have our being".[494] In this all-satisfying Presence there can be no loneliness, no lack, no suffering, and no separation.

7. Explain Omnipotence

The true meaning of the word omnipotence is all-power. It is also a name for God as the only Power in the universe. Omnipotence is the creative action of the Holy (whole) Trinity. It is also the power back of the creative Word, the authority and rulershlp of the absolute, dynamic principle of Being (God). As the power back of the Holy Spirit, it is the divine breath moving upon the face of the waters at creation, the same creative breath that made man "a living soul." Omnipotence is the dominion and authority idea, the active phase, the Father aspect of Spirit.

Omnipotence is also the will of God expressed in man through definite, purposeful ideas; it is the creative life within these ideas. It is the urge of the indwelling

---
[494] Acts 17:28

Christ seeking always to manifest its likeness. Man may at will draw upon this power in direct ratio to his faith in it. Man is often awed by the majesty of God as omnipotence and thinks that in comparison his own powers are exceedingly limited. It is man himself who limits the power of God in him. There is an inexhaustible and equal distribution of power throughout the universe, and man may have whatever degree of it his consciousness is ready to appropriate.

8. How does God Dwell in Us?

God as Spirit dwells in us as the life principle; as an offspring of God, we are spiritual beings, and out spiritual heritage is no less than the attributes (ideas) of God. God dwells in us even as we dwell in God.

We are a center of consciousness through which God-Mind expresses. "Know you not that ye are a temple of God, and that the Spirit of God dwells in you?"[495] God created us out of self; that is, God created us out of Mind substance as a perfect image of self. We were thus endowed with the holy (whole) majesty and immaculate purity of God, the transcendent One, who alone is all good, and the source of all creation.

God dwells in us as the I AM, the Christ, Jehovah, Superconscious (or Christ Mind) in the same way that life and intelligence dwell within a seed. This indwelling image is God-Mind taking form in human consciousness and seeking perfect expression as us. In this center of consciousness the ideal lives and ever seeks to manifest the likeness of itself.

---

[495] I Corinthians 3:16

9. Explain God as the One Mind

God as the one Mind is the originating source of all that is, acting through the movement of the ideas that make up Mind. Life is animation. The word animation came into our language from the Latin animus, meaning mind. The word spirit came from the Latin *spiritus*, meaning to breathe, to live. In this sense spirit and mind are synonymous terms.

In Genesis[496] we read, "In the beginning God created the heavens and the earth." God ideated, imaged the heavens (the ideal) and the earth (the mental picture of the ideal). Then in a definite plan for the universe and man, Genesis gives us the other steps, all of which are to be taken through thought.

God, the Principle of Absolute Good is alive, active as the universal Mind substance -- omnipresence -- creates and sustains good in an orderly way in man and in the universe. Substance is the totality of God and life is the action, the expression of this completeness working out a definite plan. God inspirits (inspires) all of creation with consciousness. All being, all living, all doing, all interest, all exertion, all movement is the expression of the life idea as it works in and through the passive substance or "body of God," making it active and productive.

Mind and thought are one and are inseparable. They are Principle and its way of expression. The perfection or imperfection of the manifestation is due to the character of the thought, the mental picture, that man conceives in interpreting the ideal.

---

[496] Genesis 1:1

10. What is meant by studying Mind back of nature?

Nature is considered in this question as the system of all phenomena, the physical universe. Mind is also considered in its philosophical meaning as the conscious element or factor in the universe, the underlying Spirit or Intelligence or Mind contrasted with matter. Seeking the origin, the creative cause (the idea back of the form) of mental and physical phenomena is the meaning of "studying Mind back of nature."

A fundamental premise of the Unity teaching is the equation of God with Mind, in which is involved the essence of all ideas or archetypes of natural phenomena. The ideas are conceived to be complete or perfect. Natural phenomena are in the process of evolving, unfolding, or fulfilling these inherent ideas corresponding to the degree of consciousness of the particular phenomenon.

Humankind alone among known phenomena has evolved the capacity to think and to reason with our mind beyond the physical, to seek underlying causes and operative laws (ideas) that natural phenomena might be more nearly like their spiritual patterns (ideas). Studying the Mind back of nature is the effort to know God that God might be expressed and experienced with increasing adequacy in and through His channels of expression. It is the search for Truth.

11. Are we Capable of Understanding God?

Yes, we are capable of understanding God because, created by and of God, we are of the same nature as God. As the image of God with the power to bring forth God's likeness, we are capable of understanding God, for there is no limit set to our consciousness, or understanding.

God as Absolute, formless Being, through the fusion of wisdom and love, conceived in substance the image of self that was to grow and develop into God's likeness, into God's same transcendent nature. One can no more think of God without thinking of good than we can think of a singer without a song, mind without ideas, or ideas without life, activity, expression.

Our spiritual self is infinite in nature and as a living soul, a self-conscious being, is capable of understanding infinity even though as a manifest self we may seem finite. That we are self-conscious as well as spiritual is evident. The spiritual self is related to the living God as God's child; the concrete expression or manifestation is our manifest self. Jehovah God (translated as Lord) represents the development of wisdom, and the Christ finishes the development of man through love.

12. What is our inheritance from God?

Divine ideas inherent in the nature of God is our inheritance from God, but in order to come into this inheritance we must be ready to receive it as well as to claim it. Infinite Mind or God cannot inspire us with divine ideas before our human consciousness is ready to receive them. Until that time, the ideas are of no practical use to us because they pass us by through his non-recognition. They fall by the wayside, fall on stony ground, fall where the weeds of error-thought choke them out.

Our part is to prepare our human consciousness, through denial, for the reception of divine ideas, as carefully as the agriculturist prepares the soil for the planting to be done in its season. Too often human beings fill their consciousness with thoughts of crime, disease, war, and poverty. We often cultivate these unconsciously through conversation about them, and through fear, instead of by clearing and preparing our "earth" -- the human consciousness -- for the seeds of divine ideas.

Hence, our limited beliefs prevent our coming into our "real" estate, the Christ consciousness.

13. How are divine ideas brought into manifestation?

Divine ideas are brought into expression through the divine Logos, the Word of God, (the "God said" of Genesis) which is the creative power of Divine Mind. As the Word moves through us and all creation, the ideas are made manifest according to the need of the species.

> *All the ideas contained in the one Father-Mind are at the mental command of its offspring.*[497]

Though ideas are brought into expression through the Word of God, we are a free will being must make the claim mentally in order for them to manifest in his life as the fulfillment of his needs.

> *In our true nature, our spiritual self, the Christ in us, we already have life and love and all the other divine ideas, but it is only as we consciously accept them by our thinking and feeling that they become active in our own consciousness. These qualities are then worked out in body and affairs as actual experiences.*[498]

14. From what source did Jesus feed the multitude?

Jesus fed the multitude from the substance idea in Divine Mind. The multitude numbered five thousand plus. The visible resources were five small loaves and two little

---

[497] Fillmore, Charles *Christian Healing*, p. 13
[498] Cady, Emilie *Lessons in Truth*

fishes. Andrew said, "What are these among so many?"[499] Jesus recognized the loaves and fishes as symbols of the abundance of omnipresence, the unfailing substance and rich ideas of increase. He did not allow the inadequate outer supply to blind His vision to the reality of God's all-providing essence everywhere present and instantly available as man's all sufficiency in all things. Looking up, He spoke words of thanksgiving. He looked above the seeming outer supply to the real source of all manifestation. He kept His entire attention on substance -- not on the symbols. He had faith in this all-providing resource, as well as faith that His thought and spoken word could accomplish what was necessary to feed the multitude.

In giving thanks, Jesus made use of the spoken Word of God, which fulfills the divine law of creation and increase when it is spoken with conviction. At this high level of knowing, the idea within Jesus released the Word of God into action.

The "breaking of bread" signifies constant prayer and affirmation. Jesus' keeping His attention on God as the source of the supply implies constant blessing. This account shows us the fertility of substance when the Word of God is projected into it.

15. What idea was back of Jesus' work in healing the sick and raising the dead?

The idea of life, omnipotent, omnipresent, omniscient, was back of Jesus' work in healing the sick and raising the dead. Jesus knew God as the one Mind. He also

---

[499] John 6:9

knew that Mind has ideas through which it expresses its ideals. He knew that ideas are living, eternal principles that can produce the manifestations of good when they are rightly used.

Since Mind is everywhere present and perfect, this same omnipresence and perfection must apply to the "life idea." Jesus taught, and He proved in His own body, that death of the physical form, the body, can be overcome through contact with the life idea, which in the ideal is indestructible and abundant. Having contacted the life idea, we must make ourselves consciously one with it. We must hold the idea of life in our mind and in our heart until it is accepted and becomes the ruling power in our consciousness. When the thinking faculty and the feeling nature are in perfect agreement with the Superconscious (realm of God ideas) the life idea and any of the divine ideas that make up our inheritance are free to express themselves in perfection. Finally, we must be responsive to divine love, for the love of life brings its manifestation that much more quickly. Like all divine ideas, the life idea is not for the benefit of the individual alone but for the benefit of humanity as a whole. The more unselfish the expression of life to all creation, the more the individual will be perfected and blessed as a channel.

16. How shall we do the works that Jesus did?

Jesus knew that he must be the embodiment of the one Mind, one substance, one Source, one Presence, one Power. "Wist ye not that I must be about my Father's business?"[500] Jesus recognized and claimed God as the creative power that did the work. Note these words:

> "I can of myself do nothing".[501]
> "The Father [the ideal, the perfect idea] abiding in me doeth his works".[502]
> "All power is given unto me [the ideal] in heaven and in earth,"[503]

To do the works that Jesus did, we need to
1. Seek to understand God Mind and to identify ourselves with the source of our being, God as divine substance;
2. Know and recognize that substance is expressed through ideas that at their center are endowed with the power of the cosmic ideal;
3. Learn to be still and let this perfect Mind which Jesus had, and which is ours to claim, do its perfect work in and through our whole being;
4. Have faith in its power to express its likeness through us as channels for its expression;
5. Seek to unify ourselves with the divine ideals of wisdom and love -- for without a union of these two qualities of Being there can be no perfect creation;
6. Hold to these ideals or ideas through all difficulties until they so completely dominate our human

---

[500] Luke 2:49
[501] John 5:30
[502] John 14:10
[503] Matthew 28:18

consciousness that we do indeed "have this mind... which was also in Christ Jesus".[504]

17. What and where is the kingdom of heaven?

The kingdom of heaven is out ever-expanding consciousness of the Kingdom of God within. The kingdom of heaven does not depend on location in space but is a state of consciousness that may be attained in any place. Jesus said, "The kingdom of heaven is at hand",[505] This same reference is found also in two other verses in Matthew.[506] The kingdom of heaven is recognized first within the soul of each human being, but each one must seek the Kingdom of God and begin to build his own kingdom of heaven or harmony within before he can experience it in the outer world. We are told to "seek . . . first his kingdom"[507] and our "seeking" is done through contemplation on divine ideas, through meditation, prayer, and the Silence.

To attain the kingdom of heaven, it is necessary to unfold one's understanding of the power of Truth to dispel all beliefs in the reality of sin, disease, poverty, and death. The kingdom of heaven is relative, individual Truth, a consciousness that is subject to the will of the individual depending on how much of the Kingdom of God the individual has awakened to. The kingdom of heaven is that realm within the soul where movement is taking place onward and upward, according to the highest ideals of the

---

[504] Philippians 2:5
[505] Matthew 3:2
[506] Matthew 4L17, Matthew 10:7
[507] Matthew 6:33

Kingdom of God of which the individual has become conscious. At any period in our life we may experience the kingdom of heaven, if we have so opened ourselves to the Kingdom of God that God's blessings (ideas) are made manifest in mind, body, or affairs.

18. How do we enlarge our concept of God?

We enlarge our concept of God by studying God as creative, Divine Mind from every angle. There must first be a deep desire to know God as well as to know about God. Each one, feeling this desire for God, will begin a search; be guided to books, teachers, classes, but a safe plan will always be to pray, to ask God to reveal self. If we know God as Mind, in which inhere all divine ideas, study and prayer given to the ideas of life, love, power, faith and so forth will result in illumination on the character of God. It is not enough just to study God as Mind only through ideas; these ideas must be rightly used, for they are alive and dynamic with creative power. Knowing God as Absolute Good requires that we relate the ideas that make up this good to our own life.

> *"Man has the ability to discern and understand the various factors entering into the creative processes of mind, and he is, through the study of mental laws, perceiving and accepting the science of ideas, thoughts, and words. ... he is capable of comprehending the plan and the detailed ideas of the supreme Mind".*[508]

---

[508] Fillmore, Charles *Christian Healing*, pp. 12-13

19. Why are we not always conscious of our oneness with God?

We are not always conscious of our oneness with God because somewhere in the history of the human family we have built a consciousness of separation. A writer has said that if two gateways were set before mankind, one labeled "To Heaven" and the other "To Lectures about Heaven," a large majority of persons would instinctively choose the second.

At the present state of development of the human family, the intellectual consciousness appears to be of prime importance. In developing this consciousness, many do not see the difference between intellectual awareness and spiritual consciousness. They think that to know about God and to know God are one and the same thing. For this reason, they are not conscious of their oneness with, their sameness to, God. To them God is a Being, a Father in heaven, separate and apart from themselves. God is always close; He is within us, but we do not always realize God's presence because our interest is centered largely in outer things. The fact of God's being close does not help us unless we are conscious of it. So by effort we must build up this feeling of God within us, of our oneness with Him. In doing this, we are helped by considering right values in life, placing outer conditions and things in their right relation to spiritual realities. Inherently we know the value of spiritual truths, but we need to keep reminding ourselves. This is not to imply that the intellect does not have its place, for it has -- but not as a master. Charles Fillmore has this to say:

Intellectual understanding comes first in the soul's development, then a deeper understanding of principle follows, until the whole man ripens into wisdom.[509]

20.   How are we awakened to the knowledge of God?

We are awakened to the knowledge of God by the I AM in us seeking to express itself. We may remain unaware of our spiritual nature for a very long period, but the I AM within us (God's Presence) is nevertheless ever urging us to become conscious of our oneness with Spirit. Just as the life principle within the seed is constantly urging it to develop into plant or tree to fulfill its own plan, so the I AM, or life principle within us, is urging us to develop into the manifest son of God in order to fulfill His plan for us. As the Breath of God, the Holy Spirit, moves in us we gradually become conscious of the inner prompting. At first we may recognize it only as a feeling of dissatisfaction with life as we are living it in a limited way, and the desire for a new and higher way of living becomes our goal.

As brought out in the quotation from *Keep a True Lent* above, our intellect is the forerunner of spiritual understanding. Literature, teachers, and best of all the examples of those who are alive in Truth catch the attention of the intellect. We begin to see something better than we have known before. This causes a desire to investigate and find out what others have that we have not, what transforms their lives and gives them joy instead of sorrow, health instead of sickness, peace instead of worry. Seeing a better way awakens a desire to realize it, and the earnest desire opens the way for revelation and

---

[509] Fillmore, Charles *Keep a True Lent*, p. 155

guidance in the achieving of this better way. Too often individuals get a glimpse of that which they would like to have in their life experiences but without understanding and guidance they seek in ways that are not good, often taking from others rather than seeking God and allowing His laws to bring their own to them.

We need always to remember that knowledge of God comes to each soul only through the revelation of Spirit within -- it cannot be imparted by others though much inspiration may come through the example and teachings of others. Of one thing we may be sure; revelation of the truth about God and our relation to God will come when we desire it deeply enough and are willing to seek it through contemplation of the qualities (ideas) that make up God's true character or nature, and then allow divine ideas to come alive in us through meditation, prayer, and the Silence.

21. Explain the meaning of the statement, "...in God we live, and move, and have our being..."[510] Answer a:

What we shall say in the secret place is a secondary matter. The first and most important affair is to be still and know God. "Be still and know that I am God."[511] Paul, in speaking of the innate desire for God in all of us, says that God "made of one every nation of humankind . . . that they should seek God, if haply they might feel after God, though God is not far from each one of us: for in God we live, and move, and have our being."[512]

In the silence or stillness we feel after God, and great is the blessing when we get so still that we feel the

---

[510] Acts 17:28
[511] Psalm 46:10
[512] Acts 17:26-28

Presence filling and thrilling us with life and love. In this consciousness we place the right value on the things of the world, because we become more fully aware of and appreciative of God's blessings. We know what is meant by the promise, "But seek ye first God's kingdom, and God's righteousness; and all these things shall be added unto you."[513]

The familiar Lord's Prayer,[514] will have new meaning to us when prayed in the silence. This prayer is filled with the life and the substance and the power of Jesus' realization of Truth, and it will open with a new meaning as it is prayed in the "secret place."

Answer b:

By this statement Paul was endeavoring to make clear to the people of Athens that God is a living presence and power, the cause or originating essence of all life as well as the sustenance of every living creature during its existence in a bodily form. He pointed out to them the statement made by one of the Greek poets and recorded in Christian Scripture, "For we are indeed God's offspring",[515] making plain to them that God is not a human being apart from them, nor, as verse 29 says, "like gold, or silver, or stone." Rather God is the everywhere-present intelligence, the all-pervading Spirit substance, the one Mind essence in which are inherent all the qualities or Ideas of God. It is out of this one substance through the power of Spirit moving on the ideas that beast, bird, fish, and we are created.

---

[513] Matthew 6:33
[514] Matthew 6:9-14 and Luke 11:2-4
[515] Ibid

Job stated:[516]

In God's hand is the life of every living thing, and the breath of all mankind.

The fish lives in the water and from it obtains everything needful for its existence; the bird, the animal, and the human body maintains a physical existence in the air by a natural process of breathing air substance. The soul of man lives in omnipresent Spirit substance by means of divine thought action, the Word, Spirit-breathing (inspiration), through which we are inspired by prayer with God ideas. It is the use of these ideas that enables us to express and manifest our self as a divine being instead of just a human being.

22. What is "God's will" for us?
God's "will" is the purpose, intent, plan, or law for us; and God being Absolute Good, the will is always good, because God could only plan that which is good for creation.

For us, God's will or plan is that God shall express and manifest a true spiritual nature, imaged at creation.[517]

Because our spiritual nature (called the Christ, or I AM, or our real Self), is the nature of God in us, we often refer to God's will in us as I AM, for it is the plan that we bring forth this nature. A right understanding of will does away with any tendency on our part to think that anything

---

[516] Job 12:10
[517] How I Used Truth, Lesson 1

unpleasant could be "God's will" to which we have to submit.

As brought out in the above reference from *How I Used Truth,* will does not apply to us alone, but to all species of creation, operating under the law for each species. As we learn to seek guidance in carrying out will in every area of our human experience, we begin to cooperate with the rest of creation with very satisfying results. We come to realize that will has resulted in definite laws in our world and that only obedience to these God laws can bring about the harmony, peace, and happiness we all seek. In *The Revealing Word*, the definition is:[518]

> "God's will is always perfection and all good for all; perfect health in mind and body; abundance of every good thing including joy, peace, wisdom, and eternal life"

23. What is "God's purpose"?

"Thy kingdom come. Thy will be done, as in heaven, so on earth."[519] We have learned that the kingdom of God is always, everywhere evenly present. This is a prayer that it may come into expression and be manifest in the earth, the outer, as it is in heaven, the inner. Thus it is that God's purpose is done. The great moving force that tends toward perfect expression in the universe, in us, in nature and in everything is the purpose of God. God's purpose is God's plan, purpose, intent and pleasure for us and all creation. It is very necessary in praying, "Thy will be done," to remember that God's will for us is always good. God is

---

[518] Fillmore, Charles *The Revealing Word* 87
[519] Matthew 6:10

love; God will is not that we suffer in any way, but that we come to the knowledge of God and be blessed with God's wholeness.

24. How do we come into conscious unity with God?
Answer a:

We come into conscious unity with God first by thinking about God and our relationship to God, then letting the Truth become a part of the feeling nature so that one no longer merely thinks about God, but feels God's indwelling presence.

"'Conscious oneness with the Father' means that we are able to feel — not merely think about — the Christ or God-presence within, the Source of our human consciousness. With the revelation of God as immanent in us, we come to know with deep feeling that our true nature is one with and the same as the God nature... there is a vast difference between merely being intellectually aware of Truth principles and actually knowing Truth or God and rightly using the principles. We can see, then, that we have to add feeling to our thinking in order to reach the state of knowing that is 'conscious oneness with God.'"[520]

Conscious unity with God comes from identification with God. We identify our self with God through I AM. "Be still and know that I am God."[521] We silence or quiet all that is "of the earth earthy" and contemplate that which God is. We let our human consciousness expand to encompass God's greatness, and God's power... Then we let our heart dwell on love for the "little things," the tiny insects, the blade of grass, for all are the object of love and

---
[520] See How I Used Truth, Lesson 11
[521] Psalm 46:10

care. From the greatest to the least, all are expressions of God-Being—therefore, each one of us is one with all life. Each can say for self: "I am all that God is; God is Mind; I am idea; and I live to be, to bring this idea into manifestation in all the fullness and glory of the likeness of God. I am consciously one with Spirit."

Answer b:

The claiming of what is ours in Truth we call affirmation. Jesus was bold and fearless in making the highest claims for himself. He affirmed, "I and the Father are one,"[522] and, "All things whatsoever God has are mine,[523] and so he raised himself above the prevailing thought. In this way Jesus demonstrated his oneness. He is our example; He came to teach us how to attain the realization of our oneness. We can attain this realization by following in Jesus steps, by doing as Jesus did. He said, "Judge not according to appearance, but judge righteous judgment".[524] In the realm of the manifest world all about us, many things appear true that are not true in Spirit, and we are freed from the habit of judging by appearances and established in the consciousness of the Truth of our being by the prayer of faith made in understanding.

One of the names of God Is "I AM." I AM is Being. When we enter the silence and speak the name, "I AM," it brings our being into conscious union with Him in whom "we live, and move, and have our being."[525] There is in reality but one Being. Oneness means sameness. We are to become conscious that we are unified with God, are

---

[522] John 10:30
[523] John 16:15
[524] John 7:24
[525] Acts 17:28

the same in nature as God. This consciousness comes from knowing that "I AM," from thinking, feeling and claiming that, "I am a spiritual being." As in the stillness of the soul we meditate on that which we know God is, we are to become conscious that "I AM THAT I AM."[526] God is love. In the silence I am being that which God is -- love; therefore I know, "I am love." So with all the other qualities of God of which you may think. We are to be them through thinking and, feeling these qualities or ideas within us, and then we are to make them manifest. The belief of separation of our being from God's. Being is only a part of the falsity that comes from judging by appearances. We overcome this by claiming, affirming, praying in faith, "I and the Father are one."[527]

The first step in entering the silence is to think of the presence of God; the second step is to feel oneness with God, the Good. Upon these two fundamental steps all true prayer rests, for thinking and feeling build consciousness.

25. To whom do we refer when we say: "Son of God"; "Son of man"; "son of man"?

The "Son of God" is Jehovah God, Christ, I AM, the composite Idea of God, the image of God, the Word of God, spiritual human, the ideal pattern of us in the Mind of God. This ideal is inherent in everyone as our spiritual nature.

The "Son of man" is the human being or manifest human quickened in awareness to the divinity of self. We are becoming conscious of himself as a "Son of God," and gradually expressing and manifesting the real nature. This

---

[526] Exodus 3:14
[527] John 10:30

state of becoming conscious of self as a "Son of God" is metaphorically referred to as the "new birth," "rebirth," being "born again," being "born anew."

The "son of man" is the human being, the manifest human not yet fully awakened to his spiritual nature. It is ourselves often binding self by human limitations rather than freeing self by spiritual possibilities. The "son of man" conceives of self as a species, as an object in nature, without adequate understanding of the latent inner power and character of the species to lift it to increasingly greater expression. We may be very moral in actions, yet still we holds a belief in God as apart from self.

The "son of man" becomes the "Son of man" when we are "renewed in the spirit"[528] of mind and puts on the "new nature, created after the likeness of God".[529] That is, we come to realize who we are and begin manifesting the Truth in mind, body, and affairs.

Awareness, awakening, glimpsing the spiritual possibilities of self in our evolutionary progress, is not by itself enough to lift the "son of man" to new levels of expression, although this insight is a fundamental step. The insight necessarily is to be carried into fulfillment by active pursuit of the spiritual ideal envisioned. A characteristic of God is movement. Consider the attributes equated with God, those of life, love, intelligence, power—all are suggestive of activity. A concept of the ideal of love without loving, of life without expanded living, of intelligence and power without exercising them, makes these attributes only abstract principles and not actual experiences. The "son of man" must awaken to a true relationship to God and begin to use the life, love,

---

[528] Ephesians 4:23
[529] Ephesians 4:24

intelligence, and power that are a divine heritage; then we are "Son of man," having acknowledged the Son of God as our true source and guide.

26. **When and how did you go from a view of God as transcendent to a God as immanent and transcendent?**
Answer is self-=reflective.

Chapter 3
1. **What, in your experience of spirituality, do you regard as paradoxical?**
Answer is self-reflective

Chapter 4
1. **Give both the religious and the metaphysical terms for the Holy Trinity.**
The religious terms for the Holy Trinity are:
- Father
- Son
- Holy Spirit

The metaphysical terms are:
- Mind
- Idea
- Expression

Father is the source, origin, essence, root, creator of all; Son is that which proceeds from, is begotten of the Father; like Him in nature and essentially all that the Father is. Holy Spirit is "the whole Spirit of God in action";[530] the working, moving, breathing, brooding of Spirit, made known to man through revelation, inspiration, and guidance.

---

[530] Fillmore, Charles *Jesus Christ Heals*, p. 182

Holy Spirit is the creative principle (communicated as the life and energy of creation) which animates the universe and finds a special sphere of activity in man. By its operation, man becomes not only "a living soul" but a rational being created in the image of God. The Holy Spirit is the source of the higher qualities which man develops: the indwelling Counselor, Advocate, Comforter, and Spirit of Truth.

Metaphysically interpreted, the one Mind is the source, origin, cause, substance in which all good (as ideas) inheres. Idea is that which emanates, springs forth from the one Mind; the only begotten of the one Mind, perfect as the source from which it springs. Expression is the working of the one Mind through the action of creative power moving through the Idea (Son) to develop the ideas of that Mind.

2. Explain how mind, idea, and expression are in all that appears (manifestation).

All that appears (manifests) in the external world is a symbol, an appearance resembling a causative idea. The cause of the concept of the original divine idea is found in the consciousness from which the concept or the idea comes forth. Nothing could appear externally that was not first an idea, planned and worked out in detail in consciousness. The one Creative Mind (Divine Mind) is the source, the origin, of all perfect ideas which act as first causes or spiritual patterns, ever seeking to come into manifestation through man.

A perfect idea (ideal) born in the consciousness of manifest man is like a seed. This seed grows, is developed, and mentally expressed in its fullness. The last step of the process of its development is the visible manifestation.

The original cause of the perfect idea (ideal) was the Christ Mind (Superconscious) in which it was first ideated.

The individual's consciousness (thinking and feeling), his mental sphere, may have in it a variety of groupings, each characterized by what he regards as worthy and clings to. These groupings are states of mind, or states of consciousness. But the one universal consciousness, Divine Mind, contains all the ideas that manifest man has idealized as perfect; as God consciousness, this universal consciousness contains the substance and the spiritual ideals that are the perfect patterns for all that men shall ever know.

3. **Briefly explain how understanding the metaphysical meaning of the Trinity of God helps you in daily life.**
Answer is self-reflective

4. **What is the meaning of the word Logos?**
The word logos comes to us from the Greek language. In that language it means the word or form that contains and expresses a thought, also the thought itself. As used in this lesson, it is written with a capital "L" and it means the Word of God, the Seed of God that God created out of God's own substance as "that I AM"; the image of God as Creator and First Cause of all that is. The Logos includes all the underlying principles or ideas of Being (God). In the Holy Trinity, the Logos belongs to the second phase, the Son.

The Logos, as the creative power of the one Mind, is called also the Christ, "the only begotten of the

Father".[531] The work of the Logos is to reproduce the God nature: "And the Word became flesh".[532]

Chapter 6

1. What and where is heaven? Answer a:

"Who art in heaven." This has been taken to mean "who art in the skies," but such an interpretation is misleading. Jesus says, "The kingdom of God is within you."[533] Having learned the true nature of God, we no longer think of God as separate from us. Heaven is the expanding consciousness of the kingdom of God, and is an omnipresent spiritual reality. We find it within when we find God. It is the realm of perfection and order and life and love and peace and wisdom.

Answer b:

Heaven is the poised and balanced wholeness existing in man and in the universe through a conscious realization of the presence of God — Absolute Good.

We find the word kingdom used in two ways: "The kingdom of God is within you"[534] and "The kingdom of heaven is at hand."[535]

The kingdom of God, then, must be the realm of God within the individual, the very Presence of Absolute Good or God's own nature in every person. The kingdom of heaven is the realm of harmony resulting from the right use of the ideas that make up the kingdom of God. Harmony (heaven) is always "at hand" ready to be brought

---

[531] John 1:14
[532] Ibid
[533] Luke 17:21
[534] Luke 17:21
[535] Matthew 3:2 and 4:17

into manifestation when we handle rightly the Truth ideas of God.

> *The kingdom of heaven . . . is a state of consciousness in which the soul and the body are in harmony with Divine Mind...*[536]

> *"Teachers of metaphysics find that their most difficult work is getting students to recognize that heaven is a condition of mind."*[537]

The Kingdom of God is neither a state of mind nor a condition of mind, but it is the God nature; the kingdom of heaven is that good state or condition of mind that produces in the outer life a sense of harmony, causing us to feel that we are truly "in heaven."

When we say "our Father who art in heaven" we can see that this universal Father of all, who is also our loving, individual Father, could only be harmony, wholeness, perfection. We must become conscious of and obedient to the God ideas, and make right use of them (handle them rightly), in order to dwell in this "home" of God and experience the heavenly state of joy, order, and harmony that stem from the "kingdom of God . . . within you."

Chapter 7
1. From what source did the idea-man spring? What other names are given to this idea?

The term "idea-man" as used in this lesson refers to God's idea of Himself as perfect man operating in the earthly sphere of Being. The standard set for this perfect

---

[536] *Metaphysical Bible Dictionary*
[537] Ibid, page 266

idea-man is that of a "god," an exact reproduction of the principle of perfect good which is in operation in the heavenly sphere of Being. "In the beginning God created the heavens and the earth".[538]

The source of this perfect idea-man is the one creative Mind the Father, the origin of every created thing. God, the Father, imaged Himself as a perfect man with dominion over the earth and everything in it, bringing into manifestation every needed good for "abundant living."

Perfect idea-man must form a mental concept of the nature of the earth and its inhabitants, so that he may understand the elements with which he will have to work in order to attain this mastery. The primal qualities of the God nature are wisdom and love, with which man must be acquainted in order to govern the birds of the air, the beasts of the field, the fishes of the sea, and the creeping things of the earth that God has created. Wisdom and love, which imbue us with Godlikeness, will guide us in handling this mastery aright.

According to Biblical terminology, other names given to this perfect idea-man are: Jehovah God; the Lord God; the Christ; the only begotten of the Father; the Son of God. This perfect idea-man can be called the Son of God for he is created by God in His image, and after His likeness.

2. What is meant by the term "the first-born of all creation"?[539]

First means not only that which precedes all others in the system of numbering, but also the highest, the foremost, as regards character. First-born is the "first

---

[538] Genesis 1:1
[539] Colossians 1:15

brought forth; preeminent." According to the ancient Hebrew custom the first-born in a family was the highest, the chief, and the leader. As such he inherited as a birthright his father's authority and a double portion of the father's possessions. He also succeeded to the priesthood provided he had no physical blemish.

The "first-born of all creation" is the God-idea originating in Divine Mind. However, the reference in the Scriptures to the "firstborn of all creation" is to the idea-man, the image of God, regarded as the beloved Son in whom the Father is well pleased. This idea-man is imbued with the power to develop a consciousness of the nature of God. Our "double portion" is the Presence of God and the power to form divine substance into thoughts, things, circumstances, and conditions. We are the only part of creation that can separate the elements (ideas) of God and view each one by itself.

Mind, idea, and expression in Truth are one, but in the process of producing a super-mental consciousness composed of ideas, they function separately, in a sense. The perfect human as the Idea of God is the "first-born"; then there is the mental concept of this man-idea which is expressed in manifest man's consciousness by Godlike thoughts, feelings, and words which are consciously carried into the body by the creative Word. In due season, this mind activity results in eternal life in the biological or physical body. "And the Word became flesh and dwelt among us".[540]

3. What is a "thought center"?

A thought center is an idea or an aggregation of ideas, beliefs, or concepts that is the nucleus around which

---

[540] John 1:14

substance (mind essence) gathers to form a mental structure. Thought is the act or process prompted by the one creative Mind. It does not relate alone to thinking as done by a self-conscious entity. It is any movement in the one creative Mind working toward consciousness. The essential principles of the Christ Mind, inherent in manifest man and the universe, become consciousness through these mind processes.

A center is that point within a sphere which is equally distant from every other point of its circumference, a focal point from which radiate the life and light that animate all parts of the sphere of its activity. The primal "thought center" is spiritual man, the image-likeness of God. In the Hebrew Scriptures God is named Lord God, or Jehovah God; in the Christian Scriptures God is named Jesus Christ. The Lord, or Jehovah God, functions as the "beginning" of God's ideal of us working in wisdom. Jesus Christ functions as the "fulfillment" of God's ideal of man working in love.

God's sphere of activity is man and the universe. The ideal is the pattern that is centered in God consciousness as I AM, the focal point. This pattern is to be expressed in the soul of man and manifested in his body and affairs.

4. How are thought centers formed?

Thought centers are formed by the creative power of God moving ideas toward expression through our consciousness for manifestation in the realm of form. What are called "thought centers" in the body are formed because of the experiences through which the body has passed, in its long evolutionary journey toward expression and manifestation, from a single cell to its present complex organism, we learn much through experience, and we know for ourselves only that which we experience. Before mankind had the power to reason, which is a mark of self-consciousness, our body had a feeling nature led by desire. As the biological body evolved, desire was the chief characteristic and ruled its life. In order to grow, the body desired food, so the biological cell wrapped itself around what would sustain it and cause it to expand. A repetition of this process, through countless ages, resulted in the formation of a stomach. Other organs were formed through similar processes until an organism was evolved with a highly developed nervous system and brain. Need to function preceded organization.

In the early stages of unfoldment on this earth our reasoning consciousness was expressing but dimly. The senses were paramount and instinct was the highest degree of intelligence functioning through the body. When the body was bruised or wounded, it experienced a sensation of "not good." When it found a choice morsel of food that satisfied hunger, it experienced a "good" and "very good" sensation. There was no reasoning done about it, just the establishing of reactions to sensation experienced. The cells and organs of the body were formed through these instinctive experiences, not through self-conscious thinking, as we understand thinking today, but as desires and feelings.

The manifest human feels, desires, thinks, speaks, acts, and evolves because of the movement of the creative I AM, Jehovah, or Lord God, the Son of God, spiritual mankind within seeking expression.

Chapter 8
1. When we are quickened to spiritual understanding and knows the Father or Christ (the Son, or I AM) within, what will be the result?

When we are quickened to spiritual understanding and knows the Father or Christ (the Son or I AM) within, we will be perfect both in expression and in manifestation. "I in them and thou in me, that they may become perfectly one".[541]

We will know the one Mind as the Source from which we spring and the nature of Absolute Good which we inherit as the son of God. We will know the ideal image or the divine pattern which we, as manifest man, are seeking to unfold. We will know that we do have the faith, the ability, and the energy to express this ideal with its correlated divine ideas.

As the result of all this "knowing," we will be conscious of all the good that is within us and will bring it forth into expression and manifestation. "You will know the truth, and the truth will make you free".[542] Because our unfoldment is from within outward, when we know Christ as our indwelling life and light, we begin to think, feel, speak, act, and react in a Christ-like manner.

In a way that we could understand, Jesus taught us what had been "lost" to our consciousness through the ages — that we are God's child, created in His image with the ability to express God's likeness. We have not only the example and inspiration of the life of the Nazarene, but his teachings have become living words that, when rooted in our consciousness, will grow and bear the fruit of God consciousness. This "fruit" is health of body, peace of

---
[541] John 17:23
[542] John 8:32

mind, harmonious human relations, and prosperity in all of our affairs.

2. **Explain the difference between the ideal human and the manifest human.**

An "Ideal human" is a spiritual creation of God, the man God created in His own "image".[543] Since God creates in ideas, the ideal human is non-physical, an idea involved or enveloped in God Mind, a pattern, an archetype, a creation coexistent and coterminous with God. The "Ideal human" is the Lord God, or the Christ, the I AM.

A "Manifest human" is the human being, the physical man, the man evolving, expressing, reproducing, and developing according to his individual understanding the pattern of the ideal man implanted within him.

An "Ideal human" dwells eternally in manifest man as the God-created "image" whose "likeness" manifest man is continuously unfolding and evolving. The "ideal human" is an impression of God; "manifest human" is an expression of God at the level of unfoldment of the individual soul. "Ideal human" embraces all the spiritual attributes or ideas; "manifest man" is an expresser of these attributes or ideas. "Ideal human" is the source of God ideas in humankind; "manifest human" is the user of the ideas. "Ideal human" is eternal, infinite, universal, and changeless; "manifest man" is in the process of change, evolving and unfolding his consciousness of his divine nature as a self-conscious entity.

---

[543] Genesis 1:27

3. **How does man lose his consciousness of divine harmony?**

We do not manifest harmony in life when we fail to think on divine ideas only, when we do not keep consciously in touch with I AM as the life and light of our being.

Divine harmony is the result of a consciousness that is united individually and collectively with the life principle in all creation. Consciousness is the direct knowing of each one for self, attained through thinking, feeling, speaking, and acting according to beliefs.

Very often a young people reach a time when they think the rules of his father's house place too many restraints. They feel that they know more than the father does. Therefore, they leave the father's house to seek their fortune. So it is sometimes with us in relation to our heavenly Father. As a self-conscious entity we are in an adolescent stage of development spiritually. We depend on our own present consciousness, acquired through what we have experienced, and do not turn to the Lord of life, the I AM. We go out from our Father's house (God consciousness) into a "far country" to make our own laws and to reap the results of a consciousness apart from the Lord. We lose conscious contact with the I AM and forget our own innate divinity by keeping our attention and interest on the external; thus we lose consciousness of the harmony that is our divine inheritance.

4. **How are we restored to divine harmony?**

We are restored to divine harmony through returning in consciousness (thinking and feeling) to God and learning the right use of his creative and causative power. When we get an understanding of our own threefold nature (spirit, soul, body) and his relation to Father-Mother God, then we become reestablished in our thinking, feeling, and acting to a state of agreement with the rhythm of life. We becomes an integrated and harmonious being; living in the Garden of Eden (harmony).

The Hebrew "Gan-heden" commonly rendered Garden of Eden is a compound of surpassing greatness. The word Gan means any organized sphere of activity, a garden, a body, a world, a universe. The word Heden, Eden, means a time, a season, an age, an eternity, as well as beauty, pleasure, an ornament, a witness ... When we bring forth the qualities of Being in divine order, we dwell in Eden, or in a state of bliss in a harmonious body ... The Garden of Eden is the divine consciousness".[544]

The Scriptural promise reads, "You will seek me and find me; when you seek me with all your heart"[545] and our endeavor to search for God within, with steadfastness, results in the restoration of harmony in all areas of his life.

5. What is the object of our existence?

The true object of our existence is to express all that God is in mind, body, and affairs here and now. The average person's conception of this object is that we are to be successful in material ways, to acquire prestige and position. Cognizance is not taken of the fact that achieving these things may still not be finding any real satisfaction.

The object of our existence is to demonstrate the Truth of Being.[546]

The spiritual conception of existence is that we are to fulfill self by expressing the divine attributes (ideas) that are an inherent part of our nature—the qualities of life,

---

[544] *Metaphysical Bible Dictionary*, p. 181
[545] Jeremiah 29:13
[546] Fillmore, Charles *Christian Healing*, p. 55

love, power, intelligence, and so forth. In the process of this fulfillment, position and possessions may very well come as a by-product (they frequently do), because the true meaning of existence is found in the inner values such as security, comfort, love, life. These values must in turn bring forth manifest results.

> *"Creation is not complete until it becomes manifest in the outer".[547]*

One conception of the object of our existence is to impress the world in a superficial way. The approach from a deeper standpoint is that we are to express spiritual resources (divine ideas) that are an inheritance from God in ways that make a contribution to humankind as well as to the individual. In the first viewpoint, the aim is determined only by outer results; in the other, by inner results, the "fruit of the Spirit".[548]

Jesus states as the object of His existence: "I came that they may have life, and have it abundantly".[549] We may express abundant life by coming into understanding of our true purpose in life. In expressing the true object of our existence, we become wiser, happier, more loving and positive in our approaches to life.

> *What is man that thou art mindful of him, and the son of man that thou dost care for him? Yet thou hast made him little less than God, and dost crown*

---

[547] Metaphysical Bible Dictionary, p. 1
[548] Galatians 5:22
[549] John 10:10

him with glory and honor. Thou hast given him dominion over the works of thy hands.[550]

6. Explain why we should be wise in the use of the term I AM.

I AM is the name for ideal, the Christ, the creative power of God in us (the first phase of our threefold nature). Thus, to use the powers of the I AM in an unwise way is to bring into our life experiences that which we do not want, Charles Fillmore emphasizes:

> *It is possible for us to take I AM power and apply it in external ways and leave out the true spiritual law. In our day we are proclaiming that we can use I AM power to restore health and bring increased happiness ... But some people are using this power in a material way, neglecting soul culture, building up the external without taking the intermediate step between the supreme Mind and its manifestation in the outer.*[551]

As children of God we were given the I AM powers as our spiritual heritage. With this heritage goes the responsibility of administering it wisely. It is vital, therefore, that we use the I AM powers wisely, righteously, and constructively, for that which we experience in our everyday life is the result of our use or misuse of spiritual powers. We come to see the reason for the almost magical results from sincere affirmation when we realize our responsibility in the use of our I AM powers.

We say for our body: "I AM God's life, substance,

---

[550] Psalm 8:4-6
[551] Fillmore, Charles Jesus Christ Heals, pp. 123-24

and intelligence in form." For our affairs we might affirm: "I AM prosperous, successful, and harmonious." If we are desirous of having God's revelations of Truth, we might declare: "I AM one with God's light, life, and understanding." In such statements there is no thought of powers outside of ourselves, but rather the present tense acceptance of them as available now.

Chapter 10
1. Are we limited by time, or in knowledge and power? How can we overcome belief in these limitations?

The Son is not limited in time. His throne, like the throne of God, is "for ever and ever".[552] The Son is not limited in knowledge because the entire God nature is inherent in us. Manifest human may use the light of intelligence inherent in his real Self, the Son of God, for whatever we need to know in order to express self in any state of being. In referring to the Son, Scripture says: "He reflects the glory of God and bears the very stamp of his nature, upholding the universe by his word of power".[553] The Son is therefore stamped with the seal of the Almighty.

If we have accepted falsities, limitations, in our mental processes we do not need to harbor them indefinitely. Through the power of the I AM (another name for the Son) we are able to erase, by denial, all false beliefs. Then by affirmation we are able to take on the life, light, love, and liberty that are ours as heirs of God. We learn to "walk as children of light".[554]

---

[552] Hebrews 1:8
[553] Hebrews 1:3
[554] Ephesians 5:8

2. **Explain how the Father can be in the Son, and the Son in the Father.**

The word Father is used here as a symbol of the one Creative Mind, everywhere present in its absolute purity and perfection. The word Son is used here as a symbol of the Idea of the one Mind bringing forth the entire nature of God (comprising all divine ideas). Thus the Son is both the "image" and the "likeness" of the Father. God's creative power moves through the Son, the Word (or as Charles Fillmore calls it in *Talks on Truth*,[555] "the working power of God") to create life and consciousness in all creation. The creative power of God, broadly interpreted, may be termed "thought"; however, this includes the whole gamut of life, feelings, desires, sense perceptions, scholarly intellections of self-conscious entities, to the abstract visions of the philosophers; also the life and intelligence of all creations below us, in the animal, vegetable, and mineral kingdoms.

As "thought essence" is the unformed substance of the one Creative Mind, and as this substance encompasses and supports all of its ideas ("sons"), governing all their activity, then the Father as the one Creative Mind is in all God's ideas.

The Father is the one living Mind; the Son is the one living Idea (ideal) or Word, "living" together, working together, and acting together. There can be no separation between the Father and the Son, for they are one in nature, in will, and in purpose.

Let us think of the relation of the Father and the Son in reference to our own mentality. We cannot separate an idea from the unformed mind substance —

---

[555] Fillmore, Charles Talks on Truth, p. 68

the idea is always in our mind, and our mind is always in the idea.

3. How are we begotten by the Word?

We understand "the Word"[556] to be the activity of God in every man; God's creative power; the divine essence that is immanent in every living creation, including man. Since the Word is the begetting, creating, generating factor in all creation — the impulse of life seeking expression and fulfillment — man was "begotten by the Word" when God "breathed into his nostrils the breath of life; and man became a living being".[557] One version reads, "and man became a living soul."

There is also a "begetting by the Word" in the individual consciousness of every person. We read in I Peter:[558] "You have been born anew, not of perishable seed but of imperishable, through the living and abiding word of God." This is a quickening and rebirth into spiritual consciousness when one becomes keenly cognizant of the qualities (attributes or ideas) of God within him.

Realization of the inherent creative capacities of life, love, wisdom, power, and faith, and giving expression to these capacities in experience, represent a "begetting by the Word."

4. How do we manifest Christ?

Manifest is the word commonly used to refer to that which stands forth in the outer where it is perceived by the senses. We "manifest" Christ by setting up Christ, the indwelling, the Anointed, as a standard for ourselves

---

[556] John 1:1
[557] Genesis 2:7
[558] I Peter 1:2

to live by in our every thought, word, action, and reaction. We "manifest Christ" by identifying ourselves with God-Mind, the Father — that is, by making ourselves consciously one with God-Mind. This causes us to grow spiritually in purpose, interest, use, and effect.

Identification with God takes place in our own consciousness, our mind, through the divine ideal, the I AM, and is carried out in desire, thought, word, and deed. It is God's will that man express Him in His fullness. To do this we must know ourselves to be the offspring of God, inheritor of His eternal life, love, wisdom, power (i.e., all divine ideas). We must know also that we are possessed of the ability and the understanding to bring forth these ideas.

> *Divine ideas are man's inheritance ... All the ideas contained in the one Father-Mind are at "the mental command of its offspring"*[559].

"Manifesting Christ" is bringing into visibility that which, sown as seed-ideas, has taken root in the "soil" of the human consciousness, to be unfolded in all areas of an individual's life. The visible manifestation in the flesh is the final step, the result of the "new nature".[560]

5. How do we abide in Christ?

We "abide in Christ" when we dwell consciously and continuously in the realization of the one Presence and one Power, God, the good omnipotent, active in and through us. As we carry this consciousness out into our everyday human experiences, we shall show forth or

---
[559] Fillmore, Charles *Christian Healing*, p. 13
[560] Ephesians 4:24

demonstrate the "fruits" of the kingdom of God. "He who abides in me, and I in him, he it is that bears much fruit, for apart from me you can do nothing".[561]

    When we abide consciously in the Christ, our salvation is complete. We are saved from belief in ignorance and sin, and all their effects. This is the true "atonement," the at-one-ment or redeeming of our entire consciousness that it may function as one complete spiritual unit. Jesus said, "If you keep my commandments, you will abide in my love, just as I have kept my Father's commandments and abide in his love".[562] In a true sense, if we abide (dwells consciously and continuously) in the living Word of God, Christ Jesus, then all things are already provided lavishly for us.

6. **Give in your own words five affirmations for the realization of the indwelling Christ.**
   Examples:

   "Father, I give thanks for Thy presence in me as the indwelling Christ."

   "Through prayer I come into a realization of the indwelling Christ, my hope of glory."

   "As I abide in Truth, I come to know the Christ indwelling me."

   "O Christ within me, I know Thee as my life, intelligence, supply, and support."

---

[561] John 15:5
[562] John 15:10

> *"Father, reveal Thyself to me and through me as the living Christ."*

(Note: Two of these affirmations are written in third person (about the Christ); the other three are written in second person (speaking directly to the indwelling Spirit).

7. **Give our phases as a threefold being, and explain the result if we fail to recognize this unity of our being.**

    The threefold nature is expressed as: spirit, soul, body.

8. **What is the result if we fail to recognize the unity of being, as spirit, soul, body?**

    Failure to recognize the oneness of our being as spirit, soul, body (and the place of each phase in making up the whole person) causes us to experience a sense of lack, separation, and unfulfillment. Then, our physical organism (body) will fail to manifest the health that is ours as a child of God.

    A feeling of separateness reveals itself to us in many ways. At one extreme, it may take the direction of an attempt to retire within the self, to become an introvert. The first phase, or spirit, is thought to be found entirely here, and soul and body phases are left undeveloped. A person becomes thus an introvert often seeks to escape from participation in life; he may become a recluse.

    At the other extreme, through our non-recognition of our trinity of spirit, soul, body we may give ourselves over to the view that the gratification and comfort of the body is our paramount interest; we would then become an extrovert. Or there may be a search for soul satisfaction by the intellectual pursuit of knowledge, thus developing the intellect (thinking faculty) to such an extent that anything of the spiritual side of life is ignored or counted of little value.

We need to know that the essence of our being is the Spirit of God, the source of the life, substance, and intelligence that permeates our soul and body. It is in recognizing the values of spirit, the pursuits of the soul (mind), and the development of the body that we find integration, the unity of our threefold nature bringing harmony into all levels of life.

9. **How do we identify self with the Absolute? How and what is it to acknowledge the Son?**

We establish first that the Absolute is God. Webster says of the word absolute: "Not dependent on anything else; not determined by or effected by anything outside itself; fundamental; ultimate; intrinsic; unqualified; self-contained and self-sufficient." Through our studies we have come to see that this definition applies to God as the Absolute of all existence, the self-existent One. How then do we identify ourselves with the Absolute? We are always so identified, but if we are not conscious of this oneness with God, then we need to seek quickening through prayer. We need to become alive and alert to this relationship we have with our Father-Mother God; then we are truly "identified with the Absolute."

The Son or child is a term for our own divine nature, our God-Self, the divine pattern in us; but only as we become consciously identified with God (the Absolute) can we express and manifest this nature.

To "acknowledge the Son" requires that we first identify ourselves consciously with God (the Absolute), then proceed to manifest our sonship in thought, word, and deed. Acknowledgment, so far as spiritual growth is concerned, is never merely in words, but must be the actual living of that which we would acknowledge. Thus to truly "acknowledge the Son" we must be living according to the divine pattern in all phases of our life, our business relationships, our human relationships, our social relationships.

10. What is the object of our existence?
     The true object of our existence is to express all that God is in mind, body, and affairs here and now. The average person's conception of this object is that we are to be successful in material ways, to acquire prestige and position. Cognizance is not taken of the fact that a person achieving these things may still not be finding any real satisfaction for himself.

> *The object of man's existence is to demonstrate the Truth of Being.*[563]

     The spiritual conception of existence is that we are to fulfill ourselves by expressing the divine attributes (ideas) that are an inherent part of our nature—the qualities of life, love, power, intelligence, and so forth. In the process of this fulfillment, position and possessions may very well come as a by-product (they frequently do), because the true meaning of existence is found in the inner values such as security, comfort, love, life. These values must in turn bring forth manifest results.

---

[563] Fillmore, Charles *Christian Healing*, p. 55

> *Creation is not complete until it becomes manifest in the outer."*[564]

One conception of the object of our existence is to impress the world in a superficial way. The approach from a deeper standpoint is that we are to express our spiritual resources (divine ideas) that are our inheritance from God in ways that make a contribution to humankind as well as to the individual. In the first viewpoint, our aim of is determined only by outer results; in the other, by inner results, the "fruit of the Spirit".[565]

Jesus states as the object of His existence: "I came that they may have life, and have it abundantly".[566] We may express abundant life by coming into understanding of our true purpose in life. In expressing the true object of our existence, we become wiser, happier, more loving and positive in our approaches to life.

> *What is man that thou art mindful of him, and the son of man that thou dost care for him? Yet thou hast made him little less than God, and dost crown him with glory and honor. Thou hast given him dominion over the works of thy hands.*[567]

Chapter 11
1. What is thinking? What is a structure, and what builds all structures?

Thinking is a process by which the human soul (i.e., the mind or consciousness) is able to handle abstract ideas

---
[564] *Metaphysical Bible Dictionary*, p. 1
[565] Galatians 5:22
[566] John 10:10
[567] Psalm 8:4-6

so as to form a mental "picture" or pattern. Once solidified in our mind (subconscious as well as conscious) this pattern becomes a magnet or a "mental equivalent" that is the nucleus for the outer structure. The structure will bear the character of the mind pattern of the individual doing the thinking.

> *Thought is the process in mind by which substance is acted on by energy, directed by intelligence. Thought is the movement of ideas in mind.*[568]

The creative power of God (Spirit, Divine Mind) in its action builds all structures, whether they be structures of consciousness, living organic structures of us and in animals, structures of plant life, structures in the mineral kingdom, or structures "made" by us using spiritual substance in various forms. The power that provides for the building of any structure comes from God. In the first chapter of Genesis we find an allegorical description of the great creative Mind at work. Charles Fillmore in *Mysteries of Genesis* states:[569]

> *"The record portrays just how divine ideas were brought into expression. As man must have an idea before he can bring an idea into manifestation, so it is with the creations of God. When a man builds a house he builds it first in his mind. He has the idea of a house, he completes the plan in his mind, and then he works it out in manifestation. Thus God*

---

[568] *Metaphysical Bible Dictionary*, p. 654
[569] Fillmore, Charles *Mysteries of Genesis*, p. 12

created the universe. The 1st chapter of Genesis describes the ideal creation."

The process of building all structures, whether they be on the spiritual, mental, or physical planes, follows the pattern of the Holy Trinity — Father, Son, Holy Spirit — or Mind, Idea, Expression — producing manifestation. The Word of God is the composite idea of all the elements of divinity and creation. This Word is the active agent of Spirit, guiding and directing the action so that the consciousness on earth may be the same as it is in heaven; that the abstract may be made concrete. "Thy kingdom come, thy will be done on earth as it is in heaven".[570] The resources used in the building of any structure are life, substance, and intelligence. Life (movement, animation) and substance (unformed essence containing the idea of the form) work with intelligence (light, understanding, wisdom, the knowing quality of the species) to bring forth divine ideas into form.

> *"Since man is the offspring of God, made in the image and likeness of Divine Mind, he must express himself under the laws of this great creative Mind. The law of manifestation for man is the law of thought. God ideates: man thinks. One is the completion of the other in mind."*[571]
>
> *The creative power of God moves ideas into expression and manifestation as consciousness, things, conditions, and circumstances. In the*

---

[570] Matthew 6:10
[571] Ibid 12

structure of human consciousness, the active agent of man is thought (thinking and feeling) and the spoken word of human beings.

When manifest a human being desires a certain condition in the body or in the world, we consciously directs attention toward it; we think about it with the conscious phase of mind; we feels with the emotional nature (subconscious phase of mind); we speaks the word, silently or audibly, and the manifestation comes forth. Spirit is the power that does all things; but we by our thinking, feeling, spoken word (the formative power of thought) directs the creative power of God (the Word of God) to build structures, thereby producing conditions, circumstances, and things in the world according to our own beliefs and level of soul unfoldment. "All structures are thought concentrations".[572]

2. What is the Superconscious phase of mind?

The Superconscious is the Christ Mind; the I AM; the God Presence in every person.

We refer to our threefold nature as spirit, soul, and body. The first phase — spirit — is called by many names—Christ, I AM, divine center, the "Father within," Lord, law of our being, and Super-consciousness. While Divine Mind is the realm of divine ideas for all creation, this Mind indwells us as the Superconscious or Christ Mind, and is thus the realm of divine ideas for us individually. The Superconscious is the realm of pure knowing.

The term "superconscious" indicates that the Superconscious Mind is above our conscious phase of

---
[572] Fillmore, Charles The Twelve Powers, p. 24

mind (thinking, reasoning, or intellect) and our subconscious phase of mind (feeling, emotion, or the heart). These two activities of our soul or mind are the users of the ideas of the Superconscious or Christ Mind.

We respond to the ideals of God by turning to the Superconscious or Christ Mind and laying hold of the ideas that make up our divine inheritance. Without movement of ideas in mind there could be no consciousness. The use of the ideas by our thinking and feeling will be determined by our stage of soul unfoldment, and by the needs of mind, body, and affairs.

3. What is the conscious phase of mind? What other names are given to this phase of mind?

The conscious phase of mind is the thinking faculty, the reasoning phase, the realm of conscious knowing in the individual soul. It is often termed "the intellect." In this phase, we choose, examine, judge, analyze, wills, selects, decide, form, deducts, rejects, accepts, and concludes, as we deal with the ideas received from the Superconscious.

As the realm of choice, the conscious phase of mind declares "I am I" and "You are you"; "I will" or "I will not." It is in this phase of consciousness that we may be conscious of self as an individual identity, even thinking self to be separate from God, from other human beings, and from other forms of life. But quite the reverse of this belief in separation is also possible, for the conscious phase of mind is capable of realizing that although we are a unit ourselves, we are always one with Creator, God, or Divine Mind. Thus, we come to the realization that we are also one with all human beings as spiritual brothers and sisters, and one with all other forms of life. "One God and

Father of all, who is over all, and through all, and in all".[573]

It is the function of the conscious phase of mind, or intellect, to discriminate between the general and the specific; to note differences as well as similarities in persons, religions, sciences, things, circumstances, and conditions. This phase of mind makes us a rational human being, enabling us to do rational thinking. It is this phase that allows us ultimately to know self to be the son of God. Through this function we may look out on the world of appearances, but we may also focus attention on the divine Presence, Spirit, within self. As we consciously handle the ideas to which we are heir, we may examine the how and why of life.

It is in this realm that concrete thinking is done, based upon the abstract ideas of the Superconscious. The conscious phase deals mostly with the present outlook, and because of free choice very often its judging is done from appearances instead of "righteous judgment".[574]

4. **What is the subconscious phase of mind? What other names are given to this phase of mind?**

The subconscious phase of mind is the feeling nature of each individual, as well as the receptacle of mental images (patterns) stored "in the beginning".[575] Thus we term it the seat of memory. The concrete result of our subconscious records shows forth as the physical or human body. As the lesson has already emphasized, the

---

[573] Ephesians 4:6
[574] John 7:24
[575] Genesis 1:1

subconscious phase of mind handles the involuntary activities of the organism.

The subconscious is the secondary cause, the reactive phase of mind in the individual. We call its action "the formative power of thought" as it works in substance to bring forth conditions in man's body and affairs according to the suggestions given it by the conscious phase of mind. Charles Fillmore refers to this activity of the subconscious as "secondary thinking"; when feeling takes over, there is a type of instinctive "thinking" that is the movement of ideas held in the feeling phase of the mind (subconscious).

5. How are the conscious and subconscious phases of mind related?

The conscious phase of mind (objective) and the subconscious phase of mind (subjective) are related in much the same way as the master is related to the servant. The conscious phase takes the initiative, and impresses the subconscious with divine ideas, right thoughts, or the reverse, and the subconscious will carry out the suggestions faithfully. The conscious phase sends its directives to the subconscious which must accept them and carry them out, because the subconscious has no power of its own to do its own selecting.

The conscious phase acts, but the subconscious reacts; the conscious phase makes the impression, but the subconscious produces the manifestation; the conscious phase decides what to do, and the subconscious phase does it.

Often we are pulled up short by some condition which has become unbearable. Then we may learn through study and inspiration that we have been sending wrong directives into the feeling nature, the subconscious phase of mind. If we so choose, we may use denials to cleanse the subconscious of the erroneous beliefs that have lodged there. Then we may use affirmations of Truth to refill the subconscious with true ideas from the Superconscious or Christ Mind. The conscious phase of mind records its directives, as sound is recorded on a tape; the subconscious faithfully "plays back" exactly what has been recorded.

6. Name some of the functions of the body carried on by the subconscious phase of mind.

The so-called involuntary actions are those that are controlled by the subconscious; such actions as raising and lowering the temperature of the body, making cell changes, looking after the action of the heart, the circulation of the blood, taking care of the salivary and gastric juices, superintending the breathing, digestion, assimilation, and elimination of food.

The subconscious cannot take the initiative, but it carries out faithfully the plan back of every cell of the body, the true functioning of every organ, nerve, tissue unless interfered with by the conscious phase through fear or ignorance. When the conscious phase of mind interferes with the normal functioning of the body, then the subconscious must compensate in an instinctive way and this often results in disease or illness. When the conscious phase accepts the guidance of the Superconscious or Christ Mind, then it can give right directions to the subconscious. This allows the involuntary functions to carry on their normal work of sustaining and maintaining the body in health.

7. How may one take conscious control of the involuntary functions?

One may take conscious control of the involuntary functions of the biological body through the conscious phase of mind to the extent of correcting any bad habits or inharmony which may be manifesting. When the Superconscious Mind guides the conscious thinking, it does not in any way interfere with the normal work of the subconscious. This conscious control by the conscious phase of mind, through retraining of the subconscious sphere, is the true way to healing, and much of this work can be done by affirmations. As we come more fully under the dominion of the Superconscious, the conscious phase gains understanding as to how to direct the Inner functions of the body. Under spiritual guidance, the conscious phase of mind can impress the subconscious with new habits.

It is important that we remember that we are a focal point in Universal Mind. Therefore, each of us must seek divine guidance to find the true pattern for bodily operations. When we know our body to be primarily the "temple of God" we can, through the process of denial, erase the imperfect concepts and beliefs held in the subconscious, replacing them through affirmations with the truth about the body.

When something comes to our attention that is not measuring up to the proper standard of living, our business is to make the correction, to take conscious charge of the thought currents and direct them in the way they should go to produce that which is higher and better than the present mode in which they are functioning. This means giving the subconscious better patterns from which to work.

8. From what source have many of the subconscious thought currents come?

Many of the subconscious thought currents have come into the individual's subconscious phase of mind through collective thought. We have viewed ourselves as separate, independent entities; we have looked at our earth with its thundering, lightning, solid earth, seas, wild animals, forests, and the like, and we have been overwhelmed by the stupendous proposition that we face.

The desire to live is incorporated in every cell of our biological body by God, our Creator. However, until we discover the presence and power of God in us as the same life that is immanent in all living things, even in all inanimate things, we feel ourselves to be separate entities. Then comes the feeling that we must cope, mostly by struggle, with our environment in order to make it yield to us that which is necessary for the sustenance of our body.

As mankind as a species increase in numbers, we pool our interests, learn a method of communication with each other (speech), and formed judgments based on the physical senses and past experiences. Thus the collective consciousness (subconscious of mankind as a whole) is impressed with the commonly accepted beliefs about what is necessary for us in order to live. Negative beliefs from that consciousness accepted by the individual become "mental equivalents" in our subconscious that produce similar living conditions, until they are superseded by better and higher ideas.

9. **Why do we sometimes think one thing and manifest another?**

We sometimes think one thing but manifest something different because the out-picturing in our body, life, and affairs is the result of the sum of all our thinking, feeling, acting (present and past, conscious and subconscious, good or bad). The thinking of the moment has not had sufficient time and spiritual impetus to work through the subconscious (feeling nature) into the manifest realm.

The conscious phase of mind (intellect) and the heart (subconscious phase) must work together in order to bring forth a harmonious manifestation. "Realization precedes manifestation".[576] Usually some time is required for an idea to work itself into the subconscious. Realization is not possible until the two phases of mind agree and accept the idea, so that it may blossom into the desired manifestation. Many instantaneous answers to prayer have been reported, but in such cases the work has already taken place in the mind so that realization is ready to bring forth the manifestation.

We need to remember that the conscious thought is not the sole determining factor in producing, changing, and improving manifestation; the entire consciousness must be taken into account through a process of growth, unfoldment, and development. No conscious thought is ever wasted, however, even though it may not appear to produce an instantaneous manifestation.

> *"The fulfillment ... in the world of activities may take moments, hours, days, years, centuries ... Do not think because you do not get an instant*

---
[576] Fillmore, Charles *Jesus Christ Heals*, p. 39

response to your prayers that they are not answered. Every sincere desire and every effectual prayer... is fulfilled, and will be made manifest whenever material limitations permit![577]

When the conscious and subconscious phases of mind are in harmony with the Superconscious or Christ Mind (divine ideas), we will no longer think one thing and manifest another.

10. Why is it so important to think the Truth about life?
It is very important to think the Truth about life, "For as we think in our heart, so are we".[578] The "heart" refers to the subconscious.

As we interpret life consciously and subconsciously, so we shall live life each day. If we interpret life positively, then the results in our daily living will be harmonious and will move in divine order; if we interpret life negatively, we will bring like conditions into our daily experiences.

Because of ingrained limited beliefs in the race consciousness that life begins with birth in a form and ends with the death of that form, we need to know and think the Truth about life. There are too many mistaken beliefs in regard to "the other side," too many delusions that the body is an "obstruction" and that life out of the body, in an "unobstructed universe," is where man learns the way to live. There are too many who believe that the body is like an old coat that must be discarded, instead of seeing it as the "seamless robe" of righteousness that we are to wear "forever more."

---

[577] Fillmore, Charles *Jesus Christ Heals*, p. 7
[578] Proverbs 23:7

No one can attain a consciousness of eternal life so long as we cling to the belief that the immortality of the soul is made possible by "sacrificing" the body, thus attempting to separate our trinity of spirit, soul, body.

Another teaching that needs to be cleared away is the belief that being a Christian (that is, seeking to live the Christ life) inevitably ends in martyrdom.

Until such time as we prepare the way for eternal life by getting rid of hampering beliefs in the subconscious, we are still imprisoned. As we believe in our heart, so we will interpret life, and the wrong approach to life causes us to experience confusion, frustration, sickness, poverty, and failure.

11. What line of thinking will overcome the belief in materiality?

Materiality has reference to corporeal existence in contradistinction to the spiritual; this does not mean that which is wrong, but rather that which is formed, visible, or cognizant to any of the five senses. It is when we accept the belief that only the material is real that we need to "overcome the belief in materiality."

Many persons believe that the biological body of man is the man. They believe that each body has a separate mind of its own, due to the action of the five physical senses in bringing information to the brain, where it is stored up for use. This belief is due to the teaching of primitive ancestors who had no higher knowing. Those who have such beliefs give their attention and interest largely to gratifying the appetites, passions, desires, and comforts that the fleshly body demands; therefore they are ruled by unenlightened sensation.

Mind and brain are not synonymous. God as the Life Principle activates all corporeal forms. Manifest humans as a self-conscious entity has as the center of our being the life, intelligence, and substance of Spirit, which are ours to use. Thinking is the process by which the ideas inherent in Mind substance are made active and released into daily living. All true thinking is for the purpose of knowing Truth in order that we may interpret life correctly. We then come to experience the eternal good which the one creative Mind or Spirit planned or willed for the entire universe, us included.

A materialistic conception of life can never truly interpret it. To realize the Truth is to be in harmony with the one creative Mind. If we would live a wholesome, happy life, the work that confronts us is to correct the misconceptions held in the subconscious. Through spiritual discernment we are able to perceive, receive, and conceive our true being or nature. It is only through spiritual insight and spiritual thinking that we can see ourselves and the universe as God expressing self, and thus overcome the belief in materiality as being the real.

12. Why should we hold ourselves and others, in the one all-knowing Mind?

It is vital that we hold ourselves and others as being in the one all-knowing Mind, for that is our true place as children of God, and the only way in which we are able to claim our inheritance of good. "In him we live and move and have our being" (Acts 17:28).[579]

"Hold" as used here means to judge or consider ourselves and others as being expressions of the one creative Mind which is the source and cause of all that appears in the manifest sphere of action. There is no other source that can inspire and guide each individuated unit

---

[579] Acts 17:28

except Spirit or Divine Mind. Through "that I AM" each human being is identified with the one creative Mind. A conscious recognition of this enables us to unite ourselves in consciousness with all other human beings and know that each one is a focal point expressing God Mind to the extent of their present ability to interpret life.

When we know that we are projections of Divine Mind, we are allowing this one creative Mind to express itself through creation according to its perfect plan.

13. How may all thought be brought into harmony with divine law?

All thought may be brought into harmony with divine law — the law of absolute good — through the unifying power of divine love.

"Thought" as used here means all the desires, sense perceptions, feelings, concepts, beliefs, Ideas and associations of ideas, judgments, and opinions.

"Love, in Divine Mind, is the idea of universal unity. In expression, love is the power that joins and binds in divine harmony the universe and everything in it".[580]

As the quality or idea that joins, love attracts all that is needed to bring about harmony between people and in all situations. Love, as a law itself, fulfills all the divine laws,[581] because love is the great harmonizer. If one's thoughts are confused, chaotic, unhappy, fearful, love can change them to harmony, happiness, faith, courage, and understanding. When one has sought for an answer to prayers, or a way out of problems, and we discover the Truth, it is only the quality of love for Truth, for God, that can enable us to harmonize thinking and

---

[580] Fillmore, Charles *Christian Healing*, p.130
[581] Romans 13:8

feeling. If we want to be "transformed by the renewing of your mind,"[582] we will need love to give the strength and courage needed to make the change from limited, materialistic thinking to spiritual thinking.

14. What place has order in Divine Mind and in man's consciousness?

"Order is Heaven's first law," said Alexander Pope.[583] The kingdom of heaven is consciousness being carried forward and upward according to the highest ideas of which humanity as a whole is conscious. This consciousness is termed "Christ consciousness" because it implies a state of peace and security in each individual who has so controlled and systematized the mental sphere that we have dominion over it.

Order is that faculty in our consciousness that adjusts each idea in its proper place, relating ideas to each other and relating them to the whole so that there is no friction, all working happily and joyously together for the good of the whole. Thus we may say that order is made up of right relationships — order is that which produces balance.

Order, then, must have first place in Divine Mind as well as in our consciousness, for only as ideas, persons, events move in an orderly way will the harmony or "heaven" come forth into manifestation. The first movement of order in our consciousness must be to relate self to God, to "seek ... first his kingdom" so that we may, in an orderly way, lay hold of the ideas that are our divine inheritance.

---

[582] Romans 2:2
[583] Pope, Alexander *An Essay on Man*

Chapter 14
1. Explain how our bodies are transformed.
    First we relieve the body of our former beliefs that it is merely of biological origin, that it is limited in any sense of the word. Study of spiritual principles reveals the body to be in reality the temple of God — God's life, substance, and intelligence in manifestation.

> *"The body is the meeting place of the life and substance attributes of Being, consequently body is an important factor in consciousness. Body is not matter; it is substance and life in expression".[584]*

    When denial has erased our misconception about the body, then we can accept the truth about it, namely that it is an instrument of Spirit, an ideal form based on a divine body-idea in Divine Mind. We perceive the body to be the manifestation of the God nature in the exterior world. We come to know it as an expression of the organizing power of divine love (the attracting, unifying power) united with wisdom. This revelation or vision of the body will redeem it from the belief that it is of animal origin, giving it its rightful place as a vehicle for God's life, light, and love. Affirmation, silent or audible, of the truth about the body gives us a more reverent regard for it and the bodies of all persons. "Be transformed by the renewal of your mind".[585]

    It is through our affirmation of the living Word of Truth that thoughts of life, light, and love are impressed on every cell of our body, and it is thus "saved" from corruption and death and transformed into the "body of

---

[584] Fillmore, Charles Talks on Truth, p. 158
[585] Romans 12:2

Christ." In the work that is done regarding transformation of the body, both the conscious and subconscious phases of mind must be trained.

2. What is meant by believing on Christ unto salvation?

Believing on Christ unto salvation is believing so firmly in the spiritual principles, ideas, which make up our Christ nature that they become the motivation of our thinking, feeling, speaking, and acting. The freedom we find in expressing these principles is our salvation.

Wrong attitudes and limiting concepts about ourselves bind us and keep us from experiencing the spiritual mastery we seek. Our faith is not being placed on the life, love, and intelligence constituting our Christ nature, nor on the potential of these ideals and ideas to become actual in experience. Conversely, right attitudes, the conviction that the latent good can become manifest, redeem us from limitations.

"He who is in you is greater than he who is in the world"[586] was an insight of John. The greater "he" is the Christ. This realization will meet any issue that has to be met. This is "believing on Christ unto salvation."

3. What is the way to build a consciousness of eternal life?

Life eternal, everlasting, timeless is God, the one life without beginning and without ending. This source of life is within us as the Christ, the I AM, the life principle. Here within our own being we appropriate the life idea moving from the Source, God, the one creative Mind, into expression and manifestation. "I write this to you who

---

[586] I John 4:4

believe in the name of the Son of God, that you may know that you have eternal life".[587]

God "moves" through creation as the eternal movement of His nature as life to find expression. This movement is spoken of as the Spirit of God. Every form of creation is expressing and manifesting life, the Spirit of God, according to its degree of development.

Consciousness is the direct knowing of each one for himself, attained through thinking, feeling, speaking, and acting according to his beliefs. A consciousness of anything, be it of life, of health, of peace, of prosperity, or of a negative nature such as sickness, lack, and limitation, is developed by using the tools of thinking, feeling, speaking, and acting. The difference lies in the mold or the pattern that we use as a standard for these activities. The I AM, the creative power of God, is the power that enables us to build all states of consciousness according to the thoughts provided by us. We need to remember that consciousness is never just thinking alone, but feeling must be added.

The building of a consciousness of eternal life must be done in the same orderly way in which our consciousness deals with any qualities we wish to manifest. Through study, meditation, entering the Silence, we become acquainted with tie life idea. We see its source in the Christ, or I AM, within us. We may need to use denial to erase any misconceptions we might have had about life being limited. As we use our affirmations of the eternalness of life, that is, life without beginning or ending, we begin to take on conviction that life is ours by divine right. Our whole consciousness changes; we begin to see the truth of Paul's statement in Romans, "Be transformed

---

[587] I John 5:13

by the renewal of your mind."[588] When we are faced in our outer life with challenges that seem to belie the eternalness of life, our expanded consciousness of the truth of life sustains us. We are no longer tossed by uncertainty; we have built a consciousness of eternal life as being ours now, not at some time in the future.

4. What is Christ? Explain fully how Christ is our salvation.[589]

"Christ" is the "anointed" one, a name translated from the Greek with this meaning. The Hebrew word is Messiah, the expected king, deliverer, and savior. John identified Christ with the Logos, The Word. Simon Peter identified the Christ as the "Son of the living God".[590] Paul wrote of "Christ the power of God, and the wisdom of God".[591] In modern usage the name is often used synonymously with Jesus.

The Unity teachings identify "Christ" as the spiritual human, the person created in the image and after the likeness of God. "Let us make man in our image, after our likeness".[592] "Christ" is the primal human Idea, the pattern, the archetype, the ideal, the I AM. As the spiritual essence of all mankind, the indwelling "Christ" becomes to each individual king, deliverer, and savior.

When God is defined as Divine Mind, "Christ" can be understood as the Idea, the Logos, the Word, or Divine Mind as it expresses in each of us. When God is defined as Father, "Christ" is the offspring, or the Son of God.

---

[588] Romans 12:2
[589] See Colossians 1:27
[590] Matthew 16:16
[591] I Corinthians 1:24
[592] Genesis 1:26

To us in our relationship to God, "Christ" is the divinity of our nature, the power, the life and the wisdom indwelling. In Christian thought, the one Jesus most fully identified himself with the "Christ." The two terms, as a result, have come to be often used interchangeably as referring to Jesus.

"Christ in you, the hope of glory".[593] "Christ" represents all the principles or powers of God as individuated in each human being, the image or spiritual pattern and the resources or means for developing it into manifestation, for producing only good. This is our salvation, and it comes to us as a gift from God. This is God's will or plan for us by which we are to evolve, grow, and unfold into the very likeness of God. It is available to us at all times when we are ready to accept it as our way of life.

The "Christ," in the truest sense, is the only true model that we can take. "Christ" is implanted within the heart of mankind as the pattern of the design to be worked out, as the source of ideals and the promoter of aspirations. It is our work to attain a consciousness of, acceptance of, and make use of all the spiritual powers and qualities that are in the "Christ," so that we may live to the honor of mankind and to the glory of God.

5. How is Jesus, the Christ the Savior of humankind?

Jesus, the Christ can be said to be the Savior of humankind because he sought in his ministry to draw everyone's attention to their own divine creation, and to the "saving grace" or love of God. As Way-Shower, Jesus pointed the way for everyone to seek within for the

---

[593] Colossians 1:27

"Father who is in secret".[594] Jesus became the manifestation of the principle that combines the Son of God (Christ) and Son of man (Jesus). Paul refers to this as "the fullness of the Godhead bodily".[595] The Jesus Christ principle unites the Superconscious, the conscious, and the subconscious spheres of our being, making them one. This is the true "atonement."

      Christ, I AM, is the seed idea or divine pattern of God which is implanted in every person, and contains all the elements of the God nature. Jesus represents the understanding use of this pattern; thus the Jesus Christ principle is the combination of the pattern and its application. Jesus, the Man of Nazareth, is the Way-Shower; he showed mankind the way to the understanding of our relationship to God, and the manner in which each must unfold the Christ pattern within self. Jesus taught God's Ideals which we in our belief in separation had forgotten. When we put into action, Jesus' teaching, it transforms and redeems our consciousness from belief in the reality of sin, evil, poverty, and death, directing our thought current to righteousness. It is this "tuning in" with the Almighty One that "saves" us. Thus it is not difficult for us to understand why Jesus is the Savior of mankind, both in a general way as the Teacher who pointed the way, and in an individual way as the indwelling principle in every person.

---

[594] Matthew 6:6
[595] Colossians 2:9

Chapter 15

1. How may we bring our thoughts under conscious control? Answer a:

It is no cause for discouragement if we are not able at first to enter this secret place or to close the door on the outer world. The senses are habitually active in the exterior consciousness; this habit is not overcome all at once, but by daily practice of denials, of affirmations, and of constantly aspiring toward the divine standard of thinking and feeling. It is well to have a regular time for prayer, but the mind should also be trained to "pray without ceasing,"[596] that is, the ability to turn within at all times in conscious communion with God should be sought by a continuous realization of God as ever present, "over all, through all, and in all,"[597] and waiting always in the secret place when one turns the attention there to meet God.

Answer b:

The highest way for one to bring thoughts under conscious control is by constantly aspiring toward the divine standard and daily practicing the presence of God. This may involve much denial of error (as being reality) and affirmation of the Truth, in order to train the mind to stand firm on the divine standard for right thinking and feeling.

It is possible for a person to consciously control thoughts by fixing attention on an object or on an idea, and by willfully opposing all diversions. However, resisting the forces that may distract attention takes energy and

---

[596] I Thessalonians 5:17
[597] Ephesians 4:6

wears us down, diminishing our power to produce according to the idea we hold in mind.

Desire is a great factor in making thought productive; the more intense the desire, the greater is the onward impulse of the thought and the greater is the power to produce desirable results. However, the desire must be one-pointed in order that Mind substance may assemble around the single idea to support it and give it body. When a single God idea fills the consciousness, there is no room for other thoughts to enter; one's entire interest and attention is given to it and no energy is expended in resisting other thoughts. For this reason, we take some statement of Truth into our mind, dwell on it until its inner meaning becomes a realization. Then the idea is free to do its work in and through us.

2. What is an affirmation?

An affirmation is making firm in consciousness that which is true of God and us; it is declaring as true in human experience that which is already true in Spirit.

An affirmation is a statement of Truth, spoken silently or audibly, or written for use by an individual. The word affirm comes from the Latin prefix af, an assimilated form of ad, meaning to add to or intensify, and firmare, meaning to make firm, stable. Affirmation is the claiming of what we believe (have faith) is already ours. If we have not felt our oneness with God and the spiritual principles, or laws of God, that we call divine ideas, we affirm in order to establish them as a conscious part of our mind or soul consciousness.

The constant repetition of Truth adds firmness to firmness, strength to strength, and causes a divine principle to become established in our subconscious (heart) or feeling nature. When both the conscious phase of mind (intellect, thinking faculty) and the heart (subconscious, feeling faculty) have accepted the truth behind the words of the affirmation, then the true meaning is established in our consciousness.

The power to affirm, to say "yes" to any idea, belief, or concept that comes to us, is a part of every one's divine heritage. However, too often we have misused our spiritual and mental powers and have affirmed or said "yes" to false beliefs and wrong concepts. By this wrong use of mind activity, we builds up a false standard that produces inharmony and discord in our minds, our bodies, and our affairs. For this reason we each need to be ever alert to affirm or say "yes" only to that which is true of us as an expression of God; affirm only that which we desire to see manifest in our lives.[598]

3. How are we helped by affirming Truth?

As explained, through the practice of affirming Truth, we consciously "feed" our soul with the substance of God, our "daily bread," in the form of divine ideas. As we daily affirm words of Truth, we are making our mind a storehouse of the principles of Being (God). However, our conscious phase of mind, the thinking faculty, which is constantly in touch with the outer world through the five senses, needs disciplining and help. Affirmation of Truth keeps the consciousness up to the Truth level whenever we are tempted to think or feel that which is not true. Affirming Truth (eating of our "daily bread") gives us courage and confidence to meet the experiences of daily living, and stimulates us to reach for higher goals.

The greatest help to be received from affirming Truth is that it causes us to arrive at the state of

---

[598] See Lesson 5, Lessons in Truth

consciousness where we no longer find it necessary to say actual words — we think the Truth habitually; we feel Truth habitually; we act habitually in accordance with Truth. We have identified our self with Truth until it is manifested through us both consciously and subconsciously. Just as the eating of our food each day provides the body with the various elements it needs as it goes through the processes of mastication, digestion, and assimilation, so our mind can "eat" of words of Truth masticating, digesting, and assimilating the ideas that are back of the words.

4. **Give three affirmations that help one to realize unity with God.**

    One point to be remembered is that "unity" means oneness, sameness, likeness. It is through knowing God that conscious union is made. Bear in mind that a keyword here is realize. We need more than an intellectual approach (talking about God) — we need a spiritual approach (talking to God).

Chapter 16
1. **What is the difference between spiritual understanding and intellectual understanding?**

    This subject is covered very extensively in the eighth lesson of *Lessons in Truth*.[599] We can say that the difference between these two types of understanding is the difference between that which is revealed by Spirit within and that which is apprehended through the use of the senses and the thinking faculty or intellect. Intellectual understanding may present information about God, but spiritual understanding knows God.

---

[599] Cady, H. Emilie *Lessons in Truth*, Lessons 1, 2, 5, 6 and 8

When our consciousness is attuned to Spirit we receive ideas direct from Divine Mind within our self, where all is Truth, order, and perfection. As we learn the value of these divine ideas, and learn also to use them in the right way, we attain spiritual understanding.

When our consciousness is directed only toward the external world we receive information through the five senses, which information is then handled by our intellect, or thinking faculty. It is here that we observe ideas, things, people, even beliefs about God, for the intellect or thinking is the realm of choice and judgment. Too often through ignorance we judge from the appearance of some manifestation, not from the reality. Intellectual knowledge acquired through the five senses and handled by the intellect may be good as far as it goes, but in accepting such knowledge as final we stand in danger of weakening our conscious contact with Divine Mind and putting our dependence on the external world. Unless intellectual understanding has become blended with Truth, it can fill an individual's life with restlessness and dissatisfaction, giving a sense of insecurity.

We must come to see the true relation of intellectual understanding and spiritual understanding, and perhaps the following words of Charles Fillmore found in *Keep a True Lent*[600] help to make this clear:

> *Intellectual understanding comes first in the soul's development, then a deeper understanding of principles follows, until the whole person ripens into wisdom.*

---

[600] Fillmore, Charles *Keep a True Lent*, Page 155

Chapter 17
1. **What will aid us in understanding how the one Mind creates?**

An understanding of our own mind and how it operates will aid us in understanding how the one Mind, Spirit, creates. What we term our mind is not a mental sphere that is separate from and independent of the one Creative Mind; it is the consciousness each person makes for himself, through using the one Mind essence (ideas) and the God-power, inherent in him. This one Mind essence is omnipresent and links all together as one life, one Mind, one Spirit, causing vitality and consciousness through the universe at the level of each species of creation.

The Christ Mind inherent in each and every one of us is our portion of the God substance that is for our own use. Out of this Christ Mind (Superconscious), which is ours to bring forth, we are to develop a super-mental consciousness termed the individual Christ consciousness. We are able to transform our personal mental sphere by prayer, by keeping in contact with God Mind in order to receive revelation, inspiration, and the guidance necessary to keep our life harmonious.

The human consciousness — the consciousness of humanity as a whole, of mankind as a species — may be likened to the strata of the earth. It ranges from the shifting, unstable sensations of the sensual, instinctive, intellectual, intuitional, psychical, emotional formations of our personal thoughts, to the stratum of abstract ideals. Philosophers have been prone to regard these ideals as too high for the ordinary individuals to reach in our daily living.

2. Through whom are the divine attributes, or ideas, brought into expression and manifestation?

The divine attributes, or ideas, are brought into expression and manifestation by manifest individuals. Primarily "expression" is the inner working of manifest individual's mental sphere to unfold or form a concept of the God ideas contained in his spiritual Self, "that I AM," the image of God. Man possesses the entire God nature in an undeveloped state. The elements (ideas) that make up this nature are to be released as manifest individuals gain a consciousness of them through prayer and experience. They are not to remain latent but are for our use for the unfoldment of the Godlikeness in manifestation.

God's work of creating the spiritual patterns (ideas) and providing the substance as the resource for us to use is finished. It is the manifest individual's part to get in touch with the indwelling God, our Christ self. Through prayer and meditation we gain knowledge of the essential nature of each quality or idea and learn how to co-ordinate all in an orderly way. Thus he may satisfactorily manifest these ideas to take care of the problems that confront us in daily living. We are the channel through which God-Mind flows. We may receive all that God-Mind is and give forth as fully as we receive. This constitutes obedience to the law of giving and receiving.

Chapter 18

1. Explain the meaning of the names Christ, Jesus, and Jesus Christ from the historical and metaphysical standpoint.

From the historical standpoint the terms Christ, Jesus, and Jesus Christ are names or titles applied to the Man of Nazareth, the great Healer, Teacher, Overcomer, and resurrected Lord, who according to Christian belief is the Savior of mankind. "You shall call his name Jesus, for he will save his people from their sins".[601]

As brought out in the lesson text, from the metaphysical standpoint Christ is the image of God, the Word, the Son, the Law, the pattern of perfection in each person. Christ is the I AM identity; the perfect Self of every person; the divine pattern in every person; a name for the first phase of every person's threefold nature (spirit, soul, and body).

Jesus (metaphysically) is the likeness of God; the understanding use of the Christ pattern.

Jesus Christ (metaphysically) is the radiant, living Presence, the perfected consciousness that is carrying out God's plan in every person.

2. What was Jesus' realization of oneness with God?

Jesus declared, "I and the Father are one".[602] When Philip said, "Lord, show us the Father, and we shall be satisfied," Jesus' reply was, "He who has seen me has seen the Father".[603] Jesus was keenly conscious of the character of God and of His relationship to Him. He knew that His character was one with that of God; that His identity was divine.

Jesus knew God as unlimited love, as ever-present, abundant life. He knew God as infinite wisdom and supply. He knew God as the Father, who is ever ready and willing to supply every need of the human heart. Jesus knew that as a son of God He had access to every blessing of God the Father. Jesus did not simply believe that the words He spoke were true — He knew they were true. His words had

---

[601] Matthew 1:21
[602] John 10:30
[603] John 14: 8,9

deep meaning, for they were vital, living words that carried conviction, and more important, they produced immediate results.

3. What was Jesus' custom in the matter of self-identification?

Jesus recognized Himself as God's "image" and knew that God's "likeness" was in the process of being brought forth, yet He continually affirmed that the Father within did the work.

It is a law that we manifest as that with which we identify ourselves. Jesus' custom was to identify Himself with His real or Christ self, the Son of God, the Word, the I AM, the Logos. If we would identify ourselves with God as Jesus did, then the errors of human consciousness, built up through acceptance of the concept of us as merely a biological organism, must be denied. We must refuse to use the powers of the I AM to produce conditions in mind, body, and affairs based on false conceptions.

> *We can use I AM power to restore health and bring increased happiness ... some people are using this power in a material way, neglecting soul culture, building up the external without taking the intermediate step between the supreme Mind and its manifestation in the outer.*[604]

4. Why did many of the Jews not recognize Jesus as the Son of God?

Many of the ancient Hebrews failed to recognize Jesus as the Son of God because they were expecting a Messiah who would come among them and reign like a

---
[604] Fillmore, Charles *Jesus Christ Heals*, p. 124

king on an earthly throne. They were looking for a great personality to come and lead them into racial and religious supremacy.

Since the true Messiah was then as now primarily an ideal in God-Mind, the worldly-minded people of Jesus' time were unable to discern the Christ Spirit as revealed by the Nazarene. This does not mean that these people did not have the capacity to know the indwelling Christ. It means that they had misinterpreted the Scriptures and centered their attention on the "letter" instead of the "spirit" of their own sacred writings. Many people today do not recognize the Son of God as He stands knocking at the door of their soul. Human beings are often too busily engaged in the hustle and bustle of the outer world to acquaint themselves with this Presence and Power that is within their own being — "Christ in you"[605] — or they are ignorant of its reality.

Then there are those who yearn desperately for the coming of the Savior but who "crucify" the Christ daily through putting it outside of themselves — waiting for and expecting an outer personality just as did the ancient Hebrews. The Messiah was there in the Nazarene's day Just as the Christ is here today — as the real nature of everyone waiting to come forth. If we would know the glory of the Christ or Son-of-God presence, we need only recognize the Christ within and let the Christ come forth in our everyday life in our thoughts, words, and deeds. "Observe all that I have commanded you; and lo, I am with you always, to the close of the age".[606]

---

[605] Colossians 1:27
[606] Matthew 28:20

5. What is the atonement?

The original root meaning of the verb atone was "to make at one," by reconciling differences between those who had been at variance. Metaphysically, the "atonement" is the blending and harmonious functioning of the Superconscious (realm of divine ideas in man, the realm of pure knowing), the conscious (thinking, reasoning faculty, the intellect), and the subconscious (realm of feeling, emotions, the heart).

In an unenlightened state of knowing we may have felt ourselves separated from goodness by looking upon God as "a holy Being" separate from us; feeling iniquity (inequality) in not being able to measure up to God's standard of holiness. However, Jesus of Nazareth taught at-one-ment. "I and the Father are one," he said.[607] In spite of what we think, feel, do with our inheritance of good, the important Truth taught in these lessons is that God and we are one.

Jesus, the Man, taught the relationship of God and us as Father and son. He showed the likeness to God, emphasizing inherent God nature. He encouraged people to claim and prove this oneness (at-one-ment) as he had done. He instructed them how to put away all their limited beliefs in sin and lack by the use of denials and to claim their divinity, and their oneness, by affirming it to be true.

Jesus did not make the atonement for us — He showed us how to reestablish the ideal in which we were created. Each of us must therefore put into action the mental laws that can bring about the atonement through working out our own salvation.

---

[607] John 10:30

If we are the son of God, we must be that son right now; sonship must be just as real, just as omnipresent, as the health that God has revealed through His Word. How shall we reveal our sonship to self and to others except by claiming it; by declaring that we are not a son of mortality, but a son of God.[608]

Chapter 19
1. What is meant by "asking in His name"?

"Asking in His name" is asking in the nature of the indwelling Christ, the I AM identity. It is asking in the consciousness of the power that the name Jesus Christ carries. It is asking in the "fullness of the Godhead bodily".[609] It is asking in the consciousness that all that is in Jesus Christ is in us, awaiting our recognition and acceptance.

We ask 'in His name' by asking for that which is divinely right and good. We ask 'in His name' when we ask in our own God nature, or in the consciousness of our own Christ self, the I AM within. ...

The name Jesus Christ has come to represent all that God is, expressed in and through us. However, speaking the name is more than the use of just two words — it is the actual expression of the I AM (or Son of God) nature which Jesus manifested".

"Asking in His name" makes us conscious of the power of the spoken word to give definite form to ideas. Ideas that remain unexpressed in the invisible are not of much value as blessings for manifest individuals on earth. "Asking in His name," speaking the word, clothes an idea in

---

[608] Fillmore, Charles *Talks on Truth*, p. 143
[609] Colossians 2:9

form and enables the blessings to come from the unformed into the formed realm. It opens the door between our soul and our spirit, and good flows into our life in the form required to fill any need. "Behold, I stand at the door and knock; if anyone hears my voice and opens the door, I will come in to him".[610]

2. What is true prayer? Answer a:

The subject of prayer is of vital importance to every human heart, because the hopes and the destinies of humankind depend largely upon what we believe concerning the willingness and the power of God to answer prayer. That God hears and answers those who call, millions have believed and have proved. "All things are possible to those that believe."[611]

Knowing that we are able to learn to pray with understanding and always get an answer, we can come to the study of prayer with wholehearted interest.

True prayer is conscious communion with God, actually a common union of the human consciousness with that Presence within, the principle of Absolute Good. The method of prayer is the Silence and it is reached through orderly steps in thinking and feeling.

Jesus promised, "And all things, whatsoever ye shall ask in prayer, believing, ye shall receive.[612] He gave some clear, definite instructions about how to pray, and gave The Lord's Prayer as a model. These instructions and this prayer furnish all necessary information to we pray the fervent, effectual prayer that avails much.

---

[610] Revelation 3:20
[611] Mark 9:23
[612] Matthew 21:22

First, Jesus warned against praying for the purpose of being seen and heard by others; then he taught the true way: "When you pray, enter into your inner chamber, and having shut thy door, pray to God who is in secret, and God who sees in secret shall recompense thee."[613]

The key word in this text is the word, Thou,[614] as Jesus used it. The first and most important point in the study of prayer is to understand the true character of the Presence to whom we pray. Hardly less important is it that we understand our relation to that from which the breath of life comes.

Have you prayed, yet failed to receive? Perhaps you fail to receive because you do not go to God as the Source, believing in a loving readiness to give you good things. The better our understanding of the character of God, the greater will be our consciousness of faith, and the more certainly shall we receive. Great light is thrown upon the true nature of God by the statement of Jesus, "God is Spirit; and those worshiping must worship in Spirit and Truth." This does away with the belief that God is a person and far removed from us. Spirit is Infinite Mind, always and everywhere evenly present. Paul thus describes this omnipresent One and our relation to Him: "For in him we live, and move, and have our being."[615]

Answer b:

True prayer is "conscious communion with God." When we consciously turn our attention to God within, placing our faith in Spirit (God), then we are

---

[613] Matthew 6:6
[614] We have substituted the original Aramaic version of the prayer as it gives a deeper understanding of the meaning as prayed by Jesus.
[615] Acts 17:28

acknowledging the one Presence and Power within our own being. We thus become receptive to divine inspiration in the form of God ideas, and there is no room for any limited concept to find entrance into our mind.

When our consciousness is free from worry or tension we are an open channel for the inflow of the inspiration and enlightenment of Spirit. In the book, *Lessons in Truth*, it states:[616]

> *"In eagerness 'we wait in singleness of heart' for the revelation, inspiration, or illumination from the Father. When God 'speaks' it is the movement of Divine Mind on our mind expressing divine ideas that are absorbed by our waiting consciousness. We have now come to the place where we know!"*

3. **What is the "secret place of the Most High"?**[617]
   Answer a:

   God is everywhere evenly present, but it is within us that conscious union with God is made. Jesus refers to this inner place of union as "your inner chamber," and the Psalmist calls it the "secret place of the Most High."[618] One Bible translation refers to it as "thy closet."

   Answer b:

   The "secret place of the Most High" is

   > *...a place of meeting between the Christ at the center of your being, and your consciousness — a*

---

[616] Lessons in Truth(Lessons In Truth Lesson 10 Annotation 4).Series 1 - Lesson 1 - Annotation 4
[617] Psalm 91:1
[618] ibid

> *hidden place into which no outside person can either induct you or enter himself*[619]

The "secret place of the Most High" is the name the Psalmist uses to designate the "place" within our own being where we may retire to feel God's presence and power. It is where the human consciousness merges with the divine consciousness and Spirit meets spirit (the first phase of our threefold nature). The "secret place" is the point at which we are able to silence all limited thoughts and desires that seem to entice us into sin, and acknowledge the supreme Source of our being. We are then able to contemplate our unity, oneness, and sameness with Divine Mind, the Father within.

Anything is "secret" when it is hidden; the "secret place of the Most High" is that which is hidden from all who are not in the "Most High" state of consciousness.

In our metaphysical study we find that the "secret place" can be explained simply as being the Silence, that phase of prayer when God "speaks" and we "listen" to God's revelations. In *Christian Healing*, Charles Fillmore states:[620]

> *When we pray in spiritual understanding, this highest realm of our mind contacts universal, impersonal Mind; the very mind of God is joined to our mind. God answers our prayers in ideas, thoughts, words; these are translated into the outer realms, in time and condition.*

---

[619] Lessons in Truth 9:6
[620] Fillmore, Charles *Christian Healing* 78

4. **What is the meaning of the expression "going into the silence"?**

"Going into the silence" means just what the previous annotations brought out — turning within to the indwelling Presence of God, our "inner chamber," closing the mind to all outside distractions, and waiting in stillness for God's revelation to us.

Charles Fillmore gives very definite statements about "going into the silence" in *Teach Us to Pray:*[621]

> *"The first step in scientific silence is simply to still . . . outer intellectual thoughts so that the consciousness may become subservient to the Spirit within. . . . God works in the stillness. As we come into the presence of God with prayer in the form of an affirmation of Truth... we are aware only of the soundlessness of God's word as it weaves itself in and out through the whole soul and body consciousness."*

5. **What is meant by "Enter into your inner chamber, and... shut your door"?[622] Answer a:**

"Enter into your inner chamber" — that is, turn your attention from the without to the within. "And having shut thy door, pray." To close the door is to still the five senses that connect one directly with the outer world. They will keep calling the attention without, if they are allowed to do so. Closing the eyes helps very much in closing the door to the outer world. Then "pray to God who is in secret." This inner closet of prayer is the secret

---

[621] Fillmore, Charles *Teach Us to Pray*, pages 24-25
[622] Matthew 6:6

meeting place between God and us. It is a place of stillness, of silence, so we speak of entering it as "going into the silence."

Answer b:

It is important that we realize that the instruction given by Jesus to "enter into your inner chamber" and to "shut the door" is not something mysterious but a simple turning within. The instruction telling us to "enter" also advises us to "shut the door," meaning that we are to close the mind to anything of the outer that would intrude upon this meeting with Spirit. In *Teach Us to Pray*, Charles Fillmore states:[623]

> *What we need to know above all is that there is a place within our soul where we can consciously meet God and receive a flood of new life into not only our mind but also our body . . . . Quietly entering the inner chamber within the soul shutting the door to the external thoughts of daily life, and seeking conscious union with God is the highest form of prayer we know*

Once we have entered the "inner chamber" which is God's Presence in us, it becomes a simple matter to close the mind to all that would call our attention away from the light, life, and love of God that permeates and enfolds us; yet it often requires discipline to control our thinking and feeling. The five senses need to be controlled so that the physical eyes are closed to all outer objects or situations; the physical ears no longer listen to the noises of the objective world. This also means that the mind must

---

[623] Fillmore, Charles *Teach Us to Pray*, 5, 17

be controlled so that past thought forms or psychic phenomena must not be allowed to interfere with this sacred time.

6. **What is it to "hallow" the name of God? Answer a:**
In the King James language, "Hallowed be thy name." Hallowed comes from a word that means wholeness. God's name is "I AM" which is wholeness and perfection. It should be so realized by us. "To hallow" is to make whole, sacred, pure, holy, or perfect. You are God's character, God's being, and God's expression. Are you seeking to bring forth that perfection, the reality of your spiritual nature? Stop and ask yourself these questions: "Am I, the expression of God, hallowing God's name? Am I being that which God is? Am I bringing forth in thought, word, and deed—in mind, body, and affairs—the perfection which I really am?"

Answer b:
To "hallow" the name of God means to recognize God's nature (name) as wholeness and perfection. To hallow is to consecrate and hold in reverence; to make holy, or whole. The name of God is the nature of God, thus to use the name (nature) of God only in relation to that which is good is to "hallow" the name of God.[624]

God is to each person whatever that person can conceive Him to be -- whatever the person's concept of God is. Regardless of the way one may conceive Him, God is Absolute Good in all its perfection and wholeness. The name of anything is its whole nature; it bespeaks the thing's character, its power, its authority. Therefore, when we speak of or to God we must recognize and reverence

---
[624] How I Used Truth, Lesson 3 Annotation 2, 3

Him as Absolute Good -- this is "hallowing" the name of God.

We must come to understand that God is Principle, Law, and that God bestows no new favors upon us for hallowing God's name. We simply open the door of our mind, our heart, and through this opening Absolute Good in its fullness pours into our whole being. By this "hallowing" of God's name or nature, we make contact with the highest good that we are capable of receiving and sublimate or refine our human (moral) nature so that it becomes a fit channel for the expression of our divine nature, our real Self.

7. **What is "our daily bread"?[625] Answer a:**

The lesson material brings out very clearly that according to our teaching "bread" is representative of all the divine ideas that "feed" the soul. These ideas are divine substance and the following from *The Revealing Word* covers this point:[626]

> *Bread -- Representative of universal substance. . . . Our daily bread is the sustenance for spirit, mind, and body. Some of this daily bread is appropriated in the form of food. There is substance in words of Truth, and this substance is appropriated by prayer and meditation on Truth.*

Most people feel it is vital to feed the body daily with physical food, and certain periods are set aside for mealtimes. When one becomes aware of the needs of the soul, we realize that the soul has need of its "daily bread

---

[625] Matthew 6:11
[626] Fillmore, Charles *The Revealing Word*, page 29

"in the form of divine ideas, otherwise the soul is starved for the only sustenance upon which it can really "feed."

Bread has been referred to as the "staff of life." A staff is a stick, carried in the hand, upon which one may lean for support. In Truth study, substance ("bread") is the support that God has provided for all states of our being. Life could not be made manifest unless it were "embodied," hence the necessity of substance through which to give expression and manifestation to life, to give it "body."

We are threefold beings — spirit, soul, body — and each phase of our being has need of its special food; needs to be nourished, sustained, and satisfied in order that we may be channels for the expression and manifestation of the God nature.

Let us consider other words of Scripture related to food:

> *"It is written, we shall not live by bread alone, but by every word that proceeds from the mouth of God".*[627]
>
> "He ... fed you with manna, which you did not know ... that he might make you know that we do not live by bread alone"[628]
>
> "Jesus said to them, my food is to do the will of him who sent me, and to accomplish God's work".[629]

---

[627] Matthew 4:4
[628] Deuteronomy 8:3
[629] John 4:34

"Do not labor for the food which perishes, but for the food which endures to eternal life".[630]

"I am the bread of life . . . This is the bread which comes down from heaven".[631]

From these sayings it is clear that our concern should be to feed, through prayer, upon the Word of God — the I AM — the living substance that is within every human being, providing us with the necessary sustenance for both the inner and outer life.
To sum up the meaning of "our daily bread," we say that it is the spiritual ideas, inspirations through which we enlarge our consciousness of God and God's creation. It is through "our daily bread "that we have the courage and the strength to meet our experiences at opportunities to do God's will and thus to make God manifest in the world of visibility.

Answer b:

"Give us this day our daily bread." Jesus said, "We shall not live by bread alone, but by every word that proceeds out of the mouth of God."[632] This petition, then, must have a larger meaning than is commonly believed. "Daily bread" means more than the food that is eaten physically. "Dally bread" is divine ideas that feed and nourish the soul and build states of consciousness that accords with the will of God. There is a substance in true words and no one lives life to the fullest unless we feed upon words of Truth in dally prayer and meditation.

---

[630] John 6:27
[631] John 6:48,50
[632] Matthew 4:4

"And forgive us our debts, as we also have forgiven our debtors." There is a law involved here. According to this law we cannot be forgiven until we first forgive. This would be seen more clearly if the prayer were put in the affirmative form, thus: we are forgiven our debts as we forgive our debtors.

"And bring us not into temptation, but deliver us from the evil one." All things originate in mind, and evil comes from wrong thinking. To be delivered from evil is to have the mind cleansed from all belief in evil by the Spirit in us, by prayer find meditation. In this way who are delivered from evil, delivered from the very last one of the thoughts of evil that may be in mind. So long as one false thought or belief remains, our mind needs the purifying power of the Christ Mind.

8. Explain why it is necessary to pray believing that we have received. Answer a:

It is necessary to pray believing (with faith) that we have received the good we desire, because our believing opens the door of our consciousness to receive the idea that is back of our desired good. This believing (faith) goes further than our consciousness or mind; it acts like a magnet to draw the outer forms that can fulfill our desire.

We live, move, and have our being in divine substance which is provided for our use in satisfying our longings and fulfilling our every need. All good is ours now and always has been, just as all air is ours to breathe freely.

We often refer to divine substance as the presence of God. To each of us is entrusted the power to mold this substance into the forms that fit our needs. But in order to lay hold of this substance, we have to believe (i.e., perceive through our faith faculty) that it is inherent in us as part of our divine inheritance. Through prayer we are able to appropriate this substance, in which inhere the ideas that are our "daily bread," and this appropriation should be as spontaneous and effortless as the appropriation of the air that we breathe. The mental attitude of faith, or believing, seems to correspond to the physical action of breathing air into the lungs.

The abundance that we call divine substance has always been ours, but we have lost sight of it. Because of this and our need for "daily bread," we feel the impulse to pray. When we do pray believing, our attitude becomes positive and expectant toward the answer. We are able to act as though we had already received the answer in the outer. It is through our faith, or believing, that we make way in consciousness to accept the fulfillment of all of the promises of God to us as God's beloved children. It is only our faith in God as our Source and in God's promises that we are able to mold rightly the omnipresent substance into the forms ("our daily bread") that can meet our needs.

Answer b:

One of the secrets of prayer is revealed in this promise: "All things whatsoever ye pray and ask for, believe that ye receive them, and ye shall have them." This is mysterious only until we see that it is the way of faith. "Faith is the perceiving power of the mind linked with a power to shape substance."[633] Faith shapes substance into the desired form or shape. At the tomb of Lazarus, before Lazarus came forth, Jesus said: "Father, I thank thee that you heard me. And I knew that you hear me

---

[633] Fillmore, Charles *Prosperity* Unity Books, page 43

always."[634] He knew that he had the answer, even before he saw it manifested. When he increased the loaves and the fishes, he gave thanks before he saw the demonstration. To claim the answer and to give thanks for it, unwaveringly believing in God as absolutely unfailing, even before you see the proof, is one of the greatest lessons that we learn in connection with prayer. This is the prayer of faith. With God there "can be no variation, neither shadow that is cast by turning."[635] All that God is, all that God does, all that God says, are exact law and can no more fail than following the rules in arithmetic can fail to produce the correct answer. This is the basis of our faith in prayer and this is why it is absolutely safe to claim the good God has promised and give thanks for it before we see it manifested.

9. What is meant by "holding a thought "as used in connection with prayer? Answer a:

"Holding a thought" as used in prayer means taking into the silence of our being a statement of some spiritual good that we desire to see manifest. The statement "holding a thought" is the same as "holding to the Truth," and we find further explanation of this in How I Used Truth.[636]:

> *"By this familiar statement, we mean holding words in mind that declare the reality of God, a person, a situation, or a thing until the meaning of the ideas back of the words becomes clear to our*

---

[634] John 11:41-42
[635] James 1:17
[636] How I Used Truth.[636] Lesson 8 Annotation 1, "Trusting and Resting

> *consciousness (thinking and feeling). . . . If we are 'holding to the Truth' with a sense of anxiety concerning the answer to our prayer, then we are not knowing that God is in charge. . . . When we 'let go and let God' we are releasing everything erroneous or limited from our thinking and feeling and letting our consciousness be open and receptive to the inspiration of God ideas."*

At first the thought or statement is viewed intellectually only. By affirming it over and over (silently or audibly), mentally studying its meaning, and from time to time excluding (denying) all other thoughts from our attention, we give all our interest to this statement in absorbed concentration. Meditating on the ideas embodied in each word of the statement or prayer holds the mind steadily focused and helps us attain a fuller understanding of the context of the statement or prayer — and thus we are "holding the thought" or "holding to the Truth." Meditation and concentration enable one to obtain mental control; this activity is carried on in the brain. But to reach the desired good requires more than this. It is through contemplation in the heart, or the feeling side of the soul, we come in conscious contact with the intuitional state of our being that leads to illumination. The "spirit" (i.e., the meaning) of the thought in the statement becomes alive to us, and we begin to see with the inner eye.

> *For the letter kills, but the spirit giveth life*[637]

---

[637] II Corinthians 3:6

This coming alive causes every area of our life — thinking, feeling, speaking, acting — to express and manifest the spirit of the statement.

Answer b:

Students of practical Christianity sometimes speak of "holding a thought." This means that they take some statement of Truth into the silence, repeat it over and over, and meditate upon it until they realize its meaning, until it becomes alive in consciousness as spiritual understanding. This is the way to come into understanding.

It is natural for the one who is yet in ignorance of the great all-knowing One within him to want to seek here and there of some teacher or some book for explanation of various texts of Scripture, but the only way to come into the knowledge of Truth is to seek the kingdom within. Teachers and books are helpful because they turn our attention within and help us to have faith in our indwelling Spirit.

The power to "hold a thought" is the power to concentrate upon an idea. Concentration, as used in its application to spiritual development, means the act of fixing the attention upon a central idea and drawing all the thoughts to that center. The thoughts of men require discipline. Thinking to a purpose must take the place of thinking at random. The silence gives thought discipline. Power to direct and control thought comes not from the personal will but by centering within, in I AM. Thus poise and self-control are attained in our thoughts and feelings, in realization.

10. Name and explain the eight necessary conditions of true prayer.

We must
1. Direct our prayer to God within our own being, God's Presence in us.
2. Acknowledge God as the Father-Mind which contains, constitutes, creates, sustains, and governs all that is.
3. Know that each of us is the son-idea, forever one and the same as the Father-Mind — God's image-likeness.
4. Enter the "inner chamber," the very core of our being, the innermost recess of our soul.
5. Close the door to both physical and psychical phenomena. (We are seeking Spirit, not phenomena of any kind.)
6. Seek to know, to understand the substance of Being, the kingdom of God, and the laws governing its presence and use.
7. Have faith that Absolute Good, God, is the one Presence and the one Power in the universe and that the good we especially desire is now being manifested.
8. Realize that the forgiving love of God, the love of God intelligently active in us, dissipates and dissolves all that is unlike the nature of God. We are to exercise that spirit of love by forgiving all short-comings (sins) in ourselves and in all other persons.

11. Why is it necessary to be still in order to come into a realization of Truth?

The realization of Truth cannot come to a mind that is not still, but is concerned with the exterior world. A divided mind cannot receive the revelations of God; these come only to a mind that is still, that is alert and concentrated on the "still small voice".[638] Truth is the vision, the ideal we perceive through soul insight, and if the "sight" is turned outward it is not insight. When the soul is still, we are offering God a listening and a heeding attitude. We will then receive the true guidance that can help us to go about our business in the outer world.

Prayer is the line of conscious communion between us and our Creator. In the "Secret place of the Most High"[639] within our own being, we appropriate the divine ideas that belong to God consciousness. It is in this "secret place" of prayer that we learn that the will of God is for our highest good. Only in the stillness can the full revelation come to our soul. For prayer to be effectual, we need to abide in the realization that our true place is in the one creative Mind, where all is peace and harmony. Therefore, we must learn to keep silence before God; to still the false reports of the senses that impinge on our consciousness, so that we may listen to the "still small voice" that will teach us all things — even the deep things of God.

Chapter 24
1. Give reasons for considering the Scriptures allegorical.

An allegory is a description of one thing or event, under the image of another which resembles it in properties and circumstances. In the Bible an allegory is the presentation of abstract principles under the guise of concrete forms.

---
[638] I Kings 19:12
[639] Psalm 91:1

A symbol is a visible sign, one that is conventional or traditional, of something invisible — as an idea, a quality, or an inner spiritual ideal that may not be adequately expressed in language or form. For example, the lion symbolizes courage; a nimbus enclosing a cross symbolizes Christ. Philosophers considered the ideal as being so perfect that they deemed it impossible to reproduce or duplicate the ideal in the exterior.

> *What is stated in the Book of Genesis in the form of allegory can be reduced to ideas, and these ideas can be worked out by the guidance of mental laws.*[640]

The word scriptures has come to mean any sacred writings. Before these sacred subjects were writings, they were handed down by word of mouth from one generation to another, especially in the East. The symbols used became confused with traditions. The result is symbolical allegories in which original ideas that were revealed to inspired men are mixed with events, characters, and cities. These finally became "scriptures." In these allegories and symbols there is given a plan for us to follow in order that he may live an enriched life religiously, economically, politically, and socially.

In Unity's Christian Scripture course we read:

> *A parable is a short story dealing with familiar subjects or situations, and is told for the purpose of illustrating or making clear some important truth or phase of teaching. Thus, the value of the parable is to be found not in the actual story, but in the truth*

---

[640] Fillmore, Charles *Mysteries of Genesis*, p. 9

> *or teaching which it pictorially presents. A popular definition is: "A parable is an earthly story with a heavenly meaning.*

In interpreting the allegories, symbols, and metaphors given in our Scriptures, many have done so from an undeveloped state of consciousness. They have accepted and insisted on the "letter" of the word instead of the spiritual meaning that it is intended to convey. The meaning was "veiled" behind forms, rites, ceremonies, and creeds, and was not deduced from the story that was told.

2. What phase of creation is described in the first chapter of Genesis?

The first chapter of Genesis is considered to be an allegorical description of the ideal or spiritual phase of creation—the blueprint stage. It is a record of the creation of spiritual mankind (the Jehovah, the I AM, the Christ, the Lord God, the only-begotten Son, the human created in God's image and after His likeness, the direct offspring of Divine Mind). It is considered to be a statement of the ideas upon which evolution is based. This description does not include manifest, objective, or evolutional human, the human being. Rather it deals with involution—ideas involved in creation. This creation takes place in the one creative Mind, Spirit, where God (Elohim) acts in His capacity as creative power.

We are to understand that God (Elohim) created the substance that produces the appearance (matter). God (Elohim), Spirit, creates the spiritual idea which is afterward made manifest through Jehovah God, spiritual human, the created. God created the ideas that produced creation, including ideal human, and He pronounced this creation "good" and "very good." That perfect or ideal human is the essential spiritual image in every individual, with the potential to come forth into manifestation in compliance with spiritual law.

3. What evidence have we in the Bible that this is an ideal and not a manifest creation?

The first chapter of Genesis describes the ideal creation of humankind and states that God "finished" His work in the ideal or planning stage. The second chapter makes the announcement that "there was not a man to till the ground".[641] This shows that while the spiritual human had been created as the image of God, the physical human had not yet been manifested; he had not yet evolved as a human being, as a human living in a three-dimensional form or body who could "till the ground" so that it might yield its increase.

Often words are regarded as synonymous that, strictly speaking, are not. The words expression and manifestation are examples. Expression means the pressing out or fulfilling of an idea in all its details in consciousness. It is the process of the formative power of thought, the making of an image of what is expected to be brought forth later on. Manifestation is result, the fulfillment of expression, the formed word, the living object that appears in the sphere of the senses.

"A man to till the ground"[642] would necessarily be a manifest man. It would take a natural human to work in the natural sphere of creation—a human equipped with a body or form that would make connection with and have somewhat of an understanding of nature.

---

[641] Genesis 2:5
[642] Genesis 2:5

This is the evidence that the Bible presents to us that there is first the ideal creation (expression in mind of the plan), and later on the manifestation makes its appearance.

4. Who or what is Jehovah, the Lord God of the Scriptures?

Jehovah, the Lord God of the Scriptures, is the name that is given to spiritual human, the image of God. "Then God said, Let us make man in our image, after our likeness".[643] The Lord God, or Jehovah, is God individuated in humankind as the creative power of God, the law of our being. The Lord God, or Jehovah, is the creative life principle that originates and sustains all life, all consciousness, from the highest to the lowest levels of intelligence. The Lord God, or Jehovah, is the one Presence and one Power individuated in us as our spiritual nature, our power to express and manifest our perfection as the image of God.

The one that God created in God's own image and likeness and pronounced good and very good is spiritual mankind. We are the direct offspring of Divine Mind, God's idea of perfect. This is the only-begotten Son, the Christ, the Lord God, the Jehovah, the I AM. In the second chapter this Jehovah or divine idea of perfect mankind forms the manifest human and calls his name Adam.[644]

In the *Scofield Reference Bible*, page 6, we find this definition of Jehovah or Lord God:

> *The primary meaning of the name Lord (Jehovah) is "the self-existent One" ... But Havah, from which*

---

[643] Genesis 1:26
[644] Fillmore, Charles Mysteries of Genesis, p. 12

Jehovah, or Yahweh, is formed, signifies also "to become," that is, to become known, thus pointing to a continuous and increasing self-revelation. Combining these meanings of Havah, we arrive at the meaning of the name Jehovah. He is "the self-revealing One" who reveals Himself.

The people of the Hebrew times did not recognize Jehovah, the Lord God, as the creative, executive, and causative power, the law of their being. They did not recognize this very Presence and Power of God working in and through them to bring to them the very highest good that was possible for them to have at their level of consciousness. They thought of Jehovah as their special tribal God, somewhere apart from them. They attributed to Him the power to bless and to curse, to send happiness, peace, and prosperity, and also to send floods, fires, and other forms of destruction. Sometimes we find Him pictured as a God of vengeance, visiting His wrath upon mankind; sometimes we find Him pictured as a God of lovingkindness. Sometimes He is pictured as a punisher, sometimes as a deliverer. This same concept is prevalent among many people today.

Unity's explanation of these varied concepts of the Lord God, or Jehovah, is that in the evolving soul, the human being, the creative power of God becomes a causative power as it works in our mental realm, the realm of cause and effect (the realm of man's thinking and feeling). It produces for us that which accords with our thoughts, feelings, and words. "As we think in our heart so are we".[645] in manifestation, or in other words, as we think and feel so are we in our everyday experiences.

---

[645] Proverbs 23:7

The writers of the Christian Scriptures had evolved in soul growth and had come to the place in consciousness where they caught a glimpse of the perfect working of this causative power in us, and they called it the Christ.

The Christ is the name of the perfect working of the creative and causative power of God in our spirit, soul, body, producing only good. The Christ is this self-revealing One, revealing self to us in all power, in all fullness, working and producing the image of God in the likeness of God.

5. **What and where is the "tree of life" as spoken of in the Scriptures?**

The "tree of life"[646] is a figurative expression denoting God immanent (indwelling) as the Creator and Sustainer of life in all living forms; it is the inherent life of all organisms. We also refer to it as the life principle, the I AM, the spiritual center in every person.

> *The "tree of life also in the midst of the garden" represents the absolute life principle established in our consciousness by Divine Mind.*[647]

Life is a continuous stream of energy, and emanation of God, energizing all the forms that have evolved that they may live and fulfill the purpose for which they have come forth. Inherent in the "tree of life" is the intelligence that reveals to each manifestation or form the way of life and growth and the capacity to fulfill this way. Also inherent in the "tree of life" is the law of each species

---

[646] Genesis 2:9
[647] *Metaphysical Bible Dictionary*, p. 663

by which it lives, evolves, and reproduces according to the type or pattern of its kind.

Life in its branching—as a tree—in our threefold nature, is in our spiritual nature termed the I AM, the Christ, the life principle; in our soul nature (mind, conscious and subconscious) it is the assimilation we make of the life principle and which we express psychologically; in our body nature, life is physiologically manifested and neurologically expressed in our nervous system.

6. **How should the Scriptures be "divided" in interpreting the use of the term man?**

The term man is used in the Scriptures with two references. In some instances the reference is made to manifest humans, the human being, the evolutionary person, the out-picturing of the unfolding of our soul. In other instances, it is made to the un-manifest man, our spirit, the Christ, the evolutionary image. Statements that otherwise appear contradictory are reconcilable in this framework of reference.

As an example of this, "man" is sometimes referred to as being of the earth, earthy, no health in him. Again it is referred to as the image-likeness of God, alive forevermore as the Son of God. Jesus sometimes referred to Himself from the two levels of His nature, the human and the divine. John records his saying, "I can do nothing on my own authority."[648] But Matthew quotes him stating, "All authority in heaven and on earth has been given to me."[649]

The Scriptural references to man that proclaim his limitations are made from the human viewpoint without

---

[648] John 5:30
[649] Matthew 28:18

consideration of spiritual possibilities. The references that proclaim his divine potentialities are made from the viewpoint that sees us as primarily spiritual beings, expressing and manifesting through a soul and body.

7. What does the "heart," as the term is used in the Scriptures, represent?

The "heart," as used here, represents the subconscious phase of mind, the feeling nature, the storehouse of memory and experience. The heart of anything is the part nearest the center, the more essential part of any body system — the place where life activity is carried on. "As we think in our heart, so are we"[650] may be interpreted, "As we believe in our heart or subconscious, so do we live or experience." The subconscious holds the memory of the sensations and the responses made as feelings, to conditions that were presented and through which the body passed as experiences on the evolutionary path. The sum of our feelings in regard to these experiences constitutes our emotional nature. If the heart is filled with unhappy memories of lack, sin, sickness, sorrow, and death that we have passed through it in connection with those near and dear to us, these beliefs harbored in the subconscious will act as causes to reproduce these experiences again and again until they are cleansed from consciousness.

8. How do we demonstrate the mastery and dominion which are ours as mentioned in Genesis 1:26?

Mastery and dominion are part of our divine inheritance as the image-likeness of God. Mastery and

---

[650] Proverbs 23:7

dominion are exercised as we lay hold of the power of God. "Ye shall receive power, when the Holy Spirit has come upon you".[651]

Dominion over the earth is not something that is to be acquired through physical evolution. We are created with dominion over the earth and told to subdue it. Our "earth" is primarily the human consciousness wherein we have established beliefs in "good" and "not good." We are to accept our dominion through knowing that we are God's presence on earth, the very image of God. Then we must claim our divine mastery by taking control of our own consciousness, and showing forth the likeness of God.

Jesus said, "But when the Son of man shall come in his glory, and all the angels with him, then shall he sit on the throne of his glory ... he shall set the sheep on his right hand, but the goats on the left".[652] Every human being has within consciousness the "sheep" and the "goats" which represent two types of thoughts. The thoughts, desires, and feelings that are on the positive, spiritual side are the "sheep," while the stubborn, selfish, resistant, fearful, anxious, and greedy thoughts, feelings, and desires are the "goats." These latter are to be denied or crossed out of the human consciousness where they are causing friction. When we become master over our own thinking and feeling, we comes into the glory of the Father.

We learn to demonstrate mastery and dominion when we are able to discern between the earth (consciousness) and the world (appearances), and consciously separate the "sheep" and the "goats" within ourselves by our spoken word of authority. We learn to deny the "not good" and affirm the "good," thus freeing

---

[651] Acts 1:8
[652] Matthew 25:31, 33

ourselves from belief in the reality of evil and its power over us.

9. **What is meant by the statement, "I will put my law in their inward parts, and in their heart will I write it"?**[653]

Every atom of our being has within it God's law of life. Even doctors are astonished at the marvelous way in which the various parts of the body function and are renewed; God's law is indeed in our "inward parts."

Because the involuntary functions of the body are carried on by the subconscious, that phase of mind has to have the intelligence to handle bodily functions. God has "written" or inscribed intelligent laws of life upon our heart or subconscious so that it may carry out its work. If the thinking or conscious phase does not give true patterns to the subconscious (heart), then by the law of mind action the subconscious will manifest the untrue patterns — until such time as the conscious phase of soul turns to the Superconscious for right directions to pass on to the subconscious. Then we are "transformed by the renewing of [our] mind",[654] for we have become obedient to the inspirations of the superconsclous and have impressed spiritual ideals upon the subconscious. The heart will then faithfully carry out the true law inscribed upon it.

---

[653] Jeremiah 31:33
[654] Romans 12:2

Index

Abide in Christ, 99, 330
Absolute, 9, 10, 20, 24, 26, 38, 43, 44, 55, 57, 59, 64, 99, 104, 142, 146, 147, 287, 288, 291, 293, 294, 301, 306, 315, 321, 333, 369, 375, 376, 384
Absolute Good, 293
Affirmation, 40, 61, 70, 71, 97, 120, 139, 142, 143, 144, 145, 146, 178, 220, 221, 225, 233, 234, 272, 297, 309, 326, 327, 351, 357, 358, 359, 373
Affirmations, 139, 141, 145, 147, 180, 214, 215
Allegory, 64, 68, 69, 73, 74, 75, 124, 164, 226, 385, 386
Anointed One, 354
Asking in His Name, 368
Atonement, 165, 167, 170, 201, 331, 356, 367
At-one-ment, 331
Being, 22
Being, Aspects of, 23

Believing on Christ unto Salvation, 352
Bible, 10, 12, 13, 37, 45, 61, 69, 70, 71, 87, 93, 96, 115, 128, 137, 316, 371
Birth, Second, 118
Blessing, 282
Body (Manifestation), 103
Brain, 347
Cause and Effect, 142
Christ, 168, 354, 363
Christ Consciousness, 350
Christ Life, 137, 138
Christ Mind, 39, 124, 126, 131, 133, 134, 136, 146, 171, 173, 281, 292, 314, 319, 338, 339, 342, 362, 379
Churches, 15
Co-Creation, 157, 158
Collective, 97
Collective Consciousness, 344
Conscious Mind, 110
Conscious Phase of Mind, 341
Conscious Unity, 308
Consciousness, 27, 84, 87, 91, 92, 93, 97, 108,

109, 132, 173, 211, 255, 261
Consicousness, 124, 164, 232
Conversion, 131
Creation Stories, 68
Creation, Steps of, 163
Creative Energy, 145
Creative Mind, 362
Crucifixion, 127
Daily Bread, 175, 359, 376, 378, 380
Demonstration, 255, 277, 279
Denials, 139, 141, 144, 176, 214
Devil, 48, 49, 117
Devine Ideas, 159
Divine Idea, 27, 39, 60, 95, 103, 143, 154, 162, 169, 191, 196, 205, 206, 208, 210, 212, 216, 219, 220, 225, 236, 255, 256, 275, 281, 313, 389
Divine Ideas, 85, 176, 179
Divine intelligence, 290
Divine Plan, 60
Eating, 243
Elimination, 190, 197
Eternal Life, 235, 352
Evil, 43, 44, 45, 46, 50, 143

Evil, Absolute vs Relative, 44
Evolution, 65, 91, 123, 134, 160, 161, 211
Executive Power, 161
Externalization of the Superconscious, 113
Faith, 10, 23, 31, 33, 71, 75, 94, 97, 144, 145, 149, 150, 151, 152, 153, 154, 155, 163, 184, 190, 191, 210, 211, 212, 219, 223, 225, 250, 252, 257, 266, 309, 310, 358, 370, 379, 380, 381, 383, 384
Faith Thinking, 152, 153
Faith, Blind, 150
Father, 312
Father/Mother (God), 31, 32
Feeling, 96, 142
First and Second Coming, 170
First-Born of all Creation, 63, 317, 318
Four-Sided Consciousness, 92
Fourth Dimension, 54
Free Will, 46
Genesis, 12, 33, 64, 68, 69, 70, 71, 72, 73, 74, 75, 97, 104, 163, 226,

285, 288, 293, 296,
317, 322, 329, 336,
337, 354, 386, 387,
388, 389, 391
God, 20, 287
God as Law, 25
God as Love, 27
God as Mind, 26
God as Principle, 24
God as Spirit, 23, 24, 38, 119
God as the Absolute, 26
God is, 20, 21, 22, 23, 24,
25, 26, 27, 29, 30, 31,
32, 37, 38, 43, 44, 46,
47, 49, 53, 54, 55, 56,
57, 59, 63, 66, 68, 76,
85, 88, 100, 101, 123,
128, 144, 155, 159,
177, 178, 179, 182,
185, 196, 211, 225,
226, 304, 305, 307,
308, 310, 315, 316,
370, 371, 372, 374,
375, 376, 381, 382
God's Will, 59
God's purpose, 20, 307
Grace, 29, 33, 34, 312
Hallowed, 375
Harmony, 281, 315
Harmony, Divine, 323
Healing Method of Jesus, 227
Healing, Jesus, 297

Healing, Spiritual, 222
Health, 11, 201, 203, 205, 209, 212
Heart, 15, 55, 60, 94, 109,
131, 135, 136, 149,
152, 168, 185, 190,
225, 260, 270, 274,
280, 282, 283, 285,
288, 298, 308, 324,
339, 342, 345, 346,
347, 355, 358, 359,
364, 367, 369, 371,
376, 382, 390, 393,
395
Heaven, 307, 315, 316, 378
Holy Spirit, 25, 35, 36, 37,
39, 40, 66, 99, 113,
129, 222, 233, 234,
291, 303, 312, 313,
337
Human, Ideal, 322
Human, Manifest, 322
I AM, 39, 72, 81, 82, 83,
88, 92, 134, 213, 218,
220, 225, 239, 242,
243, 250, 292, 303,
306, 308, 309, 310,
314, 319, 320, 321,
322, 323, 326, 327,
330, 338, 352, 353,
354, 363, 364, 365,
368, 375, 378, 383,
387, 389, 391, 392

Page | 399

Idea-Thought-Word, 221
Imagination, 71, 150, 190, 194
Immanent, 288, 289
Immanent/Transcendent, 30
Individuality, 115, 116
Infolded, 123
Inlet and Outlet, 213
Intelligence, 64, 207, 208, 235
Intuition, 94
Involution, 64, 65, 160, 161
James, i, ii
Jehovah, 38, 40, 66, 285, 292, 295, 310, 317, 319, 320, 387, 389, 390
Jesus, 167, 363
Jesus Christ, 169, 363
Jesus Christ Principle, 356
Jesus, Savior, 355
Judgment, 74, 190, 192
Keys to the Kingdom, 140
Kingdom of God, 53, 54, 55, 56, 57, 307, 315, 316, 384
Kingdom of Heaven, 53, 57, 58, 61, 155, 263, 300, 301
Law of Cause and Effect, 67

Law of Giving and Receiving, 267
Law of Increase, 266
Law, Divine, 32
Law, God as, 289
Law/Grace, 32
Laws, 395
Life, 12, 87, 113, 124, 190, 198, 235, 236, 277, 377, 405
Living in Two Worlds, 83, 249
Logos, 29, 39, 64, 134, 135, 226, 227, 228, 314
Lord God of the Scriptures, 389
Lord's Prayer, 305, 369
Love, 40, 74, 190, 192, 193, 209, 244, 255, 268, 282
Man, New, 136, 137
Manifest, 329
Manifesting Christ, 330
Materiality, 347
Meditation, 175, 176, 178, 181, 185, 278, 382
Mental Causes, 240
Metaphysics, i, v, 11, 201
Mind, 108, 239, 347
Mind Idea Expression, 205

Mind, Idea, Expression, 337
Mind, One, 293
Mind/Idea/Manifestation, 100
Miracles, 210
Money, 247, 251, 253, 263, 264, 265, 266, 270, 271, 272, 275
Multitude, Jesus feeding, 296
Nature, 294
New Age, 13, 129
Nonresistance, 192, 283
Nourishing, 236
Object of our Existence, 324, 334
Omnipotence, 19, 287, 290, 291, 292
Omnipresence, 30, 55, 85, 290, 291
Omniscience, 19, 287, 290
Oneness with God, 302
Order, 190, 196, 350
Paradox, 29, 30
Persistence, 216
Personality, 115, 116, 117
Planes of Life, 53
Power of Thought, 208
Praise, 184, 282
Prayer, 166, 175, 176, 177, 178, 179, 184, 185, 216, 253, 278, 279, 305, 306, 307, 309, 310, 357, 369, 370, 372, 373, 374, 376, 378, 379, 380, 381, 382, 384
Prayer Without Ceasing, 184
Principle, 376
Principle, God as, 288
Principle/Personal, 29
Process Theology, 77
Purpose, 277
Realization, 176, 183, 210, 220, 229
Receptivity, 212, 219
Regeneration, 123, 128, 129, 189, 231, 233
Reincarnation, 123, 126
Relative, 10, 146
Renunciation, 190, 197
Resistance, 51, 215
Resurrection, 14, 127, 128, 132, 169, 238, 239
Sabbath, 69, 75, 210
Salvation, 131, 132, 171, 172
Science and Religion, 57
Scripture Symbols, 36
Secondary Thinking, 341
Secret place, 304, 305, 357, 371, 372
See the Good, 280

Self-Control, 242
Self-Knowledge, 82
Self-Observation, 88
Sensation, 93
Separation from God, 46
Silence, 166, 304, 305, 308, 309, 310, 372, 373, 374, 381, 383
Silence, The, 176, 182, 183, 300, 304, 353, 369, 372
Silent Unity Method, 218
Sin, 44, 47, 48, 143
Sins of Commission and Omission, 48
Son of God, 20, 39, 132, 134, 135, 167, 172, 242, 310, 312, 317, 320, 327, 353, 354, 356, 365, 366, 368, 392
Son of man, 20, 310, 311, 312
Son, Only begotten, 289
Soul (Idea), 102
Soul Unfoldment, 135
Spirit (Mind), 101
Spirit of Truth, 40, 162
Spiritual Illumination, 135
Stillness, 385
Strength, 190, 191, 192
Subconscious Impressions, 112
Subconscious Mind, 110

Subconscious Phase of Mind, 341
Superconscious, 84, 107, 110, 111, 112, 114, 136, 170, 292, 298, 314, 338, 339, 340, 342, 362
Superconscious Mind, 111
Superconscious, 395
Symbol, 49, 64, 69, 70, 71, 93, 116, 118, 125, 132, 271, 313, 328, 386
Thanksgiving, 183, 184, 260
Thinking, 95, 153, 243, 335, 383
Thought, 11, 22, 87, 213, 221, 240, 241, 405, 406
Thought Center, 318, 319
Thought, Holding a, 381, 383
Thought, Secomdary Power, 241
Thoughts, 139, 186, 357, 358, 372, 373, 374, 379, 382, 383
Thoughts are Things, 139
Threefold Nature, 332
Tithing, 269
Transcendence, 31
Tree of Life, 391

Trinity, 35, 36, 37, 38, 39, 41, 51, 66, 67, 99, 100, 101, 103, 104, 162, 163, 207, 221, 235, 314

Truth, v, 7, 9, 10, 11, 14, 15, 16, 20, 22, 28, 40, 41, 43, 44, 50, 57, 58, 59, 61, 66, 67, 79, 82, 83, 92, 93, 94, 102, 109, 113, 114, 119, 120, 123, 125, 126, 127, 128, 132, 133, 136, 139, 144, 155, 160, 161, 162, 163, 164, 165, 170, 172, 178, 180, 182, 183, 191, 195, 201, 204, 214, 219, 220, 221, 222, 223, 224, 226, 229, 230, 240, 254, 258, 260, 262, 268, 271, 273, 280, 283, 305, 306, 307, 308, 309, 316, 357, 358, 359, 360, 361, 370, 371, 372, 373, 375, 376, 377, 378, 381, 382, 383

Truth of Being, 324

Twelve Powers, 16, 21, 25, 31, 37, 44, 49, 51, 65, 66, 88, 93, 97, 118, 121, 126, 133, 136, 139, 143, 151, 154, 160, 165, 187, 188, 405

Two Individuals, 115

Understanding, v, 10, 11, 21, 25, 26, 33, 35, 38, 40, 41, 50, 51, 59, 68, 70, 72, 73, 74, 85, 87, 94, 95, 101, 102, 124, 125, 135, 136, 145, 149, 150, 151, 152, 154, 155, 167, 171, 180, 185, 187, 190, 195, 203, 215, 227, 234, 242, 249, 250, 257, 279, 306, 309, 314, 360, 361, 369, 370, 382, 383

Understanding Faith, 149, 151, 154, 155

Understanding, Spiritual, 149, 360, 361, 372, 383

Universal Mind, 343

Wholeness, 238

Will, 72, 73, 77, 190, 195

Will, God's, 20, 166, 305, 306, 307, 308, 370, 373, 377, 378, 383

Word, 224

Word of God, 225

Word, The, 329

Words, 228

Works, Jesus', 299

Zeal, 190, 196, 197

Biography

James Yeaw is an ordained Baptist, Interfaith and Unity Minister with degrees in Psychology and Human Resource Development from California State University. He is a graduate of Unity Institute in Missouri and holds a Doctorate in Divinity from Emerson Theological Institute. With his wife, Rev. Sharon Bush, he co-ministers to a vibrant and active congregation at Unity Spiritual Center in Sun City, Arizona.

Unity Spiritual Center Publications

There is a series on the work of New Thought writers. Publications include:

- *The Impersonal Life* – Joseph Benner
- *The Game of Life and How to Play It* – Florence Scovell Shinn
- *The Power of Awareness* – Neville Goddard
- *The Twelve Powers* – Charles Fillmore
- *Lessons in Truth* – H. Emilie Cady

Unity Spiritual Center has also published material developed by the Unity School of Religious Studies, including this work: Unity Metaphysics. These publications include:

- *A Spiritual Interpretation of Hebrew Scriptures*
- *A Spiritual Interpretation of Christian Scriptures: The Gospels*
- *A Spiritual Interpretation of Christian Scriptures:*

Acts to Revelation

Other books in a series include:

- *Wisdom of the Ages (CD Rom)*
- *Thought*
- *Perception*
- *Is Unity a Cult?*
- *Discovering Unity*

See additional information and other resources at our website: www.unitysc.org

Unity Spiritual Center Online Classes

The class presented in this book and other classes are available, without charge, on Facebook. See our website for start dates and other information.
See additional information and other resources at our website: www.unitysc.org

Rev. Yeaw is available to conduct a variety of seminars on the subjects within this book. eMail: revjim@unitysc.org

Made in United States
Orlando, FL
05 March 2024